DATE DUE

MY 24 '99		
DE 7 '04		

DEMCO 38-296

Arbitrating Sex
Discrimination Grievances

Arbitrating Sex Discrimination Grievances

Vern E. Hauck

QUORUM BOOKS

Westport, Connecticut • London

Library of Congress Cataloging-in-Publication Data

Hauck, Vern E.
    Arbitrating sex discrimination grievances / Vern E. Hauck.
      p. cm.
    Includes bibliographical references and index.
    ISBN 1–56720–107–5 (alk. paper)
    1. Discrimination in employment—Law and legislation—United
States. 2. Grievance arbitration—United States. 3. Grievance
procedures—United States. I. Title.
    KF3464.H383   1998
    344.7301'4133—dc21   97–33696

British Library Cataloguing in Publication Data is available.

Library of Congress Catalog Card Number: 97–33696
ISBN: 1–56720–107–5

First published in 1998

Quorum Books, 88 Post Road West, Westport, CT 06881
An imprint of Greenwood Publishing Group, Inc.

Printed in the United States of America

The paper used in this book complies with the
Permanent Paper Standard issued by the National
Information Standards Organization (Z39.48–1984).

10 9 8 7 6 5 4 3 2 1

Copyright Acknowledgments

The author and publisher gratefully acknowledge permission for use of the following material:

Extensive material from George J. Zazas, "The Case for Establishment of Formal Standards," *Proceedings of the Thirty-Eighth Annual Meeting National Academy of Arbitrators* (Washington D.C.: BNA Books, Inc.), 1986; and Sam Kagel, "Legalism—and Some Comments of Illegalisms—in Arbitration," *Proceedings of the Thirty-Eighth Annual Meeting National Academy of Arbitrators* (Washington D.C.: BNA Books, Inc.), 1986. Used by permission of BNA Books.

To Parents and Grandparents

Contents

Preface

This book is the outcome of a project that began twenty years ago when there were not enough published arbitral discrimination awards to justify its production. Even though employment discrimination has been considered by arbitrators as far back as anyone can remember, twenty years ago there were fewer than 300 published arbitral discrimination awards available for public examination (cumulative from about 1945). Today, there are more than 1,000 published arbitral discrimination awards, easily enough awards to justify this book, which considers gender discrimination grievances, as well as a second book that considers race, religion, and national origin discrimination grievances. As might be expected, many of the problems, claims, and merits presented to labor arbitrators fifty years ago are the same as those presented today. For example, the practical solutions for sex discrimination grievances in this book document a dynamic fifty-year concern by labor arbitrators, employers, and unions for age-old conflicts centered upon gender, sexual harassment, pregnancy, childbearing, and comparable worth, just to name a few. Viewed together, the arbitral awards and court decisions analyzed in this book identify current problems, work rules, employment practices, and practical solutions for gender discrimination in the union and non-union sectors.

This book is separated into two parts. Chapters 1 and 2 of Part I consider evolving arbitral decision criteria used to determine human rights grievances. Chapter 3 details the unique features of procedure, evidence, and proofs which have evolved over the past twenty years and should be followed by the parties when arbitrating employment discrimination challenges. Because keeping proper tension between the law and the human rights clause of the labor contract is critical, many practitioners will want to read Chapter 3 before the arbitration hearing. Part II consists of Chapters 4, 5, 6, and 7. Chapter 4 contains an extensive analysis of sex discrimination awards dealing with matters such as recruitment, hiring, layoff and discharge. Chapters 5 considers performance appraisal, merit and pay systems, promotion, transfer, seniority, and training. Chapter 6 details the matter of sexual harassment, including court decisions and arbitral awards governing termination, the reasonable woman standard, welcome advances, and victim retaliation. Chapter 7 covers pregnancy and childbearing, unwed motherhood, fetal protection, maternity and family leave, and health insurance. With minor exceptions, materials in this book can be found in the abstracts of labor arbitration awards published by the Bureau of National Affairs, Inc. (BNA) and the Industrial Relations Press (IRP) publications. The on-line computer databases of both BNA and IRP were used extensively. Other materials referenced include court decisions, journal articles, and the Proceedings of the Annual Meeting of the National Academy of Arbitrators.

Acknowledgments

The number of you who supported me in this project would fill a book and I thank you one and all. First, the support issued by my wife, my son, and my family has been extensive, and each moment has been appreciated. Second, I would like to thank the entire staff at the Greenwood Publishing Group, especially Ms. Wendi Schnaufer, Ms. Marcia Goldstein, and Mr. Jason Azze. Third, it would be inappropriate to overlook the special thanks I owe to the late Camille Christie at BNA Books. Special thanks also goes to Richard Cornfield, Publisher, and other staff members at BNA Books who joined me in heartache and generously released the materials reprinted in this book following Ms. Christie's death. I also wish to acknowledge my deep indebtedness to Professor William P. Murphy; Professor Julius G. Getman; Professor James E. Jones, Jr.; Professor George A. Geistauts; Professor James Craft; the late Professor Irving Kovarsky; Professor Tom Pearce; Professor John South; Dr. James Ice; Dean William Blockman; Dean G. Hayden Green; Ms. Fannie Slatten; and the hundreds of labor arbitrators whose endeavors have provided the foundation of this book.

Abbreviations

AAA	American Arbitration Association
AIS	Arbitration in the Schools
ARB	Labor Arbitration Awards
BMS	Bureau of Mediation Services, State of Minnesota
CA	Court of Appeals
DC	District Court
EEOC	Equal Employment Opportunity Commission
GERR	Government Employee Relations Reporter
FEPC	Fair Employment Practice Committee
FEP	Fair Employment Practice Cases
FLRR	Federal Labor Relations Reporter
IND REL REP	Industrial Relations Reporter
LA	Labor Arbitration Reports
LAC	Labor Arbitration Cases (Canada)
LAIG	Labor Arbitration in Government
LAIRS	Labor Arbitration Information Retrieval System
LAIS	Labor Arbitration Information System
LRRM	Labor Relations Reference Manual
PPA	Public Personnel Administration
PSEA	Pennsylvania State Education Association
US	United States Supreme Court

PART I

FOUNDATION
AND FUNDAMENTALS

Chapter 1

Legal and Arbitral Foundations

Understanding and dealing effectively with sex discrimination grievances, the subject of this book, require the blending of two bodies of arbitral fundamentals. On one hand, the context and evolving body of arbitral thinking commonly associated with traditional grievances serve as a familiar model from which to embark upon the trail leading to the successful resolution of discrimination grievances. Practically speaking, many, but not all, of the time-tested procedures and interpretive insights applied to grievances, such as fighting or sleeping on the job, also apply to discrimination grievances. For example, the procedure is quasi-judicial in both types of cases, but, as will be discussed in Chapter 3 discrimination hearings require more procedural diligence than traditional hearings.

On the other hand, discrimination grievances are unique. And, that same uniqueness remains whether the complaint is resolved by the parties themselves, the preferred method, or turned over to an arbitrator at the culmination of the grievance process. For, unlike traditional arbitration, discrimination grievances require an additional sensitivity to the nature and often traumatic problems of the minority workers who feel compelled to seek resolution of their discrimination claims through the grievance process. The hundreds of arbitration awards cited in this book document that most minority workers face the same sorts of job conflicts as other employees, discrimination commingling and confronting the parties with an additional dimension of complexity. Thus, exploring the nature and uniqueness, as well as fashioning effective response strategies for discrimination grievances, begins with the inculcation of some appreciation for the macro forces that have driven each form of employment sex discrimination to its current status.

Naturally the specific operation of micro forces differs in detail between each form of employment discrimination at the job level and will need to be addressed by the parties and neutrals when the grievance is at hand. On a grander scale, however, there are macro linkages that interrelate and connect all forms of employment discrimination. Before embarking upon the grievance process, it is important and appropriate for the parties, witnesses, and arbitrators to be sensitive to the macro context of employment discrimination. The remedy resulting from the grievance process is much more likely to be correct when the parties are sensitive to the problem at hand.

HISTORICAL BACKGROUND

An overwhelming number of employment discrimination problems decided by legislators, judges, and labor arbitrators have dealt with racial and sexual bias. For that reason, the racial discrimination impacting blacks and women will serve to highlight the influence of the economic, political, and legal parameters forming the historical background and macro context of employment discrimination found in today's workplace. Notwithstanding, the industrial revolution and the depression impacted all forms of discrimination, but in different ways.

Economic

The Great Depression of the 1930s was a colossal economic event that changed America's guiding economic theory and set the stage for the employment opportunities that accrued to blacks and women during World War II. The nation's predepression economic philosophy was published in the well-known book by Adam Smith, *Wealth of Nations*, in 1776. Along with Malthus, Ricardo, Hume, and others, Smith developed an economic theory and system that dominated American economic thought for over a century and plays a very significant role today. According to Smith, individuals within the economic system pursue their own selfish economic interests. In so doing, large numbers of buyers and sellers are helped to interact by an "invisible hand" in such a way that the net result is a better standard of living for all.

For employment discrimination the key element in the Smithian system is a laissez-faire policy of government. Classic theory holds that government is a wasteful institution and that private industry will support a better society if left alone. The emphasis of the laissez-faire program is to eliminate economic harm by avoiding concern for the short-term plight of employment, economic growth, and inflation. Laissez-faire government takes no direct responsibility for the needs of citizens on the lower end of the economic scale, those most often discriminated against. More than that, laissez-faire government actually protects the status quo, including employment discrimination and other forms of civil rights discrimination involving voter rights and housing.[1]   It is probably not unfair to

---

[1] Irving Kovarsky and William Albrecht, *Black Employment: The Impact of Religion, Economic Theory, Politics, and Law*. Ames: The Iowa State University Press, 1970, 23.

say that laissez-faire government encourages the retention of a status quo that is aggressively hostile toward minority groups.

While inflation was not a problem, economic growth declined and the level of unemployment reached disastrous proportions in the Great Depression. In 1936, John Maynard Keynes published *The General Theory of Employment, Interest, and Money,* and demonstrated why laissez-faire theory is an inadequate technique for dealing with unemployment. Keynes's theory, which in the main still prevails, justified the need for the federal government to stabilize the economy via active spending and taxing programs that encourage economic growth, seek to lower inflation, and/or avoid large unemployment levels. The shift to Keynesian economics from laissez-faire was an important moment in the civil rights movement because government became responsible for capital investment and full employment. An active federal government interested in preventing unemployment soon found itself with the responsibility of ending employment discrimination.

Political

World War II followed on the heels of the Great Depression, and the labor shortages associated with the war effort helping to end the depression and to feed a degree of economic opportunity for women and blacks. But, it took political action in the form of a threatened march on Washington spearheaded by the predominantly black Brotherhood of Sleeping Car Porters to reveal a most embarrassing contradiction. The tight labor market and need for skilled workers in 1941 were juxtaposed by a system of employment discrimination that prohibited the complete use of blacks and women workers in war industries. In response to the threatened march on Washington, President Franklin D. Roosevelt issued Executive Order 8802, the Fair Employment Practice Committee (FEPC). And while the FEPC was made ineffective by a Congress dominated by Southern Democrats, the mere existence of the FEPC within the Office of Production and Management was a sign of emerging black power in the nation's body politic and a significant political step in the direction of fair employment.[2]

Executive Orders, *amicus curiae* briefs, and knowledge about prejudice are important, but the single most relevant political key to the elimination of employment discrimination has been the willingness, ability, and right of minority workers to vote. Economic power and political power go hand in hand. And for workers seeking fair employment, political muscle leads to economic opportunity. The Nineteenth Amendment to the U.S. Constitution was proposed on June 4, 1919 and ratified on August 18, 1920, granting the right to vote regardless of sex. Though the Fifteenth Amendment granted the right to vote regardless of

---

[2] James E. Jones, Jr., "The Development of Modern Equal Employment Opportunity and Affirmative Action Law: A Brief Chronological Overview," *Howard Law Journal,* Vol. 20, No. 1, 1977, 74-99.

race, color, or previous condition of servitude,[3] black workers were virtually without franchise after a brief period following the American Civil War until the civil rights movement of the 1960s.[4]

Legal

The foundations of employment discrimination law date back over two hundred years in the case of the Fifth Amendment, ratified on December 15, 1791, and over one hundred years in the case of the Thirteenth and Fourteenth Amendments, ratified on December 6, 1865 and July 9, 1868, respectively.[5] During the same era that the federal Constitution was being amended following the Civil War, Congress passed legislation that granted some aid to blacks: the Civil Rights Act of 1866,[6] the Enforcement Act of 1870,[7] the Ku Klux Klan Act of 1871,[8] and the Civil Rights Act of 1875.[9] But for the purposes of ending employment discrimination, the impact of post Civil War constitutional amendments and congressional legislation was set aside by the U.S. Supreme Court.

One set of monumental Supreme Court decisions was the *Civil Rights Cases*.[10] In 1883 the Court ruled that denial of access to hotels, buses, parks, and so forth does not violated the Thirteenth Amendment because citizens, such as blacks, being denied entry have freedom to go elsewhere. Similarly, the High Court found that the Fourteenth Amendment was aimed at public property only, allowing businessmen to practice employment discrimination on private property. Then in 1896 the Supreme Court took discrimination one step further when it handed down *Plessy v. Ferguson*.[11] Discrimination was institutionalized since *Plessy* approved of separate but equal public education. That is, *Plessy* had the

---

[3] Relevant portions of the Fifteenth Amendment are: "Section 1: The right of citizens of the United States to vote shall not be denied or abridged by the United States or by any state on account of race, color, or previous condition of servitude."

[4] Robert B. McKay, *Reapportionment: The Law and Politics of Equal Representation*. New York: Simon and Schuster, 1965; and Irving Kovarsky, *Discrimination in Employment*. University of Iowa: Center for Labor and Management, 1976.

[5] Relevant portions of the three amendments are: *Fifth Amendment*: "No person shall . . . be deprived of life, liberty, or property, without due process of law." *Thirteenth Amendment*: "Neither slavery nor involuntary servitude . . . shall exist within the United States . . ."; *Fourteenth Amendment*: "[N]o state . . . shall . . . deprive any person of life, liberty, or property, without due process of law; nor deny to any person within its jurisdiction the equal protection of the law."

[6] 42 U.S.C. 1981, 1983 and 1985; or 14 Stat. 27.

[7] 16 Stat. 140.

[8] 16 Stat. 433.

[9] 18 Stat. 336.

[10] 109 U.S. 3 (1883); see also *Ex parte Yarbrough*, 110 U.S. 651 (1884), *U.S. v. Cruikshank*, 92 U.S. 542 (1875), and *The Slaughter House Cases*, 83 U.S. 36 (1872).

[11] *Plessy v. Ferguson*, 163 U.S. 537 (1896).

effect of making it public policy to discriminate on the basis of race. Where the *Civil Rights Cases* passively allowed discrimination, *Plessy* encouraged government to discriminate actively. History provides that separate but equal is impossible because the whites controlled funding and spent most tax money on white needs. Taken together, the *Civil Rights Cases* first provided an environment without meaningful employment, negating the incentive to learn since no jobs were available anyway. And second, *Plessy* relegated those few blacks who were motivated to a second rate education so that they could not compete against whites in the job market.

Over fifty years passed before the Supreme Court began its historic turn away from the *Civil Rights Cases* and *Plessy*, starting small but evolving toward the concepts of equal opportunity employment. A landmark decision was *Shelley v. Kraemer*, 1948.[12] In *Shelley*, the Court considered the constitutionality of a private restrictive covenant that prohibited the sale of homes to blacks. Following portions of Justice Harlan's dissent in the *Civil Rights Cases*, the Supreme Court reasoned that the restrictive covenant was legal; however, the Fourteenth Amendment was violated when the state enforced the agreement. The importance of *Shelley* to citizens facing employment discrimination lies in the need to determine what is and what is not state involvement. *Shelley* and progeny tells the lower courts that the judicial restraint and passive enforcement of the Fourteenth Amendment under the *Civil Rights Cases* must give way to a more assertive, active, and ingenuous program to stretch the meaning of state action using the Fourteenth Amendment.[13] A far better known case, *Brown v. Board of Education*,[14] emerged in 1954, and the period of institutionalized discrimination established by *Plessy* ended.

In 1968 the Supreme Court decided that the Thirteenth Amendment is a valid deterrent to employment discrimination. Similar to *Shelley*, *Jones v. Alfred H. Mayer Company*[15] dealt with the right of a black citizen to purchase a home. However, in *Jones* the Supreme Court found that Section 2 of the Civil Rights Act of 1866 was clearly violated. Relevant portions of Section 2 require that "[a]ll citizens . . . shall have the . . . right . . . to inherit, purchase, lease, sell, hold and convey real and personal property." The important portion of *Jones* is the Court's ruling that the constitutional support for Section 2 is the Thirteenth Amendment, making the denial of the right to buy a home a remnant of slave status. Through *stare decisis* Jones ended the necessity to prove state action, a requirement of the Fourteenth Amendment, in matters of employment discrimi-

---

[12] *Shelley v. Kraemer*, 334 U.S. 1 (1948).
[13] *Norris v. Mayor and City Council of Baltimore*, 78 F. Sun. 451 (D. Md., 1948); *Barrows v. Jackson*, 346 U.S. 249 (1953); *Progress Development Corp. v. Mitchell*, 286 F. 2d 222 (C 1961); and *Todd v. Joint Apprenticeship Comm.*, 55 LRRM. 2171 (1963), reversed in part 56 LRRM. 2318 (1964). Eventually, state inaction was equated with state action on state property in *Burton v. Wilminton Park Authority*, 365 U.S. 715 (1961).
[14] *Brown v. Board of Education*, 347 U.S. 483 (1954).
[15] *Jones v. Alfred H. Mayer Company*, 392 U.S. 409 (1968).

nation. And because it doesn't require state action to find employment discrimination, the Thirteenth Amendment is a more powerful legal force against private employers, unions, and others.

Arbitration

An important arbitral issue being hammered out in the period immediately following World War II was the relationship between the labor agreement and the law. In this regard, the significant connection between employment discrimination, the labor agreement, and the U.S. Declaration of Independence was discussed by Arbitrator Clark Kerr on December 27, 1946. Resolving an interest dispute, Arbitrator Kerr selected the following clause: "no discrimination shall be practiced by either the company or the union because of sex, race, creed, color, religious belief, or national origin."[16] Arbitrator Kerr reasoned that

[s]uch a clause is common in many waterfront contracts, as well as in many other industries. These people work on the waterfront, where discrimination is not practiced. This type of clause was frequently granted by the National War Labor Board. Aside from that, our nation was founded on the belief that "all men are created free and equal."

The antidiscrimination clause selected by Arbitrator Kerr is remarkably similar to the fundamental provisions of present day human rights codes as well as the Civil Rights Act of 1964, as amended. Furthermore, despite existing popular prejudice against blacks in traditional white jobs, contractual guarantees, such as Arbitrator Kerr selected, tended to be enforced so that qualified blacks kept their jobs and unqualified employees were discharged. Arbitral opinion in 1946 was the same as today, arbitrators not requiring the employment of unqualified workers.

CURRENT LAWS AND WORK RULES[17]

The list of antidiscrimination laws and work rules with which the arbitrator and the parties must deal is rather long and growing in both length and complexity. Furthermore, the specifics of each law applicable to the grievant's complaint must be examined in light of the record provided by the parties. As detailed discussions later in this book will show, Title VII of the Civil Rights Act of 1964,

---

[16] *Luckenbach Steamship Company, Inc.*, 6 LA 98 (Kerr, 1946).

[17] The author wishes to thank Professors William P. Murphy, Julius G. Getman, and James E. Jones, Jr., for their example for organizing this section about Current Laws and Work Rules. See *Discrimination in Employment, Fourth Edition*. Washington, D.C.: BNA Books, Inc., 1979, 4-10.

as amended,[18] state law, and several court decisions are the sources of law relied upon by the parties in a majority of settings. Notwithstanding, Title VII, state law, and court decisions are just some of the possibilities that the parties must consider.

U.S. Constitution

The Fifth and Fourteenth Amendments to the federal constitution have been the basis for fair employment actions. Federal officials are barred from discriminatory conduct by the due process clause of the Fifth Amendment.[19] State officials are liable for discriminatory conduct as a result of the due process and equal protection provisions of the Fourteenth Amendment.[20] Technically, the Thirteenth Amendment, which reaches discriminatory actions by private individuals, has not been utilized directly against employment discrimination.

The Equal Pay Act

The Equal Pay Act (EPA) makes it illegal for employers and unions[21] to discriminate on the basis of sex for equal work on jobs that require equal skill, effort, and responsibility. Pay differentials based on any other factor besides gender are legal, including a bona fide seniority program negotiated between labor and management representatives. Acceptable criterion for different pay rates are seniority, merit, quality, or quantity of production.[22] Originally passed in 1963, the EPA was repeatedly amended until by 1974 nearly all state and local workers, as well as private sector employees, fell under the law.[23] Initially, the EPA was administered separately from the Civil Rights Act of 1964. Separating the administrative function is a common practice for new civil rights legislation, the same being true for the Office of Federal Contract Compliance (OFCCP) and the Equal Employment Opportunity Commission (EEOC). However, the EEOC assumed enforcement of the EPA on July 1, 1979 in order to avoid conflicting interpretations between the overlapping portions of Title VII and the EPA.[24]

---

[18] 42 U.S.C. 2000, et seq.

[19] *Hadnett v . Laird*, 4 FEP 374 (1972) .

[20] *Ethridge v. Rhodes*, 65 LRRM 2331, 1 FEP 185 (1967).

[21] *Laffey v. Northwest Airlines*, 23FEP 1629 (1980); *Donovan v. KFC Services, Inc.*, 30 FEP 1846 (1982).

[22] *EEOC v. McCarthy*, 38 FEP 536 (1985).

[23] *Marshall v. City of Sheboygan*, 17 FEP 763 (1978).

[24] *County of Washington v. Gunther*, 25 FEP 1521 (1981; see also *Hodgson v. Brookhaven General Hospital*, 9 FEP 579 (1970) and affirmed at 9 FEP 793 (1972); *Briggs v. Anderson*, 40 FEP 883 (1986).

The Civil Rights Act of 1964

Title VII outlaws discrimination on the basis of color, religion, sex, or national origin by employers with fifteen or more employees, union, and employment agencies. Title VII makes it unlawful to discriminate against employees in hiring, firing, compensation, terms, condition, or privileges of employment or to segregate or classify any individual employees in a way that deprives them of employment opportunities or status.[25]   The Pregnancy Discrimination Act amended Title VII in 1978, making it necessary to treat pregnant women on the basis of their ability or inability to work. While race and color are always covered, bona fide occupational qualifications (BFOQ), such as the specific need for an male actor or female actress,[26] allow discrimination on the basis of gender in hiring, employment, referral, training, and advertising.

The Civil Rights Act of 1991

Signed by President Bush on November 21, 1991, the 1991 Act provides appropriate remedies for intentional discrimination, codifies the concepts of "business necessity" and "job related" enunciated by the Supreme Court in *Griggs v. Duke Power Company*, confirms statutory authority and guidelines for adjudication of disparate impact suits under Title VII, and modifies the impact of Supreme Court decisions such as *Ward's Cove Packing Company v. Antonio.*[27] A substantial part of motivation for adopting the Civil Rights Act of 1991 appears to have been concern for the impact of *Ward's Cove* by the leader of the civil rights movement. Title III of the 1991 Act contains provisions to protect the rights of certain government employees so that they are free of race, color, religion, sex, national origin, age, or disability discrimination. Title III has been given the short title of "Government Employee Rights Act of 1991." In 1994 the Supreme Court decided that the portion of the Civil Rights Act of 1991 that extends Section 1981 to all phases of the employment relationship does not apply retroactively to conduct occurring before November 21, 1991, a decision which reduced employer liability.[28]

---

[25] *Teamsters v. United States*, 14 FEP 1514 (1977) and *American Tabacco Company v. Patterson*, 28 FEP 713 (1982).

[26] *Fernandez v. Wynn Oil Company*, 26 FEP 815, the same principle holds for the need for a female nurse's aid in a nursing home mostly for women, see *Fesel v. Masonic Home* 17 FEP 330 (1978).

[27] *Ward's Cove Packing Company v. Antonio*, 49 FEP Cases 1519, 490 US 642 (1989).

[28] The Civil Rights Act of 1991, PL No. 102-106, became effective November 21, 1991. *Rivers v. Roadway Express*, U.S. SupCt. No. 92-938 (1994). The Government Employee Rights Act of 1991, PL No. 104-1, became effective January 23, 1996.

Executive Orders

Federal, state, and local executive orders generally parallel Title VII, though there are some significant differences. Presidential Executive Order 11246 outlaws race, color, religion, sex, and national origin discrimination by government contractors and subcontractors; in the same vein, Executive Order 11478 outlaws discrimination in federal employment. Executive Order 11246 requires affirmative action by government contractors to ensure equal employment opportunity. Executive Order 11141 bans age discrimination but has limited enforcement capability.   Physical handicap discrimination is also covered by federal executive order. State and local executive orders operate much the same as federal orders, but with less financial backing, and frequently near the cutting edge of change in employment discrimination law.[29]

The Vietnam Era Veterans' Readjustment Assistance Act of 1974

This act, 38 U.S.C. 2012, requires that contractors or subcontractors with federal contracts amounting to $10,000 or more take affirmative action to employ or advance in employment "special disabled veterans and veterans of the Vietnam Era." Veterans are to be given employment referral priority, and since 1982 contractors must annually report the number of employees within the coverage of this act to the Secretary of Labor.

Title IX of the Education Amendments of 1972

Title IX prohibits sex discrimination in any educational program or activity receiving federal financial assistance. The U.S. Supreme Court found the Educational Amendments of 1972, as amended, to apply to both employees and students who are working in or going to school at institutions of learning that are covered by Title IX. That is, Title IX makes it illegal to practice gender discrimination with respect to employment and many other activities in federally funded educational programs.[30] Since federal financial assistance can be found in most public and many private educational institutions, the reach of this law is extensive. Title IX is often cited, for example, as a cornerstone for the rise of women's athletics in sports previously dominated by men, or in sports formally open to men only.   The Civil Rights Restoration Act of 1987 (CRRA) requires entire institutions, not just subdepartments, to comply with Title IX.[31]

---

[29] Minneapolis, Minn. program concerning A.I.D.S.; see *AIDS Policy & Law*, 26, 6.

[30] *North Haven Board of Education v. Bell*, 28 FEP 1393 (1982); see also *Franklin v. Gwinnett County Public Schools*, 59 FEP 213 (1992).

[31] CRRA overturned *Grove City College v. Bell*, 465 U.S. 555 (1984).

State and Local Fiscal Assistance Act

Administered by the Federal Office of Revenue Sharing (ORS), the State and Local Fiscal Assistance Act (SLFAA), as amended, requires state and local governments receiving federal funds to comply with equal employment opportunity law or be denied revenue sharing money. The SLFAA prohibits job discrimination on the basis of race, color, national origin, sex, age, handicap, or religion. Either federal or state court or federal administrative agency may find fund recipients in violation of SLFAA, in which case the ORS is required to initiate administrative cutoff procedures. Complaints may be filed by a private party, by a state or local administrative agency, or by the ORS.

State and Local Fair Employment Practice Laws

Arbitrators frequently find themselves dealing with state law because Title VII requires that job discrimination charges be deferred for initial action to those designated state and local agencies that have enforcement standards comparable to the EEOC. Virtually all states and many local jurisdictions, such as the District of Columbia, have fair employment practice laws that forbid discrimination by employers, unions, and employment agencies on the basis of race, color, religion, sex, or national origin.[32]   Additionally, many states and local jurisdictions also ban discrimination based on age, handicap, marital status, and a host of other categories, including physical appearance, sexual preference, and political affiliation not covered by federal law. While Title VII applies to firms with fifteen or more employees, state and local human rights laws frequently apply to much smaller employers than is covered by federal law. Some states and local governments have no minimum number or employees or size requirement at all, other states and local governments requiring as few as one employee to be covered. Many local jurisdictions, such as borough, county, or city governments that have instituted their own ordinances outlawing employment discrimination have patterned their local law after Title VII or the one of the various state fair employment laws applicable to the local government.

Labor Laws

The Railway Labor Act[33] and the National Labor Relations Act (NLRA)[34] are separate laws, though the determinations of the Railway Labor Board and the National Labor Relations Board (NLRB) frequently parallel one another. And

---

[32] *Colorado Anti-discrimination Commission v. Continental Air Lines*, 1 FEP 25 (1963).
[33] 45 U.S.C. 151.
[34] 29 U.S.C. 151.

with respect to employment discrimination, the NLRB has found that employers who discriminate based on race, color, religion, sex, or national origin, standing alone, may not be in violation of the law unless it is found that the employer has inhibited employees in exercising their self-organizational rights.[35] Turning to union action, the Supreme Court has expressed confidence in the ability of the grievance arbitration process to resolve discrimination complaints.[36] The Supreme Court has also ruled that unions falling under the Railway Labor Act may not engage in racial discrimination against employees who are or are not in the unit,[37] a ruling adopted by the NLRB.[38] A union engaging in discrimination is subject to unfair labor practice proceedings which could result in revocation of the union's certification.[39]

Work Rules

Some work rules outright ban discrimination in employment; other work rules stress affirmative action to eliminate job discrimination. First, prohibitions against discrimination are found in 94 percent of the nation's collective bargaining agreements.[40] Labor contracts normally contain a broad statement (a) that the employer will comply with federal, state, or local antidiscrimination laws or (b) that discrimination on the basis of race, color, creed, sex, national origin, or age, for example, is a violation of the labor agreement. Second, some union and some nonunion employers have developed work rules against employment discrimination and grievance arbitration procedures that operate much the same as, but separate from, a labor agreement.[41] Third, affirmative action programs are highly individualized, depending on the type and size of the company, the status of minority groups within the company, the recruiting area, and a variety of other factors. In general, affirmative action work rules attempt to create a company culture hospitable to the hiring and retaining of minorities.[42] That is,

---

[35] *Jubilee Mfg. Co.*, 82 LRRM 1482 (1973); however, employers must bargain in good faith over the elimination of discriminatory conditions of work, *Farmer's Cooperative Compress*, NLRB, 78 LRRM 1465 (1971); and employers must not inflame employee racial prejudices during an antiunion campaign, *Sewell Mfg. Co.*, NLRB, 50 LRRM 1532 (1962).

[36] *Emporium Capwell Co. v. WACO*, 9 FEP 195 (1975).

[37] *Steele v. Louisville & Nashville R.R. Co.*, 15 LRRM 708 (1944); *Tunstall v. Locomotive Firemen*, 15 LRRM 715 (1944); and *Railroad Trainmen v. Howard*, 30 LRRM 2258 (1952).

[38] *Pioneer Bus Co.*, NLRB, 51 LRRM 1546 (1962).

[39] *Handy Andy Inc.*, NLRB, 94 LRRM 1354 (1977).

[40] Staff, *Basic Patterns in Union Contracts*, 10th ed. Washington, D.C.: The Bureau of National Affairs, Inc., 1983, 112.

[41] James E. Youngdahl, "Arbitration of Discrimination Grievances," *The Arbitration Journal*, Vol. 31, No. 3, September 1976, 145.

[42] *CUNY, Baruch, Student Services Department, CUNY* 000291 P-77-97 (Stutz, 1977) and *CUNY, Brooklyn, Mathematics Department, CUNY* 000279 P-76-84 (1976).

jobs are analyzed, policy is written, and practices are implemented by employers to eliminate employment discrimination. And where employers deviate, unions use the grievance arbitration process to force management into complying with the company's own affirmative action plan.[43]

ADVERSE IMPACT, DISPARATE IMPACT, AND DISPARATE TREATMENT

The terms "adverse impact" and "disparate impact" are almost always used interchangeably by civil rights practitioners. Whether this free interchange between the two terms is technically correct is debatable. Some legal scholars argue that the term "adverse impact" as used by the Supreme Court in *Griggs v. Duke Power Company*[44] refers to both disparate impact and disparate treatment.

Adverse Impact

The landmark Supreme Court case regarding employment discrimination, *Duke Power*, was decided in 1971. *Duke Power* was overturned by *Ward's Cove Packing Company v. Antonio* in 1989.[45] *Ward's Cove*, however, was set aside by the Civil Rights Reform Act of 1991, the 1991 law reestablishing the fundamental principles in *Duke Power*. According to the Court, employment practices that have an adverse impact on the employment opportunities of any race, sex, or ethnic group and are not justified by business necessity violate Title VII and Executive Order 11246. For its part, the EEOC will regard the actions of an employer that violate the so-called four-fifths or 80 percent rule as evidence of adverse impact from hiring, promotion, and other employment decisions. The 80 percent rule compares hiring rates for different groups, and frequently used in affirmative action programs. But affirmative action aside, the detailed meaning of *Duke Power* and progeny bifurcate into the concepts of disparate impact and disparate treatment.

Disparate Impact

Discrimination claims stressing the disparate impact doctrine involve "employment practices that are facially neutral in their treatment of different

---

[43] *Metropolitan Waste Control Commission*, BMS 8908.33 (Gallagher, 1989); *Struck Construction Company*, 74 LA 369 (Sergent, 1980); *Boston School Committee*, 774 GERR9 & DIG 105868 (Bornstein, 1978); and *Hollander and Company*, 64 LA 816 (Edelman, 1975).

[44] *Griggs v. Duke Power Company*, 3 FEP 175 (1971).

[45] *Ward's Cove Packing Company v. Antonio*, 49 FEP Cases 1519, 490 U.S. 642 (1989).

groups but that, in fact, fall more harshly on one group than another and cannot be justified by business necessity."[46] This disparate impact standard, outlined in *Duke Power*, must be satisfied by employers as a first line of lawfulness.

An employer who does not intentionally discriminate may still violate Title VII if minority workers suffer from the discriminatory consequences of the employer's actions or policies. The courts may, for example, order women to be promoted over equally qualified men to remedy the effect of an employer's discrimination against women collectively. And, once disparate impact has been proven, employers who choose between equally qualified male and female applicants find the courts taking a dim view of subjective judgment and outdated methods of evaluation.[47] The employer's promotion criteria must objectively evaluate each applicant's tenure, job knowledge, and experience.[48] Proof of disparate impact is often decided on the basis of statistical evidence[49] and employers are exonerated if their percentage of minority employees is proportional to the geographical labor market[50] and labor force.[51]

Taking the case of race discrimination and promotion, for example, the court is likely to find a violation of the law, disparate impact, where past employment practices continue to exclude a disproportionate percentage of the same race from promotion. The court may conclude that Title VII has been violated if a disproportionate percentage of protected employees are kept from gaining the necessary experiences for promotion;[52] the standards for promotion used by foremen are subjective;[53] or the employer manipulates work assignments detrimentally so that output figures inhibit the promotion of protected employees.[54]

Disparate Treatment

Disparate treatment arises when an employer has treated an individual less favorably than other employees simply because of race, color, religion, sex, or

---

[46] *Teamsters v. U.S.*, 431 U.S. 324 (1977); *American Tobacco Co. v. Patterson*, 28 FEP 713 (1982).

[47] *Albemarle Paper Company v. Moody*, 10 FEP 1181 (1975); see also William H. Warren, "*Albemarle v. Moody*: Where It All Began," *Labor Law Journal*, Vol. 37, No. 10, October 1976, 609.

[48] *Rich v. Martin Marietta Corp.*, 11 FEP 211 (1975).

[49] *Albemarle Paper Company v. Moody*, 10 FEP Cases 1181 (1975); *Griggs v. Duke Power Company*, 3 FEP Cases 175 (1971); *Sprogis v. United Air Lines*, 3 FEP 621 (1971).

[50] *Hazelwood School District v. U.S.*, 15 FEP 1 (1977) and *Vuyanich v. Republic National Bank*, 24 FEP 128 (1980).

[51] *Rich v. Martin Marietta Corp.*, 11 FEP 211 (1975).

[52] *Klapac v. McCormick*, 640 F2d 1361 (1977).

[53] *Rowe v. General Motors Corp.*, 4 FEP 445 (1972).

[54] *Taylor v. Safeway Stores, Inc.*, 11 FEP 449 (1975).

national origin.[55] Discriminatory intent with respect to individual employees must be proven in disparate treatment cases and can be inferred from the employer's different applications of the same employment policy.[56] Disparate treatment is determined through the three step allocation of burdens and order of presentation of proof enunciated in *McDonnell-Douglas v. Green*.[57]

First, the applicant must prove a prima facie case of discrimination as judged against the preponderance of evidence standard. According to *McDonnell-Douglas*, prima facie discrimination exists if: the applicant belongs to a minority group; the candidate applied and was qualified for the job for which the employer was seeking applicants; despite being qualified, the applicant was rejected; and, after the applicant's rejection, the position remained open and the employer continued seeking applicants.

Second, if prima facie discrimination is proven, the employer must articulate a legitimate nondiscriminatory reason for rejecting the candidate, though the articulated reason need not be convincing to the judiciary to move to step three.[58] Third, if the employer articulates a legitimate reason for rejection, the applicant must prove by a preponderance of evidence that the employer's rationale is merely a pretext for intentional discrimination.

Returning again to race discrimination and promotion, for example, the court is likely to find disparate treatment where the employer's rationale for rejecting a black applicant includes projected inconvenience, annoyance, or extra expense.[59] The court might conclude that Title VII has been violated if: the employer's decision to promote a white supervisor is based on the belief that employees will feel uncomfortable working with a black supervisor, or just possibly more comfortable working for a white supervisor;[60] the standards for making promotion recommendations used by foremen are subjective;[61] the employer uses an employee's unlawful act as an intentional pretext to discriminate against a black worker when deciding promotions, employment discrimination bring conveniently blamed upon the victim by management;[62] or the employer's failure to promote the woman can be statistically regarded as disparate treatment, even though no disparate impact occurs.[63] The existence of disparate impact is not required in order for the court to determine the existence of disparate treatment.

---

[55] *Furnco Construction Company v. Waters*, 17 FEP 1062 (1978); *Wright v. National Archives and Records Service*, 21 FEP 8 (1979).

[56] *Keene State College v. Sweeney*, 18 FEP 520 (1978).

[57] *McDonnell-Douglas v. Green*, 5 FEP 965 (1973).

[58] *Texas Department of Community Affairs v. Burdine*, 25 FEP 113 (1981).

[59] *Griggs v. Duke Power Company*, 3 FEP Cases 175 (1971).

[60] *Haan v. Andrus*, 25 FEP 502 (1981).

[61] *Rowe v. General Motors Corp.*, 4 FEP Cases 445 (1972).

[62] *McDonnell-Douglas v. Green*, 5 FEP Cases 965 (1973).

[63] *Furnco Construction Company v. Waters*, 17 FEP Cases 1062 (1978).

AVOIDING LITIGATION AND/OR ARBITRATION

It is simplistic, but in general, litigation and/or arbitration is avoided by taking preventive action before employment discrimination occurs. Many employers and unions take advanced corrective action by following the Uniform Guidelines on Employee Selection Procedures,[64] voluntarily implementing affirmative action plans that give preference to minorities and women.[65] In *Steelworkers v. Weber*,[66] the Supreme Court agreed that an employer who found a conspicuous imbalance in the labor force could establish a plan containing goals and timetables for hiring, training, and promoting minorities and women, even though discrimination had not been proven. *Weber* provides some help to employers and unions about permissible affirmative action plans:

1. The affirmative action must be in connection with a "plan."
2. The plan must be remedial to open opportunities in occupations closed to protected classes under [Title VII]; and in order to make such a determination the parties are required to make self-analysis to determine whether and where conspicuous . . . imbalances exist.
3. The plan must be voluntary.
4. The plan must not unnecessarily trammel the interests of [the majority].
5. The plan must be temporary.[67]

Permissible affirmative action plans are usually helpful, but grievances arise whether or not affirmative action is voluntarily pursued. And when a grievance arises, litigation and arbitration are best avoided by setting proper investigation, documentation, and review processes in motion, determining the facts of the case, examining legal and arbitral decision making, and seeking to settle grievance by compromise or by convincing the party in the wrong to abandon an indefensible position.

A new set of difficulties emerge when the grievance process ends in arbitration. The courts have taken the position that the various laws, such as Title VII, the State Human Rights Law, or a Local Human Rights Ordinance for resolving civil rights disputes operate independently.[68] To be precise, in *Alexander v. Gardner-Denver Company*[69] the Supreme Court ruled that a grievant who lost a

---

[64] 29 CFR 1607 (1979); 401 FEP Manual 2231.

[65] Courts have approved affirmative action programs. See *U.S. v. Allegheny-Ludlow Industries*, 11 FEP 167 (1979). Courts have required hiring quotas to eliminate discriminatory conduct, see *Morrow v. Crisler*, 7 FEP 586 (1974). The EEOC will issue "consent decrees" to obtain pledges of affirmative action from employers and union violating Title VII.

[66] *Steelworkers v. Weber*, 20 FEP 1 (1979).

[67] David P. Twomey, *A Concise Guide to Employment Law: EEO & OSHA*. Cincinnati: South-Western Publishing Company, 1986, 62.

[68] *Cooper v. Philip Morris, Inc.*, 4 FEP 943 (1972); an adverse ruling before a local or state human rights board does not bar a subsequent Title VII action.

[69] *Alexander v. Gardner-Denver Company*, 7 FEP 81 (1974).

complaint pursued through the grievance arbitration process in a valid collective bargaining agreement was not barred from seeking remedy under Title VII. According to the Court, Title VII rights and collective bargaining rights are distinctly separate and must be pursued separately. Put another way, the grievant has a legal right to "two bites at the apple." Furthermore, a grievance arbitration proceeding does not "toll" the statute of limitation requirements under Title VII.[70]

Despite possible double jeopardy, discrimination complaints have been submitted in increasing numbers to labor arbitrators since *Gardner-Denver*.[71] An important explanation of this phenomenon hinges on the law itself. *Gardner-Denver* establishes that a court may give great weight to an arbitral decision provided the arbitrator gives full consideration to four fundamental relevant factors that should exist if the courts are to give an arbitral decision full consideration.[72] These four "relevant factors include the existence of provisions in the collective bargaining agreement that conform substantially with Title VII, the degree of procedural fairness in the arbitral forum, adequacy of the record with respect to the issue of discrimination, and the special competence of particular arbitrators." The challenge faced by the parties and labor arbitrators wishing to make the grievance process viable is how best to satisfy the requirements of Footnote 21 in *Gardner-Denver* while at the same time seeking to avoid an improper interpretation of the labor agreement.

SUMMARY

Whether labor arbitrators should decide discrimination complaints is probably academic. Over the years opponents have often argued that labor arbitrators are not qualified, that the possibility of judicial review of an award erodes the institution of arbitration, and that discrimination awards are biased against the grievant. Proponents point out that many labor arbitrators are qualified, that arbitration is sensitive to the parties' needs, and that arbitration has actually supported the judicial system, saving the parties both time and money, and that on balance he benefits of arbitrating discrimination cases outweigh the costs. Practically speaking, the task faced by the parties is how best to achieve the just requirements of *Gardner-Denver* when a discrimination complaint arises. For regardless of which position is taken, the fact remains that discrimination complaints have existed and been submitted in increasing numbers to labor arbitrators since the closing days of World War II.

---

[70] *Electrical Workers, Local 790 v. Robbins & Myers, Inc.*, 13 FEP 1813 (1976).
[71] Staff, *Labor Arbitration Reports, Cumulative Digest and Index*. Washington, D.C.: Bureau of National Affairs, Inc., Sections 106 and 107, all volumes.
[72] *Stozier v. General Motors Corp.*, 635 F2d 424 (1981).

Chapter 2

Blending Law and Arbitral Practice

Alexander v. Gardner-Denver makes it possible for a grievant with an employment discrimination complaint to lose the grievance under the collective bargaining process and still win the case under Title VII. This possibility exists because the Supreme Court decided that group-oriented collectively bargained rights should be pursued separately from individually oriented Title VII rights. But while the possibility of "two bites at the apple" cannot be avoided altogether, *Gardner-Denver* establishes that a court may give great weight to an arbitral decision provided the arbitrator gives full consideration to the employee's Title VII rights. And by giving full consideration to the grievant's Title VII rights during the grievance process, the parties stand a solid chance of avoiding a reversal of the arbitral decision.

MAKING *GARDNER-DENVER* FUNCTIONAL

In conformance with Footnote 21 in *Gardner-Denver*, discussed in Chapter 1, neutrals follow any one of three approaches when interpreting discrimination grievances. One approach is exemplified in *Basic Vegetable Products.*[1] Arbitrator Gould assumed the authority equal to that of federal judges under Title VII. Using broad powers, he considered all aspects of applicable law, reinstated the grievant with fifty percent back pay, and granted reasonable attorney fees. A major advantage of Arbitrator Gould's approach is that every aspect of the civil rights law is openly considered and determined, making it a simple task for courts to give great weight to the arbitrators award under the guise of Footnote 21 in *Gardner-Denver*. That is, by complying with and deciding civil rights law, Arbitrator Gould increased the likelihood of a binding award. The difficulty with

---

[1] *Basic Vegetable Products*, 75 ARB 8239 (Gould, 1975).

Arbitrator Gould's method is that the courts may overturn the arbitrator's award because the arbitral decision hinges on the law rather than the labor agreement.

It is generally conceded that the authority of an arbitrator stems from the collective bargaining contract, and courts should not question arbitrators authorized to interpret the agreement.[2] However, when the agreement does not provide guidance or when Title VII conflicts with the agreement, the authority of the arbitrator is less certain and the *Steelworkers Trilogy*[3] of 1960 and progeny provides only limited guidance. The *Gardner-Denver* decision by the Supreme Court provides a partial answer to this dilemma. The arbitrator is required, as called for in *Steelworkers*, to follow the terms of the agreement and not civil rights law. Thus, if there is conflict between the contract and Title VII, the arbitrator, according to the Supreme Court, must follow the agreement. But, where the contract is silent or the contract requires following the law, the arbitrator can, and perhaps must as Arbitrator Gould did, turn to Title VII.[4]

The second approach differs from Arbitrator Gould's only in that the arbitrator does not assume the same authority as a federal judge. Following this mode, Arbitrators Boals[5] and Koven[6] considered relevant law so that, if adjudication occurred, the courts could give their award great weight. But, after careful discussion of the law, Boals and Koven based their decisions squarely on interpretations of the collective bargaining agreement. This second approach has the advantage of signaling the court that the arbitrator has examined all law in accordance with Footnote 21, but keeps the award within the scope of traditional arbitral authority embodied in the labor contract.

The third general approach is followed by a vast majority of arbitrators. They do not openly mention, discuss, or consider civil rights law in the arbitration award. Instead, as bona fide experts have agreed for nearly two decades, most neutrals decide discrimination cases by employing a multiplicity of traditional arbitral decision rules on a situation-by-situation basis.[7] In *South Bend Tool & Die Company*,[8] for example, the employer was justified in discharging a black janitor who had a record of unsatisfactory performance. Arbitrator Traynor did not mention civil rights law when he concluded that the grievant had not been

---

[2] *Milwaukee Area Technical College*, 40 AIS 8 (1973).

[3] *Steelworkers v. Warrior & Gulf Navigation Company*, 363 U.S. 574 (1960); *Steelworkers v. Enterprise Wheel & Car Corporation*, 363 U.S. 593 (1960); and *Steelworkers v. American Manufacturing Company*, 363 U.S. 564 (1960).

[4] *Bowen v. U.S. Postal Service*, 459 US 212 (1983) and *Hines v. Anchor Motor Truck*, 424 U.S. 554 (1976).

[5] *Southern Gage Company*, 68 LA 7555 (Boals, 1977).

[6] *County of Santa Clara*, 71 LA 290 (Koven, 1978).

[7] Marlin M. Volz and Edward P. Goggin (eds.). *How Arbitration Works, Fourth Edition 1985-87 Supplement*. Washington, D.C.: Bureau of National Affairs, Inc., 1988; Harry T. Edwards, "Arbitration as an Alternative in Equal Employment Disputes," *The Arbitration Journal*, Vol. 33, No. 4, December 1978, pp. 23-27; and Morris Stone and Earl R. Baderschneider (eds.). *Arbitrating of Discrimination Grievances: A Case Book*. New York: American Arbitration Association, 1974.

[8] *South Bend Tool & Die Company*, 68 LA 536 (Traynor, 1977).

discriminated against; that the grievant's work record justified discharge, regardless of race; and that the grievant had been warned of the consequences of his conduct. The advantage of this third approach is that the arbitrator's decision falls clearly within the bounds of the labor agreement. The disadvantage is that the court may not afford the arbitrator's decision great weight because, at first glance, very little objective evidence exists in the arbitral award to show that the criteria of Footnote 21 have been satisfied.

KEEPING AWARDS IN TENSION WITH THE LAW

Assessing the desirability of arbitrating discrimination grievances gives rise to two key questions which must be answered in the affirmative each time a discrimination grievance is arbitrated. Question one asks, was the result of the award, standing alone, in compliance with the civil rights law existing at the time the award was rendered?[9] Question two, does the arbitrator's award satisfy the requirements of Footnote 21 in *Gardner-Denver*? A carefully controlled scientific examination by a panel of experts sought to answer these two fundamental questions on the bases of published arbitration awards, the experts evaluating thirty-seven randomly selected arbitration awards containing discrimination disputes. The panel of experts found that the three approaches followed by arbitrators, such as Gould, Boals, Koven, and Traynor, almost always resulted in an arbitration award that was in proper tension with civil rights law.

Compliance with Civil Rights Law

Looking at the first question, the expert review panel unanimously agreed, felt certain, that the result of the award was in compliance with the law in twenty-seven of the cases (nearly 73 percent) regardless of which of the three general approaches was chosen by the arbitrator for handling discrimination grievances.

The panel of experts also agreed unanimously, but with less certainty, that the result of the remaining ten awards (27 percent) was in compliance with the civil rights law. The panel's uncertainty in this group of cases stemmed from the law itself, not the arbitrator's award. Like much of the legal process, civil rights law has been evolutionary and had not yet been determined by either the courts or the legislature when arbitrators rendered their awards in eight of the cases. To be specific, the law was not clear regarding unique questions associated with handicapped workers,[10] affirmative action plans and implementation of affirma-

---

[9] Vern E. Hauck, "The Efficacy of Arbitrating Discrimination Complaints," *Labor Law Journal*, Vol. 35, No. 3, March 1984, 175.

[10] *Masonite Corporation*, 62 LA 558 (1974).

tive action plans,[11] the Fair Labor Standards Act,[12] burden of proof,[13] racial harassment,[14] maternity leave,[15] and instances of possible or actual lead poisoning to an unborn fetus.[16]

In two instances the panel felt the merits contained in the grievance confronted the arbitrator with the necessity to decide issues that could arguably be at odds with the law. The panel agreed that the arbitrator-in-point had more likely than not decided correctly in both cases. It has been a long-standing rule, dating to *Duke Power*, that unqualified workers needn't be hired, promoted, or retained. And, both cases concerned the promotion of black employees into jobs for which they were unqualified, making the result of the two arbitration awards correct even though the employer may have violated some portion of existing civil rights law. For example, in *Joy Manufacturing Company*[17] the arbitrator agreed with the employer's judgment that the grievant was unqualified for promotion. The expert review panel noted that one of the employer's multiple decision criteria was potentially illegal. The qualifying test given the grievant was not clearly shown to be job relevant. And, in *Georgia Power Company*,[18] a court may have concluded that Title VII was violated since the foreman making the judgment against promotion gave direct testimony validating his own subjective bias against blacks. Similar to *Joy Manufacturing Company*, however, *Georgia Power Company* remained on somewhat safe ground since the foreman's judgment was only one of several criteria relied upon when management decided to deny promotion to the black worker. Had the decision been based upon the foreman's judgment alone, the arbitrator may have decided for the Union.

Compliance with *Gardner-Denver*

Turning to the second question, the panel's in-depth analysis validates that almost all arbitration awards comply with the four relevant factors in *Gard-*

---

[11] *State of Ohio, Department of Human Services*, 96 LA 673 (Fullmer, 1991); *City of Pontiac*, 93 LA 1067 and 94 LA 14 (Daniel, 1989); *Reynolds Electrical and Engineering Company, Inc.*, 89-1 ARB 8025 (Morris, 1988); *District of Columbia, Department of Finance and Revenue*, 91 LA 1 (Hockenberry, 1988); and *City of Detroit*, 79-2 ARB 8597 (1979).

[12] *Evans Products Company*, 70 LA 526 (1978).

[13] *Jacksonville Shipyards, Inc.*, 68 LA 1091 (1977).

[14] *U.S. Steel Corporation*, 70 LA 146 (1977).

[15] *Bristol Borough School District*, 70 LA 143 (1978); the law was clarified by P.L. 95-555, The Pregnancy Disability Amendment to Title VII.

[16] *Olin Corporation*, 79-2 ARB 8460 (1979); the law was subsequently clarified by *Wright v. Olin Corporation*, 30 FEP 889 (1982) and *Zuniga v, Kleberg County Hospital*, 30 FEP 650 (1982).

[17] *Joy Manufacturing Company*, 70 LA 4 (1977); for clarification see *Griggs v. Duke Power Company*, 401 US 424 (1971).

[18] *Georgia Power Company*, 75 LA 181 (1980); for clarification see *Rowe v. General Motors Corporation*, 457 F2d 348 (1972).

ner-Denver's Footnote 21. First, the majority of awards reviewed included references to antidiscrimination provisions in the applicable labor contract. Second, though shaky, the evidence in the awards suggests the existence of a more than adequate degree of procedural fairness. Indeed, procedural adequacy may prove to be of secondary concern since justice under civil rights law is a normal by-product of arbitral conclusions. Third, discrimination was discussed in every award reviewed, usually in the parties' positions and less frequently in the arbitrator's opinion. Finally, the results of an overwhelming majority of the awards reviewed in the study were judged in compliance with Title VII, documenting the competence of particular arbitrators to determine discrimination questions. It is interesting to note, however, that the law has changed with time and several of the arbitration awards judged in compliance would violate today's civil rights law.

HOW DISCRIMINATION GRIEVANCES DIFFER

The general theory of labor contract interpretation has been reviewed and analyzed in exhaustive detail since at least the end of World War II, an endeavor that continues because the field of labor arbitration must adjust with the changing needs of the parties.[19] Probably the best-known arbitral decision making studies suggest that arbitrators reach their awards by combining a multiplicity of decision rules that have evolved from the law. These legal decision rules predict, among other things, that arbitrators will follow specific rather than general contact language, that arbitrators will give meaning to the intent of the parties who negotiated the agreement, and that arbitrators will make their decisions on the basis of the issue, the contract, and the record.

Other research ties the legal decision rules to decision models that are activated by composites of cues.[20] One such model by Gullett and Goff argues that arbitrators have built a body of widely held belief systems which shape decision making in individual cases.[21] Gullett and Goff formulate a Bayesian type flow chart (yes-no) decision model using fifteen decision rules common to arbitration. Their model depicts that arbitrators formulate judgments on the basis of contract

[19] Jean T. McKelvey (ed.), "The Profession of Labor Arbitration" in papers from the *First Seven Annual Meetings of the National Academy of Arbitrators.* Washington, D.C.: The Bureau of National Affairs, Inc., 1957; Arnold M. Zack and Richard I. Bloch, *Labor Agreement in Negotiation and Arbitration.* Washington, D.C.: The Bureau of National Affairs, Inc., 1983; Marvin F. Hill, Jr., and Anthony V. Sinicropi, *Evidence in Arbitration.* Washington, D.C.: The Bureau of National Affairs, Inc., 1986; Robert J. Thornton, and Perry A. Zirkel, "The Consistency and Predictability of Grievance Arbitration Awards," *Industrial and Labor Relations Review,* Vol. 43, January 1990, 294-307.
[20] Paul Prasow and Edward Peters *Arbitration and Collective Bargaining: Conflict Resolution in Labor Relation,* 2nd ed. New York: McGraw-Hill, 1983.
[21] C. R. Gullett and W. H. Goff, "The Arbitral Decision-Making Process: A Computerized Simulation," *Personnel Journal,* Vol. 59, No. 8, 1980, 663-667.

language, past practice, precontract negotiations, past arbitral rulings, and the common law of arbitration. And by answering yes or no the user of the Gullet and Goff flow chart is led to an arbitral conclusion.

A number of other studies illuminate a variety of aspects of arbitral decision making. For instance, Drews and Blanchard[22] subjected 120 arbitration awards to factor analysis and identified five clusters of grievances that arbitrators normally face: central issues, job assignments and promotions, union rights and activities, supervision and working conditions, and coercion. Bass[23] reports a study of demographic characteristics of 146 arbitrators judged by their peers as effective decision makers. Edwards[24] and Coulson[25] researched the experience of arbitrators with discrimination cases, outlining decision-making difficulties and proper procedures. Oppenheimer and LaVan[26] focused on case outputs by a group of arbitrators. They noted that Unions are frequently more likely to a public sector grievance when discrimination is judged by an arbitrator.

Cain and Stahl[27] probed beyond the surface of legal reasoning and found that all arbitrators are probably quite consistent in the application of their respective decision policies. Cain and Stahl found that arbitrators decide most grievances on the basis of seven cues: management rights and efficiency, clear language of the contract, past practice, fairness, effect on the worker, negotiating history, and prior awards. When subjected to statistical analysis, these seven cues combine into a three-cue model showing that arbitrators are actually guided, in order of priority, by considerations for:

1. Management Rights
2. Equity = Fairness + Effect on Worker
3. Stability = Contract Language + Past Practice + Negotiating History + Prior Awards

The theory of labor arbitration in employment discrimination intertwines with and parallels the general theory of labor contract interpretation suggested by Gullett and Goff or Cain and Stahl. That is, arbitrators have changed emphasis and modified the general theory of labor contract interpretation in order to meet the needs of parties facing discrimination complaints. Figure 2.1 illustrates this juxtaposition. While the general theory of labor contract interpretation remains dominant, both theories emerge from the same, or nearly the same, social, politi-

---

[22] D. W. Drews and R. E. Blanchard, "A Factorial Study of Labor Arbitration Cases," *Personnel Psychology*, Vol. 12, 1959, 303-310.

[23] Bernard Bass, *Organization Psychology*. Boston: Allyn and Bacon, 1965.

[24] Harry T. Edwards, "Arbitration of Employment Discrimination Cases: An Empirical Study" in *Proceedings of the 28th Annual Meeting of the National Academy of Arbitrators*. Washington, D.C.: The Bureau of National Affairs, Inc., 1976, 59-92.

[25] Robert Coulson, "Title Seven Arbitration in Action," *Labor Law Journal*, Vol. 27, No. 3, 1976, 141-151.

[26] Margaret Oppenheimer and Helen LaVan, "Arbitration Awards in Discrimination Disputes: An Empirical Analysis," *The Arbitration Journal*, Vol. 34, No. 1, 1979.

[27] Joseph P. Cain and Michael J. Stahl, "Modeling the Policies of Several Labor Arbitrators," *Academy of Management Journal*, Vol. 26, No. 1, 1983, pp. 140-147.

cal, economic, and legal foundations. For example, the Commercial Arbitration Code, the Norris-LaGuardia Act, the Wagner Act, the Taft-Hartley Act, the Landrum-Griffin Act, the Civil Rights Act of 1964, the *Steelworkers Trilogy* of 1960, and *Gardner-Denver* can be located in the foundation of either theory.

Continuing with Figure 2.1, judicial interpretation of civil rights legislation has mandated that labor arbitrators revise long-standing arbitral hearing processes as a prerequisite to opening the employment discrimination hearing, a matter detailed in Chapter 3. Once the hearing is underway or when the record is closed, the arbitrator must combine the labor contract with legal precedent applicable to employment discrimination complaints. The last portion of Figure 2.1 models the existence of a unique body of arbitral decision policy that consistently governs employment discrimination awards.

ARBITRAL DECISION RULES

Very few arbitral decisions turn upon the application of one or two long standing decision rules. The contract and the needs of the parties are unique, even fluid at times, requiring arbitrators to tailor their decisions to the individual requirements called for by the law of the shop and each labor agreement. Indeed, it is difficult to find general agreement among arbitrators that any standard body of arbitral decision rules exists at all. Instead, arbitrators make their decisions by combining a multiplicity of evolving decision criteria. But, which evolving decision rules are used for deciding sex discrimination grievances? And, how are these evolving rules frequently combined by arbitrators as they decide and write their gender discrimination awards?

The myriad of evolving decision criteria being written about and available complicates the problem of identifying which sets of these evolving principles are actually used by arbitrators in discrimination grievances.[28] To simplify this identification problem, thirty legal decision rules commonly used by arbitrators during the past five decades, as shown in Table 2.1, were selected and used by a panel of experts who conducted a detailed structural analysis of published discrimination awards.

Individual Decision Rules

Thirteen of the thirty evolving rules selected for analysis were found in more than 48 percent of the discrimination cases reviewed. Two rules, intent of the parties and burden of proof, were present in every case, though often at an ob-

---

[28] Frank Elkouri and Edna A. Elkouri, *How Arbitration Works*, 3rd ed. Washington, D.C.: The Bureau of National Affairs, Inc., 1973; Paul Prasow and Edward Peters, *Arbitration and Collective Bargaining*. New York: McGraw-Hill, 1970; and Ray J. Schoonhoven (ed.), *Fairweather's Practice and Procedure in Labor Arbitration*, 3rd ed. Washington, D.C.: BNA Books, Inc., 1991.

scure level. Thus in every discrimination award under study the arbitrator determined the mutual intent of the parties by examining the terms of the labor contract and deciding between the parties' opposing interpretations of disputed language.[29] Decision rules are virtually always combined by labor arbitrators.

Figure 2.1
Stages in Employment Discrimination Arbitration Process

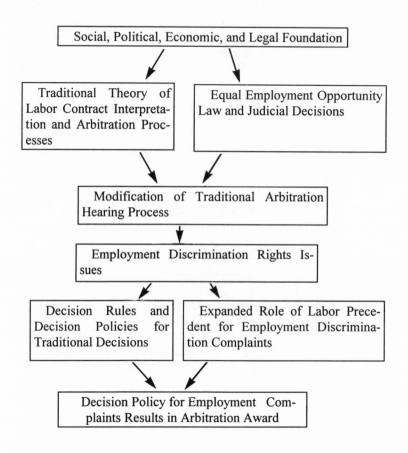

---

[29] *Metropolitan District Commission*, 64 LA 1988 (1975); *Continental Telephone Company*, 68 LA 882 (1977).

Table 2.1

Evolving Arbitral Decision Rules Found in Discrimination Awards

Cluster No.	Decision Rule	Percentage of Use Frequent	Seldom
1	Company Manuals and Handbooks		13.5
	Doctrine of Implied Obligations		13.5
	Major-Minor Test		8.1
	Parol Evidence Rule		2.7
2	Language Is Clear and Unambiguous	59.5	
	Industry Practice	48.6	
	Prior Settlements as an Aid to Interpretation	75.7	
	Precontract Negotiations		10.8
3	Interpretation in Light of the Law	73.0	
	Specific v. General Contract Language	89.2	
	Normal & Technical Usage		16.2
	Doctrine of *Ejusdem Generis*		8.1
	Reason and Equity		21.6
4	Construction in Light of Context	67.6	
	Custom and Practice of Parties	70.3	
	Arbiter Refuses to Substitute His Judgment for Mgmt's.	64.9	
	Reasonable and Prudent	86.5	
5	Issue, Contract, and Record	78.4	
	Awarding Back Pay Needs More Justification		10.8
	No Consideration to Compromise Offers	8.1	
6	Agreement to Be Construed as a Whole	56.8	
	Avoidance of Harsh, Absurd, or Nonsensical Results		10.8
	To Express One Thing Is to Exclude Another		8.1
	Promissory Estoppel Doctrine		8.1

Continued Cluster No.	Decision Rule	Percentage of Use Frequent	Seldom
Non-clustering Decision Rules			
	Intent of the Parties	100.0	
	Burden of Proof	100.0	
	Avoidance of a Forfeiture		2.7
	Experience and Training of Negotiators		2.7
	Interpretation Against Party Seeking Language		10.8
	Past Practice Cannot Be Nullified by Sweeping General Provisions		100.0

Note: Knuder-Richardson twenty cluster reliability's ranged from .36 to .79 with a mean of .58; Rate/Re-rate reliability's ranged from .69 to .97 with a mean of .87.

In almost 90 percent of the discrimination cases reviewed, arbitrators employed the decision rule that specific contract language governs over general contract language.[30] For example, one arbitrator following specific contract language could not find sex discrimination where an employee's attitude made her unqualified for promotion and a memorandum of agreement did not require the employer to select the most senior employee for a supervisory position.[31] A closely associated rule was identified in 60 percent of the cases, arbitrators basing their awards upon language that is clear and unambiguous.[32] The heavy use by arbitrators of these two rules may be due to their desire to remain safely within the bounds of the contract, avoiding extra-contractual decisions, and their authority as specified by the law in *Steelworker's Trilogy* and progeny.

Seventy-eight percent of the arbitrators based their discrimination grievance decision solely on the issue, the contract, and the record; and arbitrators made their civil rights interpretations in light of the law in 73 percent of the cases. While both of these rules appeared simultaneously in 45 percent of the cases, one or the other usually dominated in the arbitrator's written opinion. *Bristol Borough School District*[33] was an exception. Arbitrator Belsky denied maternity sick leave because the denial was in line with applicable interpretations of Title VII (in 1978) and did not conflict with the collective bargaining agreement.

Title VII outlaws discrimination against an individual because of race, color, religion, sex, or national origin, except when justified by *business necessity*.[34] Despite its importance, employers were seldom judged in light of the business

---

[30] *ITT Continental Baking Company*, 72 LA 1234 (1979); *Brown County Mental Health Center*, 68 LA 1363 (1977).
[31] *Stayton Canning Company*, 75 LA 2 (1980).
[32] *Ibid.*
[33] *Bristol Borough School District*, 70 LA 143 (1978).
[34] *Teamsters v. U.S.*, 431 US 324 (1977); *American Tobacco Company v. Patterson*, 102 S Ct 1534 (1982), a seniority clause is illegal only when intentional discrimination is proved.

necessity exemption concept.[35] However, 86 percent of the time arbitrators did look to see if management's action was reasonable and prudent, a decision rule sometimes connected with business necessity. In *Olin Corporation*,[36] for example, Arbitrator Knudson found that the employer reasonably disqualified females of childbearing age from some jobs since even the Occupational Safety and Health Administration (OSHA) admitted that removal of pregnant employees from lead exposure is advisable. That is, Arbitrator Knudson's award adopted the advice given by OSHA at the time (1980) when he ruled it a necessity to disqualify most women from jobs involving exposure to lead poisoning because of potential injury to an unconceived fetus. Arbitrator Knudson's decision also included another rule appearing in 65 percent of the awards; he refused to substitute his judgment for management's judgment.[37]

Several detailed readings of each case indicate that parol evidence frequently plays a difficult-to-detect part in determining discrimination grievances. Under this rule, all previous oral understandings are contained in the collective bargaining contract and cannot be presented to modify or change the written agreement.[38] The rule does not preclude parol evidence that explains an ambiguity or establishes the interpretation of contractual terms having a particular trade meaning.[39] Arbitrators presented with admissible parol evidence in discrimination grievances frequently turned to one of five evolving concepts to clarify the contract: prior settlements as an aid to interpretation[40] (76 percent), the custom and practice of the parties[41] (70 percent), industry practice[42] (49 percent), construction in light of context[43] (68 percent) and agreement to be construed as a whole (57 percent).

Decision Rule Combinations

Returning to Table 2.1, most arbitrators agree that the legal decision rulesare normally applied in combination. Arbitrators use groups, or clusters, of legal decision rules to evaluate information and make judgments about discrimination

---

[35] Two clear exceptions are *Georgia Power Company*, 75 LA 181 (1980); and *ITT Continental Baking Company*, 72 LA 1234 (1979).

[36] *Olin Corporation*, 79-2 ARB 8460 (Knudson, 1979).

[37] *South Bend Tool & Die Company, Inc.*, 68 LA 536 (1977).

[38] Henry C. Black, *Black's Law Dictionary*, 5th ed. St. Paul, Minn.: West Publishing Company, 1979, 1006.

[39] *Brigham Apparel Corporation*, 52 LA 430 (1969).

[40] *Olin Corporation*, 79-2 ARB 8460 (1979); *International Paper Company*, 77-2 ARB 8564 (1977); and *Hurley Hospital*, 78-1 ARB 8266 (1979).

[41] *Reynolds Metals Company* 74 LA 1121 (1980); *Air California*, 67 LA 1115 (1976); and *Colt Industries*, 71 LA 22 (1978).

[42] *American Airlines*, 77-1 ARB 8167 (1977).

[43] *Continental Telephone Company*, 68 LA 882 (1977); *California Sample Service Company, Inc.*, 70 LA 338 (1978); and *Weyerhaeuser Company*, 70 LA 1 123 (1978).

complaints. That is, when faced with similar civil rights grievances and problems, labor arbitrators consistently applied similar groups of evolving decision
rules or emerging standards to resolve employment conflicts. Statistical analysis
of the thirty legal decision rules in Table 2.1 provided six groups, or clusters, of
legal decision rules that arbitrators regularly combine, depending upon the issue
at hand, to reach their determinations in discrimination grievances.[44] The six
combinations of legal decisions rules that operate together and frequently
emerged are:

Combination One: Management's action is weighed in terms of
                        equity to the worker and the language of the
                        contract. Employee benefits are commonly
                        assigned on the basis of the decision rules
                        grouped in this combination when the contract
                        is silent (see Table 2.1, Cluster No. 1).

Combination Two: Management's action is examined on the basis
                        of reasonableness and conformity with the
                        parties' past practices. Decision rules in
                        this combination are often used to interpret
                        parol evidence (see Table 2.1, Cluster No. 2).

Combination Three: Management's action is examined on the basis
                        of reasonableness and conformity with the
                        contract and the law. Decision rules in this
                        combination often focus on the rendering of
                        awards that do not give an unfair advantage to
                        one party (see Table 2.1, Cluster No. 3).

Combination Four: The arbitral award is justified in terms of
                        the language of the contract, the impact on
                        the parties, and the parties' past arbitral
                        awards. Decision rules in this combination are
                        often used to interpret the law of the shop (see
                        Table 2.1, Cluster No. 4).

Combination Five: The arbitral award is justified in terms of
                        the language of the contract and the equity to
                        the parties. Decision rules in this combination
                        commonly emphasize the assignment of the burden
                        of proof and the elimination of immaterial and
                        irrelevant evidence (see Table 2.1, Cluster No. 5).

---

[44] Benjamin Fruchter, *Introduction to Factor Analysis.* New York: D. Van Norsstrand
Company, 1954. The thirty rules were placed in an intercorrelation matrix and subjected
to multiple cluster analysis using the Tyron-B coefficient procedure. Kuder-Richardson
20 cluster reliability's ranged from .36 to .79 with a mean of .58; rate/rerate reliability's
ranged from .69 to .97 with a mean of exactly .87 and a median of .885.

Combination Six: The arbitral award is justified in terms of
the parties' negotiating history and equity to
the grievant. Decision rules in this combination
focus on the four corners of the labor
agreement (see Table 2.1, Cluster No. 6).

The individual decision rule data in Table 2.1 suggest that decision rule combination number four is the most popular, followed closely by decision rule combinations number two and three. Decision rule combination one was rarely identified as being used by arbitrators as a basis for deciding civil rights grievances, possibly because arbitral discussion of the parol evidence rule was obscure.

Logic suggests that the unique body of decision policy governing arbitral decision making in discrimination cases has much in common with the arbitral decision policy found in traditional arbitration awards. To test this logic, the thirty legal decision rules listed in Table 2.1 were statistically compared to see if any of the seven cues proposed by Cain and Stahl could be found in discrimination awards.[45] Eight cues were found, one more than Cain and Stahl identified: management rights, reasonableness, clear language of the contract, past practice, fairness, effect on the worker, negotiating history, and the law. The law is the eighth cue not found by Cain and Stahl.

The actual decision policies followed by labor arbitrators for deciding discrimination complaints were determined and verified by subjecting the eight cues to higher order statistical analysis. While three cues were prioritized in Cain and Stahl's study of tradition arbitral decision policy, two cues emerged dominant for discrimination cases. The two cue model indicates that arbitrators prioritize and are consistently guided in discrimination cases by considerations for:

1. Equity = Management Rights + Fairness + Negotiating History;
2. Management Rights = Reasonableness + Effect on the Worker +
                              Contract Language + Past Practice + the Law.

Beneath the surface, management rights is a significant connecting link for arbitrators confronted with discrimination grievances. But, stability is not a significant policy-setting force among arbitrators deciding discrimination grievances. Instead, the needs of the parties for rapid settlement of discrimination complaints are being served by an arbitral decision policy that consistently emphasizes equity as the number one priority, equity ranking more significant statistically than any other consideration. This dominant concern for equity can be traced through both the higher order statistical analysis similar to that followed by Cain and Stahl and the cluster analysis evolving from Table 2.1. Clearly, the

---

[45] Vern E. Hauck and John C. South, "Arbitrating Discrimination Grievances: An Empirical Model for Decision Standards," *Policy Studies Journal*, Vol. 16, No. 3, Spring 1988, p. 511.

arbitrator's dominant concern for equity in human rights grievances stems from the law, sensitivity to the existence of employment discrimination at places of work, and the parties' preference for fair play. Notwithstanding, the application of historically familiar arbitral decision making criteria to civil rights grievances is a fact of life.

SUMMARY

Statistical support exists for the contention that labor arbitrators reach conclusions about discrimination complaints based largely on interpretative decision rules traditionally used to decide questions such as seniority, discharge, and promotion. The cases analyzed in this chapter indicate that some evolving arbitral decision rules are applied more often than others but that arbitrators do not have a single predictable rule or set of rules which can be followed to decide discrimination grievances. The intent of the parties, burden of proof, specific versus general contract language, reasonable and prudent, and interpretation in light of the law were among the evolving contract interpretations rules most frequently mentioned by arbitrators to justify their discrimination awards. Among other things, the present findings indicate that discrimination grievances will typically involve the labor arbitrator with considerable ambiguity, parole evidence, and the interpretation of contract terms rather than civil rights law. Concern for the wisdom of arbitrators deciding discrimination grievances pales beside the cases examined in this chapter. Almost all arbitration awards comply with the four relevant facts in *Gardner-Denver's* Footnote 21. First, the majority of awards reviewed included references to antidiscrimination provisions in the applicable labor contract. Second, though shaky, the evidence in the awards suggests the existence of a more than adequate degree of procedural fairness. Indeed, procedural adequacy may prove to be of secondary concern since justice under civil rights law is a normal by-product of arbitral conclusions. Third, discrimination was discussed in every award reviewed, usually in the parties' positions and less frequently in the arbitrator's opinion. Finally, the results of an overwhelming majority of awards reviewed are in compliance with Title VII, documenting the competence of particular arbitrators to determine discrimination questions.

Chapter 3

Procedure, Evidence, and Proof

Arbitration has proven most useful to the parties when hearing procedures are legalistic but informal, evidence is provided in a structured but informal manner, and the burden of proof is correctly enforced in an informal way. That is, the arbitral forum has proven itself to be less meaningful and less useful to the grievant and the parties whenever the process starts looking too much like a courtroom. Similarly, the grievant and the parties seem to prefer that discrimination grievances be handled in a manner that can be characterized as rigorous but informal. Take care, there are key procedural, evidentiary, and proof allocations which must be observed in discrimination grievances in order to satisfy the requirements of *Gardner-Denver's* Footnote 21.

THE CONDUCT OF THE PARTIES

The professional responsibility of the advocates in arbitration has been a topic of discussion before the National Academy of Arbitrators (Academy) for many years. And from time to time, there have been formal attempts to establish written guidelines for the advocates. In 1951, for example, the Academy, the American Arbitration Association (AAA) and the Federal Mediation and Conciliation Service (FMCS) adopted the *Code of Ethics and Procedural Standards for Labor-Management Arbitration.*[1] Part III of the 1951 Code devoted itself to the *Conduct and Behavior of [the] Parties.* But in 1974 the Joint Steering Committee with representatives from the Academy, the AAA, and the FMCS elected to drop Part III of the 1951 *Code of Ethics and Procedural Standards for Labor-Management Arbitration* because Part III had served its purpose and was no longer helpful to the parties or to the arbitrator.

---

[1] *Code of Ethics and Procedural Standards,* 15 LA 961.

In his 1985 address to the Academy, George H. Cohen looked back at Part III of the 1951 Code and concluded that

the 1974 decision of the Joint Steering Committee was prompted, in part, by the experiences of Messrs. Garrett and Seward – and their fellow Academy members, as well – during the 25-year post-Code period when the arbitration of labor-management disputes increasingly became a fact of life. Insofar as the Code of Conduct for the Unethical Behavior of Parties is concerned, the Committee undoubtedly subscribed to the Will Rogers school of homespun philosophy: If it ain't broke, don't fix it. Finally, I am likewise confident that the Committee recognized that perhaps a more effective alternative existed if it were lawyers whose conduct had to be policed. An attorney's conduct is subject to scrutiny by the bar associations of the states in which he or she is admitted. Various forms of discipline can be imposed from suspension to disbarment.[2]

As Mr. Cohen noted, the precise problem foreseen by the 1951 Code drafters came true. Enforcement of Part III turned out to be impractical. That is, Part III of the 1951 Code was dropped, and has never been readopted, because the parties' conduct did not need correcting and because the 1951 Code could not be enforced at the arbitral forum.[3] The arbitrator could, of course, have elected to enforce the Code by withdrawing from the hearing or penalizing (finding against) one of the parties for acrimonious, bitter, or ill-mannered conduct. However, such approaches to enforcement are fraught with difficulties, particularly if the arbitral penalty were to be leveled against an otherwise deserving grievant.

Rule 3 of the Model Rules of Professional Conduct of the American Bar Association[4] was last amended on February 12, 1990, and is the model for advocacy conduct urged by the American Bar Association (ABA). While ABA model rules are advisory only and individual jurisdictions operate independently, virtually all jurisdictions have adopted a standard for professional advocacy conduct that is the same as the ABA model or is at least in keeping with the ABA model. And in each instance, applying the bar association code of conduct to arbitration will contribute toward the attainment of an adequate record and a degree of procedural fairness in keeping with Footnote 21 in *Gardner-Denver*. Furthermore, lawyers who fail to comply with the applicable code of professional conduct are subject to discipline at the hands of their local jurisdiction, frequently the state bar, up to and including suspension or debarment.

In his paper titled "The Case for Establishment of Formal Standards," George J. Zazas summarized the important features of the ABA model code:

---

[2] George H. Cohen, "The Professional Responsibility of the Advocates, Part II," *Proceedings of the Thirty-Eighth Annual Meeting National Academy of Arbitrators*. Walter J. Gershenfeld, ed. Washington, D.C.: BNA Books, Inc., 1986, 109.

[3] Jean T. McKelvey, ed., "The Profession of Labor Arbitration," *Selected Papers From the First Seven Meetings, National Academy of Arbitrators, 1948-1954*. Washington, D.C.: BNA Books, Inc., 1957, 147.

[4] *American Bar Association Model Rules for Professional Conduct* (1995). See Especially ABA Model Rules 3.1 through 3.9.

[a]dvocates are admonished not to maintain cases or assert defenses known to be without merit. They should strive to expedite and not delay the proceeding. The tribunal should be treated with candor. Facts and law should not be misstated nor should evidence, oral or documentary, be offered which is known to be false. The opposition is to be treated fairly. Its access to evidence should not be obstructed nor should evidence be altered, destroyed or falsified. The impartiality of the tribunal must be respected. Advocates should not seek to influence the tribunal in any improper way and should avoid ex parte communications. Disruptive conduct is to be avoided. These are the salutary principles and are as applicable to arbitration as they are to judicial proceedings. To them should be added at least two other subjects which have special application to labor arbitration.

The first of these is the responsibility of the advocate in arbitration to the underlying collective bargaining relationship of the parties. . . . Second is the question of the advocate's obligation to avoid participation in a breach of the duty of fair representation by the union.[5]

Every examination of proper advocacy conduct leads to the unavoidable conclusion that arbitration, much less arbitration involving discrimination, cannot work unless the parties approach the process with integrity, candor, and respect.[6] Over one thousand awards were reviewed in the preparation of this book, only one award contained any evidence of improper conduct by the parties. In *Department of Veterans Affairs*,[7] Arbitrator W. Crozier Gowarn, Jr., chastised a union representative in writing for engaging in ex parte communications after the hearing and for submitting an unauthorized post-hearing brief.

THE RESPONSIBILITY OF THE PARTIES

The success of arbitration is due in some measure to its flexibility and relatively narrow focus upon the needs of the parties and their contractual relationship. One difficulty, however, which emerges as soon as arbitration is utilized in discrimination grievances is the need of the parties to enforce the legal rights of the grievant, an undertaking that goes beyond collective bargaining claims that evolve around a breach of contract. Title VII complaints involve a potential breach of law and the Supreme Court expressed its concern for the viability of the arbitration process for the resolution of statutory issues. In *Gardner-Denver* the Court observed that

the fact-finding process in arbitration usually is not equivalent to judicial fact-finding. The record of the arbitration proceedings is not as complete; the usual rules of evidence

---

[5] George J. Zazas, "The Case for Establishment of Formal Standards," *Proceedings of the Thirty-Eighth Annual Meeting National Academy of Arbitrators*. Washington, D.C.: BNA Books, Inc., 1986, 111.

[6] *Department of Veterans Affairs, Medical Center, Denver*, 94 FLRR 2-1062 (Wollett, 1993).

[7] *Department of Veterans Affairs*, LAIRS 21072 (Gowan, 1992).

do not apply; and rights and procedures common to civil trials, such as discovery, compulsory process, cross-examination, and testimony under oath, are often severely limited or unavailable.

When the parties elect to undertake the arbitration of a discrimination grievance, it is their responsibility to engage in a fact-finding process that seeks to limit and overcome the usual shortcomings of arbitration cited by the High Court. The benefits of a thorough investigation of all discrimination complaints were documented in *Brin Northwestern Glass Company*, 1994.[8] Arbitrator Mary Beth Koehler dismissed the union's racial discrimination claim because the employer had investigated the discrimination complaint in a timely and thorough manner, found no evidence of race discrimination, and because the grievant had worked two more years following the discrimination complaint before being discharged for excessive tardiness.

At about the same time the Supreme Court issued *Gardner-Denver* in 1974 some pioneering parties, such as the International Woodworkers of America, Local 515 and Weyerhaeuser Company, began adopting special procedures for the handling of employment discrimination disputes.[9] In 1976 Harry T. Edwards set forth a model arbitration procedure to deal with employment discrimination cases.[10] Today after thirty years of experience with arbitrating discrimination grievances, the utility of much of the pioneering efforts and Edwards' far-reaching vision is apparent. To be specific, the multitude of cases reviewed in this book document the practical nature of a significant portion of the work of these early pioneers. Most employers and unions have elected not to adopt any special procedures for the handling of gender discrimination disputes, opting instead to handle sex discrimination as well as other forms of employment discrimination grievances within the normal grievance framework of the parties' labor contract. Nevertheless, much of what Edwards tendered in his proposed model is what has, over time, taken place. Said Edwards:

> The first question that must be considered in devising an arbitration procedure to deal with employment discrimination cases has to do with the type of cases that should be arbitrated. The Supreme Court in *Gardner-Denver* stated that "the policy against discriminatory employment practices can be best accommodated by permitting an employee to pursue fully both his remedy under the grievance-arbitration clause of a collective bargaining agreement and his cause of action under Title VII." Implicit in this statement is the suggestion that arbitration of employment discrimination cases should never be discouraged. However, this is a naive view.

---

[8] *Brin Northwestern Glass Company*, BMS 9501.33 (Koehler, 1994). See also *Georgia Pacific Company*, 100 LA 622 (Singer, 1993), and *Department of Natural Resources, State of Minnesota*, LAIG 4780 (Cole, 1993).

[9] James E. Youngdahl, "Arbitration of Discrimination Grievances," *The Arbitration Journal*, Vol. 31, No. 3, September 1976, p. 145.

[10] Harry T. Edwards, "Arbitration of Employment Discrimination Cases: A Proposal for Employer and Union Representatives," *Labor Law Journal*, Vol. 27, No. 5, May 1976, p. 265.

There are a number of cases where the legal issues are so complex or novel, or where the class of plaintiffs is so large, or where both the union and employer are charged as co-defendants, that it would be inappropriate on public policy grounds to allow a private jurist to decide the legal issues posed in these cases. Furthermore, in many of these same cases, it is very likely that the issues in dispute will be litigated in a court of law even when arbitration has been employed, so no good purpose is served by forcing or even encouraging the parties to waste time in arbitration.

Probably the only group of employment discrimination cases that should be handled in arbitration are those involving a claim that the company allegedly violated the contract and the "law" while enforcing or applying the terms of the collective bargaining agreement; in other words, situations in which an employee files a grievance alleging that the company has done something that may be viewed as both a breach of contract and a breach of law. Such cases might include, for example: (i) a claim that an employee was discharged without "just cause" and in violation of Title VII or (ii) a claim that an employee was improperly denied a promotion under the seniority provisions of a collective bargaining agreement and in violation of Title VII.

In all such cases, the legal and contractual issues will be closely intertwined and normally the same facts will be relevant to decide both issues. . . . All other cases involving claims of employment discrimination should be explicitly excluded from arbitration.[11]

Edwards recommended that six classes of employment discrimination cases be specifically exclude from arbitration, even going so far as clearly limiting arbitral authority to decide these six types of grievances in the collective bargaining agreement.[12]

ADVOCATE COMPETENCY

There is little evidence that employers or unions engage in dishonest or bad faith processing of grievances, including reprehensible conduct involving discrimination cases. Nevertheless, gross error in the investigation and representation of employee grievances has been known to happen and has resulted in the upset of arbitration awards. In *Hines v. Anchor Motor Truck*,[13] for example, the Supreme Court decided that both the employer and the union erred in the investigation and processing of discharge grievances involving seven employees. For its part, the employer improperly discharged the employees and, for its part, the union failed to fully investigate all the facts and adequately represent the grievants at the arbitration hearing. Because they both erred, the court required the parties to share equally any back pay due the seven employees. *Anchor Motor Truck* found that the union had breached its duty of fair representation, and the employer shared financial responsibility for the outcome.

The principle of the parties' joint liability when an employee is improperly represented during the grievance process was further enunciated by the Supreme

---

[11] *Ibid.*

[12] *Ibid.*

[13] *Hines v. Anchor Motor Truck*, 96 Sup. Ct. 1048 (1976).

Court in 1983. In *Bowen v. U.S. Postal Service*[14] the court apportioned the financial liability of the parties to an improperly discharged employee in accordance with their share of wrongdoing. The *Bowen* remedy required that the union pay $30,000 and the employer $23,000 when the union failed to comply with its statutory duty of fair representation. But, the principle of joint liability is somewhat muted on two counts. *De Costello v. Teamsters* provides a statute of limitations so that an employee must file a breach of fair representation claim within six months of the union's alleged mistake.[15] Second, the courts allow unions a wide range of reasonableness in the exercise of their duty of fair representation. Proving arbitrary or bad faith conduct by the union in processing grievances is possible, but not without difficulty. So long as the union investigates and processes grievances the same for all employees, the parties can be reasonably safe to assume that a negotiated solution to a grievance will not be overturned even when the solution is unacceptable to an individual employee.[16] The union has a duty to represent employees fairly and the employer is well advised, even encouraged by financial liability, to assist the union in its quest. And in the case of Title VII complaints, *Gardner-Denver* increases the burden upon the parties to provide the grievant a fair opportunity.

In Title VII grievances a duty of competent representation is added to the duty of fair representation. While negligence, careless grievance handling, or incompetence may pass muster in many other types of grievances, misplaced grievance forms, missed time limits, and/or inexperienced advocates must be avoided in Title VII disputes. Clearly, Footnote 21 in *Gardner-Denver* calls upon the parties to ensure that the grievant in a discrimination complaint is treated fairly and without hostility, not subjected to unwarranted "horse trading" during the early steps of the grievance process, and provided with a competent advocate.[17] The courts are much more likely to afford an arbitrator's award great weight when the advocates are experienced with arbitration and familiar with the Title VII rights of employees. The safest approach is for the parties to appoint lawyer advocates schooled in Title VII, allowing the grievant the right to bring his/her own attorney if desired.

TRANSCRIPT REQUIREMENTS

Whether or not to require transcripts for all arbitration hearings is frequently debated by advocates and arbitrators. Because transcripts are expensive, or the parties request it, the vast majority of arbitrators do not require a transcript of the hearing. Instead, most arbitrators keep notes and tape the hearing, stipulating that the tape recording is an extension of the arbitrator's notes. On the

---

[14] *Bowen v. U.S. Postal Service*, 459 U.S. 212 (1983).

[15] *De Costello v. Teamsters*, 462 U.S. 151 (1983).

[16] *Vaca v. Sipes*, 386 U.S. 171 (1967).

[17] James D. Holzhauer, "The Contractual Duty of Competent Representation," *Chicago-Kent Law Review*, Vol. 63, No. 2, 1987, p. 255.

other hand, the cost of not requiring a transcript potentially far outweighs any no transcript savings, particularly in Title VII disputes. In his 1985 address to the Academy, Sam Kagel placed the transcript at the foundation of the arbitrator's award, called for informal but legalistic hearing processes, and declared the wisdom of requiring transcripts. Arbitrator Kagel stated:[18]

> As you are aware, in *Alexander v. Gardner-Denver*, the Supreme Court stated that it would not defer to arbitration decisions in cases where arbitrators have ruled against grievants claiming discrimination. But, it is significant that the Court in Footnote 21 stated that weight could be accorded arbitration decisions if certain relevant factors were present, among them an "adequate record." An arbitrator's notes, or even tapes, would not, in my opinion, be such an "adequate record" so as to satisfy a court. I am familiar with cases where transcripts of arbitrations, when introduced in such court proceedings, have led to the dismissal of actions under *Alexander*. And, at least in such instances, the courts have deferred to the arbitrator's decision. . . .
>
> A transcript then is essential to aid the arbitrator in making a decision based on the record, and to provide protection against attacks that may be made on his decisions.

Arbitrator Kagel's advice should be followed in Title VII disputes. Arbitrator Kagel advises that all arbitration hearings, including those not considering a civil rights challenge, should include an official transcript. And in matters of employment discrimination, the parties and the arbitrator should require that an official transcript be taken at all arbitration hearings. Failure to do so may result in failure to satisfy Footnote 21 in *Gardner-Denver*.

PROTECTING GRIEVANT'S RIGHTS

The potential conflict of interest between the grievant, the employer, and the union in human rights grievances evolves from bedrock, from the very theory of labor arbitration. The earlier stages of the grievance process are designed to allow the parties the opportunity to uncover the truth about the employee's complaint and to resolve differences through negotiation and/or compromise. But once the threshold is crossed into arbitration, the parties become adversarial. Each side is out to win.

The adversary system common to arbitration is based on so-called fight theory. And under fight theory, the truth is best presented when the opposing parties strive as much as ethically possible to present evidence and argument favorable to their side. As described by Paul Prasow and Edward Peters in 1983, "we obtain the fairest decision . . . when two men argue, as unfairly as possible, on opposite sides, . . . [for then] . . . it is certain that no important consideration will altogether escape notice." The untrustworthiness, chicanery, partisan zeal, crude

---

[18] Sam Kagel, "Legalism – and Some Comments on Illegalisms – in Arbitration," *Proceedings of the Thirty-Eighth Annual Meeting National Academy of Arbitrators*. Washington, DC: BNA Books, Inc., 1986, pp. 184-185.

reasoning, and irrational testimony which is frequently present at court and in arbitration stems from the essential nature of fight theory.[19]

In contrast with fight theory, which has roots in English-speaking countries, "truth" theory rests upon a concept of judicial inquiry frequently found in Continental Europe. In accordance with truth theory, the court might, for example, appoint an investigator who examines evidence and asks questions to determine the facts. The investigating magistrate then submits the objective facts to the court, the court possibly giving the magistrate's report great weight.[20] The balance between the fight and truth doctrines is acute in labor arbitration. And if doubt exists, the scales should be tipped in favor of the truth theory approach in matters of discrimination covered by the labor agreement.

Nowhere is the need for fairness and accuracy in decision making more important than in grievances falling under the *Gardner-Denver* mandate expressed in Footnote 21. Once again *Anchor Motor Truck* illustrates the point. Recall that the arbitrator ruled in favor of the employer in *Anchor Motor Truck*, sustaining the discharge of seven truck drivers for the alleged falsification of motel receipts. Further investigation after the arbitral decision, however, revealed that the discharged truck drivers had been deceptively overcharged for room rent by a motel clerk who pocketed the difference between the motel's normal rate and the bogus higher rate he charged the drivers. Keeping in line with the requirements of the *Steelworkers Trilogy*, the lower courts elected to support the arbitrator's decision so that the incorrectly discharged truck drivers remained off the Anchor Motor Truck payroll. But despite its earlier finding in the *Steelworkers Trilogy*, the U.S. Supreme Court overturned the arbitrator's decision in *Anchor Motor Truck* and ruled in favor of the truck drivers who were improperly discharged. The utility of fight theory yielded to an investigation process, falling within the scope of the truth approach, in *Anchor Motor Truck* that produced a fair, reasonable, and correct outcome. It seems reasonable to assume that a court that would overturn an arbitral decision under the circumstances of *Anchor Motor Truck* would be equally willing to overturn an unfair arbitral award falling within the scope of labor contract requirements governing civil rights.

Anchor Motor Truck makes it the responsibility of all individuals involved with the grievance process, witnesses, advocates and arbitrators, to find and tell the truth. Particularly in Title VII cases, it is the responsibility of the arbitrator and the parties to ensure that important questions are asked; that significant facts are placed upon the record; that legal standards are properly investigated and applied to the merits of the case; that all material and relevant matters are placed upon the record;[21] and, that the grievant is afforded the opportunity to confront

---

[19] Paul Prasow and Edward Peters, *Arbitration and Collective Bargaining: Conflict Resolution in Labor Relations, Second Edition.* New York: McGraw-Hill, 1983, 250-251. Quotes from Jerome Frank, *Courts on Trial: Myth and Reality in American Justice.* Princeton: Princeton University Press, 1950, 80.

[20] *Ibid.*

[21] *TRW, Inc.*, 92-2 ARB 8562 (Fullmer, 1992), and *Spectrulite Consortium, Inc.*, 101 LA 1134 (Hilgert, 1993).

his accuser in cases of race discrimination.[22] Indeed more so than in other forms of arbitration, the arbitrator and the parties must move affirmatively and aggressively in discrimination cases to protect the rights of the grievant.

ROLE OF THE WITNESS

The role of the advocates and the witnesses is to present the arbitrator with the facts. By telling the truth, witnesses enable arbitrators to make their decision on the basis of the complete record, often weighing testimony about discrimination in conjunction with other persuasive evidence.[23] For example, in *Department of Corrections, State of Michigan*,[24] Arbitrator Michael P. Long set aside the white grievant's three day suspension when a black co-worker testified that he was not offended when the grievant called him "alfalfa" anymore than the white grievant was offended when the black grievant called him a "tomato picker." The grievant's unchallenged testimony that he had apologized to the offended black employee also caused Arbitrator Long to mitigate the three-day suspension. To tell the parties to avoid misleading the arbitrator is probably a waste of time, for seldom is the case that anyone testifying before an arbitrator tells a bare-faced lie. Frequently, however, the facts are unintentionally distorted in a way that clouds the arbitrator's record, possibly facilitating an erroneous award and causing long-term injury to the parties. The greater danger is that an important material witness will not be called to testify.[25]

Distortion of the record by well intending witnesses is most often the by-product of one or a combination of several philosophical motivates. First, the witness may view himself as a mere conduit of information, an educator. The ethical dilemma of a narrowly defined educator role lies in the absence of a moral standard. The witness may be asked to divulge critical knowledge to a cause the witness feels personally to be unjust. Second, the witness may view himself as an advocate. In this mode the witness is more likely to give testimony that is cleverly edited, shaded, exaggerated, or glossed over. The advo-

---

[22] *Fernald Environmental Restoration Management Company*, 104 LA 596 (Cocalis, 1995), and *County of Orange*, 20 LAIS 3899 (Darrow, 1993).

[23] *American National Can Company*, BMS 9306.2 (Bognanno, 1993), and *Special School District 1*, BMS 9206.6 (Swenson, 1992).

[24] *Department of Corrections, State of Michigan*, LAIG 5107 (Long, 1995). See also *Reynolds Metals Company/ Alreco Metals, Inc.*, 99 LA 239 (Kahn, 1992) and *ITT – Continental Baking Company, Inc.*, 8 LAI 2831 (Springfield, 1981).

[25] Howard S. Sacks and Lewis S. Kurlantzick, "The Problem of the Missing Witness: Toward an Educator-Facilitator Role for Labor Arbitration," *Industrial Relations Law Journal*, Vol. 5, No. 1, 1982, p. 87. The educator-facilitator role is the most effective approach for arbitrators to use when attempting to gain the testimony of an otherwise missing material witness. See also *Huron Forge & Machine Company*, 75 LA 83 (Roumell, 1980); *Furr's Inc.*, 72 LA 960 (Leeper, 1979); and *U.S. Postal Service*, 66-2 ARB 8073 (Schulman, 1966).

cate witness might mislead on behalf of the greater good, such as elimination of perceived discrimination. Third, some witnesses are paid to give testimony. In this type of situation the witness may select information that is helpful to those who are paying the bill, but which distorts the true facts. Finally, the witness may view himself as being in harmony with the position of the party who has asked him to testify. While a witness in this circumstance faces no ethical dilemma, pressure may develop for the witness to overstate the facts. The danger is that otherwise ambiguous data appears to be clearer than is altogether the case.[26]

Witnesses who appear before arbitrators should expect to give testimony that is factually correct, honest, and impartial. A witness may legally withhold information, as in the case of privileged communication at court, but should avoid the partiality and manipulation sometimes urged by advocates. For what it is worth, all witnesses should be sworn by the arbitrator, but advocates are not required to take the oath, nor to promise to tell the truth. A promise to tell the truth is not binding at arbitration; witnesses cannot be held in contempt.

Expert witnesses appearing before arbitrators, or working behind the scenes during preparation for arbitration, should play the same role as they are expected to play before the court. Essentially, expert witnesses in discrimination cases should be governed by the helpfulness standard outlined in the Federal Rule of Evidence 702, becoming acquainted with the disputed facts, reviewing relevant scientific literature, and emphasizing research findings that are not known to the arbitrator.[27] Two court decisions illustrate the application of the helpfulness role for expert witnesses.

Subjective prejudice explanations of behavior by members of a minority group have been shown by expert social psychologists to be incorrectly attributed to laziness or lack of intelligence rather than to the disadvantages evolving from discrimination.[28] In *Alexander v. University of Washington*,[29] the expert witness explained attribution theory. The overworked black employees denial of promotion was incorrectly attributed to a lack of managerial skills. But in fact, this competent black worker had taken on an additional work load despite the lack of adequate resources. In *Price Waterhouse v. Hopkins*,[30] the expert

---

[26] Michael J. Saks, "Expert Witnesses, Nonexpert Witnesses, and Nonwitness Experts," *Law and Human Behavior*, Vol. 14, No. 4, August 1990, pp. 291-313.

[27] Jane Goodman and Robert T. Croyle, "Social Framework Testimony in Employment Discrimination Cases," *Behavioral Sciences & the Law*, Vol. 7, No. 2, pp. 227-241. The Federal Rule of Evidence 702 states: "If scientific, technical or other specialized knowledge will assist the trier of facts to understand the evidence or to determine a fact in issue, a witness qualified as an expert by knowledge, skill, experience, training, or education, may testify thereto in the form of an opinion or otherwise."

[28] T.F. Pettigrew, "The Ultimate Attribution Error: Extending Allport's Cognitive Analysis of Prejudice," *Personality & Social Psychology Bulletin*, Vol. 5, 1979, pp. 461-476.

[29] *Alexander v. University of Washington*, No. 85-2-15427-4 (King County Sup. Ct., Washington, 1988).

[30] *Price Waterhouse v. Hopkins*, 109 S. Ct. 1775 (1989).

witness explained the impact of stereotyping that subtly infects decision making. Expert testimony in *Hopkins* aided the Supreme Court in its recognition that generalized discrimination, in the form of stereotyping, is relevant in the proof of disparate treatment. Further, evidence of discrimination against one group, such as blacks, is allowable to support a claim of discrimination against another group, such as women.[31]

EVIDENCE

Whereas statutes mandate the production of evidence in court, the discovery requirements placed upon arbitration result from the Federal Arbitration Act, some state law, and from interpretations of the National Labor Relations Act (NLRA) by the National Labor Relations Board (NLRB).[32] Arbitral subpoena power, for example, was decided by the NLRB and the Supreme Court in 1967.[33] Using the Federal Rules and Civil Procedure as a broad model, the NLRB and the Court established in *NLRB v. Acme Industrial Company* that the employer's obligation to bargain in good faith includes the duty to provide the union with properly requested information necessary to evaluate and process grievances.[34] The union's duty to bargain in good faith also includes the obligation to provide the employer with properly requested information.[35]

The right of the union to make reasonable requests or to subpeona relevant information from the employer before the arbitration step in the grievance process is also supported by the NLRB's application of Sections 8(a) and 8(d) of the NLRA.[36] Notwithstanding, as a practical matter subpeonas are seldom mandatorily imposed in arbitration because of the necessary court delay. But,

[w]hether information is relevant or not depends upon the facts in each case. Accordingly, a determination of whether the employer must furnish a specific type of information to the union will depend primarily upon the circumstances surrounding the request at the time it is made. Virtually any type of information might be considered relevant to a union grievance when coupled with the proper set of circumstances. Thus items such as wage and benefit data; job evaluation information and job descriptions; records pertaining to productivity, productivity levels and standards (including incentive wage sys-

---

[31] Freshman, Clark, "Beyond Atomized Discrimination: Use of Acts of Discrimination Against 'Other' Minorities to Prove Discriminatory Motivation Under Federal Employment Law," *Stanford Law Review*, Vol. 43, No. 193, November 1990, p. 241. The legal theory of disparate treatment under *Hopkins* may have been extended to disparate impact cases in *Watson v. Fort Worth Bank and Trust*, 108 S. Ct. 2777 (1988).

[32] The policy of the NLRA is frequently paralleled by the Railway Labor Act.

[33] *NLRB v. Acme Industrial Company*, 385 U.S. 432 (1967).

[34] Gavin S. Appleby, "The Practical Labor Lawyer," *Employee Relations Law Journal*, Vol. 10, No. 4, Spring 1985, pp. 736-744.

[35] *Detroit Newspaper Printing and Graphic Communications Union*, 233 NLRB 994 (1977) and 598 F. 2d 267 (D.C. Cir., 1979).

[36] *Western Massachusetts Electrical Company v. NLRB*, 589 F.2d 42 (1st Cir., 1978).

tems); general employee information on unit employees, non-unit employees and former employees; time study data; plant access to conduct independent time studies; financial data, including business volume, earnings and sales data; business relationships; sub-contracting information; physical plant layout; customer information; time records and work assignment information; absenteeism records; attendance data; accident damage reports; employment application and driving records; handwriting analyses; employee information related to hiring, transfer, layoff and discharge; employer association membership roster; records reflecting work done at a company's new facility; names of witnesses to an incident resulting in employee discipline; information related to removal of equipment; and EEO data all have been held relevant under a particular set of facts.[37]

[T]he employer must inform the union of any expected delay in complying with its request and present justifiable reasons for the delay, or risk an adverse finding because of a delay. Justifiable reasons for delay may include other work responsibilities of the person assigned to gather the information and the burdensome volume of information requested. . . .[38] Employers' defenses to the production of information, based on deferral, nonarbitrability, waiver, availability and confidentiality, frequently have been rejected.[39]

While Sections 8(a)5, 8(b)3, and 8(d) of the NLRA support its application, the practical use of subpoena power in arbitration is negated by the length of time it takes to process and enforce an unfair labor practice charge through the NLRB.[40] The one-and-one-half-year average time it takes to process an unfair labor practice charge calling for subpoena enforcement is probably too much delay in a discrimination grievance for an arbitral decision to satisfy the Footnote 21 requirements of *Gardner-Denver*. The employer's need to guard the confidentiality of EEO records provided to the union should be satisfied by deleting references to irrelevant names. Notwithstanding, the NLRB has required *Lucky Markets, Inc.*[41] to comply with a union's reasonable request for statistical information about employees transferred or placed in management training positions as part of a bona fide affirmative action program. The union had requested to know the employees' race, sex, marital status, and names.

Statistical evidence, as requested in *Lucky Markets, Inc.* and *Department of Commerce, Patent & Trademark Office*,[42] is a common basis for either a disparate impact or disparate treatment challenge; however, arbitrators are seldom asked to consider disparate impact. Relevant statistical evidence can establish a prima facie disparate treatment case if the employee shows a profound disparity.

---

[37] Linda J. French, "Arbitral Discovery Guidelines for Employers," *UMKC Law Review*, Vol. 50, No. 2, Winter 1982, pp. 145-149.

[38] *Ibid.*, 151.

[39] *Ibid.*, 161.

[40] Gary Furlong, "Fear and Loathing in Labor Arbitration: How Can there Possibly Be a Full and Fair Hearing Unless the Arbitrator can Subpoena Evidence?," *Willamette Law Review*, Vol. 20, No. 3, Summer 1984, pp. 535-566.

[41] *Lucky Markets, Inc.*, 251 NLRB 836 (1980).

[42] *Department of Commerce, Patent & Trademark Office*, LAIRS 21867 (Blackwell, 1994). See also, *Naval Air Rework Facility, Norfolk*, LAIRS 13579 (Whyte, 1981); *County of Hennepin, Medical Center*, BMS 9209.24 (Jacobowski, 1992); and *Nuclear Regulatory Commission*, LAIRS 21293 (Leeper, 1993).

For example, an employer's failure to promote either sex can be statistically regarded as disparate treatment, even though no disparate impact occurs.[43] When statistical evidence relevant to a disparate treatment claim is used the sample size should be adequate, the data should concern the challenged practice and pool of employees, and care must be taken to ensure that the party using the statistical evidence carries the burden of proving the claimed relevance.[44]

Some analysts argue that statistical evidence of disparate treatment loses much of its probative value because these cases deal with intentional discrimination against an individual employee and are very fact-specific.[45] Furthermore, discharge cases taken before an arbitrator most often turn upon whether the employer has "just cause" to terminate the employee and statistical evidence is of limited help in determining a just cause discipline.[46] That is, 83 percent of all labor agreements require that discharge be undertaken for "cause" or "just cause,"[47] and evidence of discharge for just cause does not often appear in statistical form. The collective bargaining concept of just cause is an irrelevant concern under Title VII. Instead, human rights law requires that employers not discriminate and doesn't say anything about the employer's need to have a just cause for discharging employees.

Besides statistical data, circumstantial and direct evidence are of value in proving or disproving employment discrimination. Circumstantial evidence is based upon inference, the likelihood that a set of circumstances will be present when another set of circumstances is present.[48] Examples of circumstantial evidence that might cause the court to conclude the existence of disparate treatment are: the employer's decision to promote a male supervisor based on the belief that employees will feel uncomfortable working with a woman supervisor;[49] when the standards for making promotion recommendations used by foremen are subjective;[50] and when the employer uses an employee's unlawful act as an intentional pretext to discriminate when deciding promotions.[51]

Direct evidence is without inference and is always relevant if it establishes the fact to be proved. Employees who offer direct evidence of employment discrimination testify from firsthand knowledge which, if accepted, resolves the

---

[43] *Furnco Construction Corp. v. Waters*, 438 US 567 (US SCt, 1978) and *Wright v. National Archives and Records Service*, 609 F2d 702 (CA-4, 1979).

[44] Craig H. King, "Employment Discrimination: The Burden of Proof," *Southern University Law Review*, Vol. 13, No. 1, Fall 1986, pp. 98-99.

[45] *U.S. Pipe*, 100 LA 1014 (Krislov, 1993). See also *Cleveland Plain Dealer*, 94-1 ARB 4078 (Morgan, 1993) and *Southern Connecticut Gas Company*, 94-1 ARB 4096 (Lieberman, 1993).

[46] *Nix v. WLCY Radio Rehall Communications*, 738 F2d. 1181 (11th Cir., 1984).

[47] *Basic Patterns in Union Contracts, Tenth Edition*. Staff Editors of Collective Bargaining Negotiations & Contracts. Washington, D.C.: BNA Books, Inc., 1983, 6.

[48] *Radomsky v. U.S.*, 180 F.2d 781 (9th Cir. 1950).

[49] *Hagan v. Andrus*, 651 F.2d 622 (CA-9, 1981).

[50] *Rowe v. General Motors Corp.*, 457 F.2d 348 (CA-5, 1972).

[51] *McDonnell Douglas Corp. v. Green*, 411 US 792 (1973).

factual proposition of the case. For example, the testimony of an employee who actually hears, not secondhand, another employee make a discriminatory statement or a written document containing discriminatory statements would constitute direct evidence. In *Trans World Airline v. Thurston* [52] the Supreme Court decided that the disparate treatment test of employment discrimination enunciated in *McDonnell Douglas* is not applicable when the employee presents relevant direct evidence of discrimination. Falling into step with *Trans World Airline*, Arbitrator William J. Berquist reasoned it best for the union to prove its claim of race discrimination against *Northern States Power Company*[53] by presenting direct evidence in the form of statements made by the employer or through other statements that clearly show the existence of racially discriminatory motives in the employment environment. Arbitrator Berquist ruled that the union could win its race discrimination charge with direct evidence and/or by providing a prima facie proof of intentional employment discrimination.

BRIEFS

Unless the case is particularly complex or unusual, arbitrators and advocates do not feel compelled to write posthearing briefs. But in employment discrimination cases, the parties and the arbitrator should (a) practically always require posthearing briefs and (b) practically always require that the briefs include the citation of relevant cases. In this regard the late Arbitrator Peter Seitz wrote:

To be sure, there are cases that present novel and highly unusual questions of the interpretation and application of collective bargaining agreements. An arbitrator faced with such a question for the first time may welcome reference to a decision of a highly respected arbitrator in order to be informed of the reasoning that led to his conclusions.

. . . nevertheless, it has been and remains the practice of many advocates, in their briefs, to avalanche their arbitrator with citations and quotations from the decisions of their brethren. There may be some arbitrators who are impressed and overwhelmed by this briefing tactic, but I doubt it. I believe that most experienced arbitrators would agree that they are more likely to be persuaded by a cogent and convincing argument than by a legion of citations of doubtful authority gleaned from the footnotes of Elkouri and Elkouri.[54]

The significance of practically always requiring a brief and citations for employment discrimination grievances is not overstated. Most often these are thorny cases in which the advocates have a vested interest in avoiding lengthy

---

[52] *Trans World Airline v. Thurston*, 105 S.Ct. 613 (1985). See also Charles A. Edwards, "Direct Evidence of Discriminatory Intent and the Burden of Proof: An Analysis and Critique," *Washington and Lee Law Review*, Vol. 43, No. 1, Winter 1986, pp. 1-35.

[53] *Northern States Power Company*, BMS 9508.15 (Berquist, 1995).

[54] Peter Seitz, "III. The Citation of Authority and Precedent in Arbitration (Its Use and Abuse)," *The Arbitration Journal*, Vol. 38, No. 4, December 1983, pp. 59-60.

legal proceedings. Furthermore, the contractual terms of labor agreements that
outlaw employment discrimination are interwoven with matters of law, statutory
and judicial. The willingness of the courts to give an arbitrator's award great
weight, per Footnote 21 in *Gardner-Denver*, will most assuredly hinge in part
on whether or not the issues, facts, and legal concerns placed before the arbitrator match with the requirements of fair employment law. The post hearing
brief will aid the court in evaluating whether the parties and the arbitrator considered all relevant statutory and case law as well as the contract when presenting and rendering an arbitral award regarding employment discrimination.[55]

BURDEN OF PROOF

The distinction between disparate impact and disparate treatment presented in
Chapter 1 should be reviewed in conjunction with the order and burden of proof
now discussed. The courts apply a preponderance of evidence proof to establish
a Title VII violation; similarly, arbitrators require the party with the ultimate
burden of proof to provide a preponderance of evidence in order to achieve a
favorable award.[56]   Once again, most arbitral awards regarding employment
discrimination involve disparate treatment matters, and   *Texas Department of
Community Affairs v. Burdine*[57] is an important link in the line of progeny beginning with the *McDonnell Douglas*[58] criteria for proving disparate treatment.
After reiterating that the litigant making a disparate treatment challenge retains
the ultimate burden of persuasion at all times, *Burdine* reaffirms the levels of
proof desirable within the context of the ultimate burden.

Listed in descending order of rigor, the common levels of proof are: proof beyond a reasonable doubt,[59] clear and convincing proof, preponderance of evidence proof, and burden of production.[60] The burden of production is not a
proof in the same sense as the other three proof. Rather, the burden of production is operationally the same as the articulation standard placed on the employer by the Supreme Court in *McDonnell Douglas*; both the burden of pro-

---

[55] Tim, Bornstein, "To Argue, To Brief, Neither or Both: Strategic Choices in Arbitration Advocacy," *The Arbitration Journal*, Vol. 41, No. 1, March 1986, pp. 77-81.

[56] *Henkel Corporation*, 104 LA 494 (Hooper, 1995); *Department of Human Services,
State of Ohio*, 19 LAIS 2083 (Feldman, 1992); *Police Department, City of New York*, 20
LAIS 3242 (Meyer, 1992); *Veterans Administration, Medical Center, Jackson*, LAIRS
19139 (Murphy, 1989); and, *Office of Hearings and Appeals, Social Security Administration*, LAIRS 16440 (Jaffe, 1984).

[57] *Texas Department of Community Affairs v. Burdine*, 101 S. Ct. 1089 (1981).

[58] *McDonnell Douglas Corp. v. Green*, 411 US 792 (1973); *Furnco Construction Corp.
v. Waters*, 438 US 567 (US SCt, 1978); *Board of Trustees of Keene State College v.
Sweeney*, 439 US 24 (S. Ct., 1978); and *Burdine*.

[59] Applies to criminal cases.

[60] Henry C. Black, *Black's Law Dictionary, Fifth Edition*. St. Paul, Minn.: West Publishing Company, 1979, p. 178.

duction and the articulation standard are met when legitimate evidence is introduced by the employer even though it may not convince the judiciary.

In *Burdine*, the applicant proved prima facie discrimination by a preponderance of the evidence. She was a qualified minority applicant who applied for the position and was rejected. The position remained open and a male subordinate was subsequently selected. Several careful readings of the case show that the district court, court of appeals and Supreme Court agree that prima facie discrimination existed in *Burdine*. However, the legal standard for a prima facie case is flexible and is not the only consideration for finding a disparate treatment violation of Title VII. The Supreme Court then moved to the second *McDonnell Douglas* criterion for deciding disparate treatment. The court decided between two vastly different interpretations of the burden of proof appropriate at this stage of legal inquiry. It reversed the court of appeals because the burden of proof required by the lower court was greater than the simple articulation (i.e., burden of production) standard established by *McDonnell Douglas*.

The appeals court found for the applicant, taking the position that "if the employer need only articulate, not prove a legitimate non-discriminatory reason for his action, he may compose fictitious, but legitimate, reasons for his actions."[61] Put another way, the possibility that a mere articulation would enable the employer to compose fictitious but legitimate barriers against promoting a qualified, or equally qualified, female applicant led the appeals court to impose on the employer an interim burden of proof similar to the preponderance of evidence carried by the employee. The Supreme Court reasoned that the result of the burden of proof proffered by the court of appeals is contrary to the wish of Congress since it obligated the employer to hire the plaintiff. The Supreme Court agreed with the district court's application of the second *McDonnell Douglas* criterion. According to the line of cases followed in *Burdine*, the interim burden of proof requires the employer to articulate rational legitimate reasons for not promoting the applicant. Again, articulation implies that the employer need not actually prove that the proffered rationale motivated the rejection. To be specific, the *McDonnell Douglas* standard for lawful articulation was achieved in *Burdine* because the employer testified that the promotion decision was based on consultation with trusted advisors; that a legitimate evaluation of the applicant's relative qualifications was made; that the rejected acting project director did not work well with the other employees; and that work efficiency and productivity by subordinate employees in the job environment would improve if the equally qualified male were made project director. The equally qualified female was rejected for promotion in *Burdine*.

Burdine has not been extended to disparate impact cases.[62] Clearly, the degree of objectivity required of supervisory evaluations in situations of disparate im-

---

[61] 608 F.2d 563 (CA-5, 1979).
[62] *Johnson v. Uncle Ben's, Inc.*, 628 F.2d 419 (CA-5, 1980); vac'd. and rem'd. (US S.Ct., 1981).

pact is not applicable to the disparate treatment issue advanced in *Burdine*.[63]
That is, each of the proffered rationales for rejecting the female applicant in
Burdine contains subjective judgment that might not be acceptable under the
disparate impact doctrine.[64] For example, the decision to reject *Burdine* hinged
on opinions about her relative qualifications, a belief that she did not work well
with subordinates, and a belief that she caused inefficiency. Subjective judgment
exists in most management decisions and normally leads to the promotion of
clearly qualified applicants and the rejection of clearly unqualified applicants.
But, when an applicant is borderline, seemingly equally or slightly more qualified, the possibility looms that unconvincing subjective opinion will lead to the
rejection of a qualified worker. In sum, the articulation standard makes relatively subjective evidence a practical basis for refusing to promote an equally
or maybe slightly more qualified applicant without violating the law.[65]

Turning to a speculative issue, it may be situational whether arbitrators will be
in concert with the Supreme Court regarding an employer's claim that an applicant is unqualified for promotion. Arbitrators apply an ultimate burden of persuasion proof to determine their awards, except in unusual circumstances. An
arbitrator's assignment of the burden of proof normally has some similarity with
the burden of proof set by legislatures and followed by the courts for disparate
impact cases. It appears likely, then, that in disparate impact grievances arbitrators will reach conclusions similar to those of the court, particularly when
questionable evidence is used to substantiate the qualifications of an applicant
seeking promotion. However, the level of proof usually followed at arbitration is
more in tune with the court of appeals interpretation of *McDonnell Douglas* than
with the district court position adopted by the Supreme Court in *Burdine*. In
matters of disparate treatment, the danger may be that arbitrators will assign a
burden of proof upon management that is different than the law requires.

SUMMARY

Two of the requirements in Footnote 21 of *Gardner-Denver* are particularly
germane to the conduct of the parties, the evidence provided, and the proof presented in discrimination complaints. The court will determine whether or not to
give great weight to the arbitrator's decision based, in part, upon (a) "the degree of procedural fairness in the arbitral forum" and (b) the "adequacy of the
record with respect to the issue of discrimination." Among other things, *Gard-*

---

[63] The connection between the *Burdine* standard of proof for disparate treatment cases
was roughly equated for disparate impact cases by *Wards Cove Packing Company v.
Antonio*, 109 S.Ct. 2115 (1989), the *Wards Cove* standard being set aside by The Civil
Rights Act of 1991.

[64] *Ablemarle Paper Company v. Moody* 422 US 405 (1975) and *Washington v. Davis*,
426 US 229 (1976).

[65] *Gillespie v. Board of Education of North Little Rock*, DC Ark, (1981); and *Evans v.
Baldrige*, DC (1981).

ner-Denver makes it essential for the parties to supply the arbitrator with all facts and arguments, and to behave professionally. The parties' conduct must add to, not subtract from, the procedural fairness and clarity of the arbitral forum. Delays, unwillingness to turnover relevant materials, and other dirty tricks have no place in any arbitration, but especially in those involving any form of discrimination. The use of attorneys competent with discrimination law is urged for discrimination grievances.

PART II

TOPICAL ISSUES

Chapter 4

Employment Status

Many published reports regarding sex discrimination are quick to point out that the word sex was inserted into Section 703 of Title VII one day before the House passed the act. The theory goes that congressmen opposed to Title VII thought that by adding the word sex they would kill the entire legislation. These same reports usually note that without legislative hearings and little debate, the courts have not had the benefit of a descriptive legislative history from which to determine congressional intent in matters of sex discrimination. But while the lack of a congressional record is a historical fact, it is also a fact that the number of court decisions and reported arbitration awards concerning sex discrimination exceeds all others. One wonders why Congress came so close to missing the boat. Employment status deals with alleged discrimination faced by workers attempting to gain and keep their job. Sex discrimination complaints involving recruitment, hiring, demotion, layoff, and discharge exemplify the type of disputes falling into the employment status category.

TREND SETTERS

Looking back for a moment, women have been shaping the nature of anti-discrimination law for decades. For example, an important issue being hammered out by women workers in the period following World War II was the relationship between the labor agreement and the law. In this regard, the significant connection between employment discrimination, the labor agreement, and the U.S. Declaration of Independence was noted by Arbitrator Clark Kerr on December 27, 1946.[1] Resolving an interest dispute, Arbitrator Kerr selected the following clause: "no discrimination shall be practiced by either the company or

---

[1] *Luckenbach Steamship Company, Inc.*, 6 LA 98 (Kerr, 1946).

the union because of sex, race, creed, color, religious belief, or national origin."
Arbitrator Kerr reasoned that

[s]uch a clause is common in many waterfront contracts, as well as in many other industries. These people work on the waterfront, where discrimination is not practiced. This
type of clause was frequently granted by the National War Labor Board. Aside from that,
our nation was founded on the belief that "all men are created free and equal."

The antidiscrimination clause selected by Arbitrator Kerr is remarkably similar
to the fundamental provisions of present day human rights codes as well as the
Civil Rights Act of 1964, as amended. Furthermore, despite existing popular
prejudice against female employees in traditional male jobs, contractual guarantees, such as Arbitrator Kerr selected, tended to be enforced so that qualified
senior females kept their jobs and unqualified employees were discharged.

In 1983 the U.S. Supreme Court decided that, except for a narrow set of circumstances, sex discrimination stands on the same footing as race discrimination
under Title VII.[2] This relationship between race and sex discrimination under
Title VII has been extended to other statutes governing sex discrimination. For
example, the Equal Pay Act and Title VII are interrelated, though with different
remedy. Both Acts make it unlawful to discriminate, limit, segregate, or classify
employees on the basis of gender.[3] Distinctions in hiring, classification, promotion, tenure, sex stereotypes[4] and working conditions based upon sex are illegal,
unless the distinction falls under the narrowly defined bona fide occupational
qualification (BFOQ) exception.

Title VII does not require a desexualized workplace.[5] Gender discrimination
does not occur when an employee is turned away or not promoted due to lack of
qualifications.[6] It is not a violation of Title VII when an employer selects a male
over a female with approximately the same qualifications.[7] The statutes cover
sex discrimination against men as well as women,[8] but do not apply when a male
gives preferential treatment to his paramour.[9] Having sex with another employee
is not a legal basis for employment decisions unless the female participant in a
real or suspected inter-employee liaison is singled out for punishment or given
preferential treatment.

---

[2] *Arizona Governing Committee v. Norris*, 32 FEP Cases 233, 103 S.Ct. 3492 (1983).
[3] *Schnellbaecher v. Baskin Clothing Company*, 7th Cir. (1989). The Equal Protection
Clause of the US Constitution may apply when a state agency is assailed for sex bias; see,
Conlin v. Blanchard, 51 FEP 707 (6th Cir. 1989).
[4] *Lipsett v. University of Puerto Rico*, 54 FEP 230 (1st Cir. 1988).
[5] *Ellison v. Brady*, 54 FEP 1346 (9th Cir. 1991).
[6] *Dillon V. Coles*, 36 FEP 159 (3rd Cir. 1984).
[7] *Texas Department of Community Affairs v. Burdine*, 25 FEP 113, 450 US 248 (1981)
and *Heerdink v. Amoco Oil Company*, 54 FEP 909 (7th Cir. 1990).
[8] *Martinez v. El Paso County*, 32 FEP 747 (5th Cir. 1983) and *Loeffler v. Carlin*, 39 FEP
1089 (9th Cir. 1985).
[9] *DeCintio v. Westchester County Medical Center*, 42 FEP 921 (2nd Cir. 1986).

RECRUITING AND HIRING

An employer, labor union or employment agency[10] that engages in sex bias during any phase of the recruiting or hiring process violates Title VII unless sex is a BFOQ. For example, a help-wanted advertisements placed under separate male and female headings is considered illegal.[11] But, a newspaper ad for a "young man" which does not prevent females from applying for the job is fine.[12] It is legal to follow the same preemployment procedures for men and women, such as physical examinations.[13] And, it is legal to ask the same preemployment information from male and female job applicants so long as the requested information is job relevant.[14] For example, an employer may not ask female applicants whether they intend to get pregnant and quit, nor may any employee in a position of authority ask a woman whether her husband objects to her being away on business with men.[15] However, an employer may ask family oriented questions of females provided a sex stereotype does not become the basis for hiring,[16] as in the instance of child care responsibilities interfering with travel requirements.[17]

The BFOQ exception to Title VII allows employers, unions, and employment agencies to consider the sex of the applicant where gender is a necessary requirement for the job.[18] The courts have allowed BFOQ exemptions from Title VII in women's professional sports as well as in acting.[19] Prison security or inmate privacy rights,[20] foreign customer preference for working with males,[21] a

---

[10] *Barnes v. Rourke*, 8 FEP 1113 (MTenn Dist. 1973) and *Kaplowitz v. University of Chicago*, 8 FEP 1131 (NIll Dist. 1974). See also *Platner v. Case-Thomas Contractors Inc.*, 53 FEP 940 (11th Cir. 1990).

[11] *Pittsburgh Press Company v. Pittsburgh Commission on Human Rights*, 5 FEP 1141, 413 US 376 (1973); see also *Capaci v. Katz-Besthoff*, 32 FEP 961 (5th Cir. 1983), and *Hailes v. United Airlines*, 4 FEP 1022 (5th Cir. 1972). Employment agencies are treated the same as employers under Title VII.

[12] *Banks v. Nuen-Norwood*, 15 FEP 1571 (8th Cir. 1977).

[13] *Wroblewski v. Lexington Gardens, Conn.*, Conn. Sup. Ct. (1982).

[14] *Griggs v. Duke Power Company*, 3 FEP 175, 401 U.S. 424 (1971).

[15] *Barbano v. Madison County*, 54 FEP 1288 (2nd Cir. 1991), and *King v. Trans World Airlines*, 8th Cir. (1984).

[16] *Bruno v. City of Crown Point*, 57 FEP 623 (7th Cir. 1991).

[17] *Goicoechea v. Mountain State Telephone and Telegraph Company*, No. 82-3001 (9th Cir. 1983).

[18] *Gifford v. Achison, Topeka & Santa Fe Railroad Company*, 34 FEP 240 (9th Cir. 1982).

[19] *Graves v. Women's Professional Rodeo Assn. Inc.*, 53 FEP 460 (8th Cir. 1990), considers professional women's sports; *Norris v. Arizona Governing Committee for Tax Deferred Amnisty & Deferred Compensation Plan*, 32 FEP 233 (US SupCt, 1983), considers professional acting.

[20] *Torres v. Wisconsin Department of Health and Social Services*, 48 FEP 270 (7th Cir. 1988).

bogus need of the police force to wield a sledgehammer or to "run someone in,"[22] a desire for female only flight attendants,[23] and the need for football coaching ability[24] do not justify BFOQs. A height requirement that excludes 87 percent of the female applicants and only 20 percent of the male applicants from police work is suspect.[25] Minimum height,[26] weight,[27] and strength[28] requirements may be imposed upon females and not males where an employer can prove that there is no other less discriminatory alternative. That is, when there is a legitimate business need for minimum height[29] and strength,[30] an employer is entitled to a Title VII BFOQ exemption.

Some jobs require more physical strength than others and employers are justified in seeking employees who can accomplish necessary physical tasks. But according to Arbitrator Irwin M. Lieberman, *Braniff Airways, Inc.* violated contact provisions requiring all hiring, transfer, and promotions be made without regard to sex by disqualifying a female worker on the belief that she could not perform the physical duties of a customer service agent. The union prevailed because the grievant's right to due process was nullified by the employer and because evidence of the grievant's inability to handle the physical requirements of the positions was inconclusive. Arbitrator Lieberman favored the union because the job had been denied to females by contract until recently; because no female remained in the air freight position, despite several attempts by the company to place a woman in the grieved position; because the company interviewer told the grievant that no female "in her right mind" would want the position, given the historical inability of women to perform the work; and because the employer had sociopsychological motives for engaging in gender discrimination.[31]

Employment policy that forbids or restricts the hiring of married women or women with young children without creating the same conditions for men is not

---

[21] *Fernandez v. Wynn Oil Company*, 26 FEP 815 (9th Cir. 1981).

[22] *King v. New Hampshire Department of Resources & Economic Development*, 15 FEP 669 (1st Cir. 1977); *U.S. v. Gregory*, 50 FEP 1568 (4th Cir. 1989).

[23] *Diaz v. Pan American World Airways*, 3 FEP 337 (5th Cir. 1971).

[24] *Arizona Department of Law, Civil Rights Division v. Unified School District*, 33 FEP 1135 (Ariz. CtApp. 1983).

[25] *Blake v. Los Angeles*, 19 FEP 1441 (9th Cir. 1979).

[26] *Costa v. Markey*, 30 FEP 593 (1st Cir. 1982).

[27] *Dothard v. Rowlinson*, 15 FEP 10, 433 US 321 (1977).

[28] *Weeks v. Southern Bell*, 4 FEP 1255 (5th Cir. 1972); see also *Bowe v. Colgate Palmolive Company*, 6 FEP 1132 (7th Cir. 1973), and *Long v. Sapp*, 8 FEP 1079 (5th Cir. 1974).

[29] *Boyd v. Ozark Air Lines*, 17 FEP 827 (8th Cir. 1977).

[30] *EEOC v. Ryder/P.I.E. Nationwide*, 42 FEP 929 (West North Carolina Dist. 1986).

[31] *Braniff Airways, Inc.*, 66 LA 421 (Lieberman, 1976). See also *Toledo Blade Company*, 79-2 ARB 8601 (Dworkin, 1979); *Anheuser-Busch, Inc.*, 81-1 ARB 8058 (Seitz, 1980); and *Tonawanda Union Free School District*, 134 AIS 2 (Babiskin, 1980).

allowed by Title VII, veterans preference being one exception.[32] Another exception to this rule occurs when it can be shown that the restriction is related to job performance.[33] For example, state requirements establishing minimum teacher certification standards are related to job performance and the school district is not practicing sex discrimination by refusing to hire an unqualified teacher.[34] While the employer need not hire unqualified females or males, direct evidence in the form of oral statements by management that no women should be named to a technical deanship constitutes a violation of Title VII.[35] In another vein, an employer may not refuse to hire or seek to terminate an unwed mother unless the same policy applies to unwed fathers.   However, an employer may hire an unwed father, but not an unwed mother, where a BFOQ exists.[36] A recently married female may not be required to change her name on personnel forms unless a counterpart rule is applied to men.[37] The airline policy requiring stewardesses to be unmarried or to be terminated when they marry was outlawed by the Supreme Court over twenty years ago.[38]

A BFOQ exemption for a female only Counselor position at *Western School District*[39] was denied by Arbitrator Richard L. Kanner. The grievant, a male, was not considered by the District because the employer maintained that gender constituted a BFOQ when the position was established as well as for filling the position. The District wanted to hire a woman. Arbitrator Kanner ruled that the employer had stepped beyond the boundary of the parties' management rights clause, failed to consider the grievant's qualifications and seniority, and violated the no discrimination provision in the labor agreement. Arbitrator Kanner directed the District to consider the grievant's qualifications to do the work and the grievant's seniority when examining the male grievant's application for the female Counselor position.[40] Arbitrator Kanner did not concur with the position of the District regarding the BFOQ exemption.

In *Spencer Foods, Inc.*[41] Arbitrator Clifford E. Smith reviewed the company's employment application and interview process. Arbitrator Smith spelled out ap-

---

[32] *Personnel Administrator of Massachusetts v. Feeney*, 19 FEP 1377, 442 US 256 (1979) and *Brown v. Puget Sound Elec. Apprenticeship Trust*, 34 FEP 1201 (9th Cir. 1984).

[33] *Phillips v. Martin Marietta Corporation*, 3 FEP 40, 400 US 542 (1971).

[34] *Chambers v. Wynne School District*, 53 FEP 840 (8th Cir. 1990); see also *Lamphere v. Brown University*, 49 FEP 1464 (1st Cir. 1989).

[35] *Burns v. Gadsden State Community College*, 53 FEP 1165 (11th Cir. 1990).

[36] *Chambers v. Omaha Girls Club*, 45 FEP 698 (8th Cir. 1987).

[37] *Allen v. Lovejoy*, 14 FEP 1194 (6th Cir. 1977).

[38] *Sprogis v. United Airlines*, 3 FEP Cases 621, 404 US 991 (1971).

[39] *Western School District*, 94 LA 681 (Kanner, 1990).

[40] *Babcock and Wilcox Company, Diamond Power Specialty Co. Division*, 66 LA 729 (High, 1976); see also *Lykes Brothers Steamship Company*, 79-2 ARB 8563 (Turkus, 1979) and *PCL Packaging, Ltd.*, 11 LAC(3d) 333 (O'Shea, 1983).

[41] *Spencer Foods, Inc.*, 64 LA 1 and 191 AAA 12 (Smith, 1974). See also *Smithfield School Committee*, DIG 102269 (Liguori, 1977).

plication and interview guidelines useful to all employers who seek compliance with federal, state, and local human rights law.

The Arbitrator has studied carefully the record of the arbitration hearing as well as the brief submitted by each party. We must evaluate the behavior of Mr. Christenson and the Company in general to determine whether the Company's posture toward these two applicants was in any way different than that afforded male applicants. The employment process must treat all applicants fairly and equally without regard to race, creed, color, sex, age or nationality. This is required by State and Federal law, as well as by Article 4 of the Agreement which further forbids discrimination on the basis of membership in the Union.

We find it quite significant that both applicants wrote on their application form, in response to the question regarding the type of job desired, the words "Any" and "Night clean-up," while the other wrote "Any or Night clean-up" and then circled "night clean-up." We find it difficult to understand how Mr. Christenson then concluded these applicants were interested only in part-time work on night clean-up.

We find the applications completed by the grievants to be sufficiently clear regarding the type of work desired. We further find that Mr. Christenson should have obtained the desired and necessary information on the 18th of February. An employment interview is conducted by the Company representative, and it remains the responsibility of the Company representative to conduct this interview fairly and in such a manner that the needed information for determining applicant qualifications for open positions is obtained. This requires that the interviewer make no assumptions about an applicant without questioning the applicant to confirm or deny the assumption. The applicant is usually not familiar with the job or the job specifications and it is again the responsibility of the interviewer to conduct an interview so as to obtain all the facts necessary to select employees based only on their qualifications to perform the job. . . . The Company failed to show that the employment process utilized was, in fact, similar to that followed by all applicants.

We are also disturbed by the Company position that if there was in fact a misunderstanding, then the two applicants must "contact" Mr. Christenson for an interview. . . . We find the company's requirement to be unduly oppressive and, thereby, discriminatory. We do not deny the Company the right to obtain more information. However, the Company has the responsibility to take the initiative and to contact the applicants, explaining its need for additional information, and requesting they return for further interviewing. There was no testimony to show that this approach would have been followed if the applicants were male.

One final point made by Arbitrator Smith dealt with the relevance of the Company's concern with the applicant's current employment with another employer. Here again, Arbitrator Smith evaluated the grievant's employment status and ruled in favor of the union. Arbitrator Smith awarded the grievants back pay:

The Company indicated in its brief that "neither Raper nor applicant Lauritsen gave him [Mr. Christenson] any indication that they were intending to terminate their respective employment elsewhere." We don't see this to be relevant. The record does not indicate that Mr. Christenson asked for this information, but if he had, it would have had no relevance in determining the applicant's *qualifications* to perform a specific job. An applicant, once offered a job with an organization, must then determine whether to accept the position and terminate other employment as may be necessary.

The grievants' back pay awarded by Arbitrator Smith was to be calculated at the base labor rate from the date in the hiring process when they were discriminated against, less earnings from other employment while out of work.

In a case involving the City University of New York, Queens, Arbitrator Thomas G. S. Christensen split his decision because of a general nondiscrimination clause which the union claimed to prohibit sex bias in hiring.[42] Arbitrator Christensen ruled that management's failure to appoint the grievant was not a matter of academic judgment, but rather an arbitrary exercise of authority. Arbitrator Christensen agreed with management that no one in authority had appointed the black grievant to the lecturer position she performed between September 15 and October 27; and, Arbitrator Christensen agreed with the union's allegation that its prima facie discrimination challenge was unanswered by the employer. Arbitrator Christensen returned the case to the parties for discussion of why the university refused to appoint the grievant to a lecturer position.

DISCIPLINE AND UNFAIRNESS

The right of employers to discipline employees for cause is not amended by the civil rights law. An employee who engages in the false use of company resources[43] or who has a record of excessive absenteeism[44] cannot claim gender bias in order to avoid discharge. It is, however, paramount that employers afford all employees due process when examining the record and before issuing discipline. That is, where inconsistencies in the record reflect a lack of procedural due process by the employer,[45] such as where the burden of proof falls upon the employer to show that the risk to an unborn fetus warrants termination,[46] the courts are willing to overturn discharge. The courts have found sex discrimination and denied summary judgment[47] or reinstated employees when an employer's claim of nondedication to work, absence of commitment, lack of experience, and/or probationary status is a pretext for discrimination.[48] Circumstantial evidence of a salary disparity and an employer's unwillingness to correct the situation[49] or direct evidence in the form of a regional manager's remarks to su-

---

[42] *CUNY, Queens, SEEK Program*, 7 AIS 22 (Christensen, 1970). See also *Commonwealth of Massachusetts*, LAIG 3152 (Jacks, 1982), and *Rath Packaging Company*, 11 LAI 603 (Hoffmeister, 1984).

[43] *Taylor v. Houston Lighting & Power Company*, S. Texas Dist. (1990).

[44] *Johnson v. Burnley*, 54 FEP 944 (4th Cir. 1989), and *Swanson v. Elmhurst Chrysler Plymouth Inc.*, 50 FEP 1082 (7th Cir. 1989).

[45] *Jones v. Jones Brothers Construction Corp.*, 50 FEP 548 (7th Cir. 1989).

[46] *EEOC v. Service New Company*, 52 FEP 667 (4th Cir. 1990).

[47] *Sorlucco v. New York City Police Department*, 54 FEP 398 (2nd Cir. 1989).

[48] *Chamberlin v. 101 Reality Inc.*, 54 FEP 101 (1st Cir. 1990).

[49] *Gray v. University of Arkansas*, 50 FEP 1112 (8th Cir. 1989); see also *Williams v. Giant Eagle Markets, Inc.*, 51 FEP 1841 (3rd Cir. 1989).

pervisors that too many women had been hired[50] is sufficient support for the courts to overturn discipline.

The courts have concluded that the employer properly disciplined a female employee for violation of the company nonfraternization policy,[51] for personal conflicts with other employees,[52] and where a sexual assault charge was dismissed years before the moment of discipline.[53] An employer's failure to give preferential treatment to women does not constitute gender bias, nor is it improper for an employer to issue discipline for just cause after saying a female employee should "quite and let husband take care of her."[54] An employer may discharge a female employee for budgetary considerations unrelated to gender.[55] The denial of tenure was not due to sex discrimination where a female faculty member was granted more time and funding for research than male faculty.[56] To sum, the courts require even handed discipline of male and female employees with similar work records, the same standard of fairness applying at arbitration under labor agreements. While it is difficult to prove that a particular supervisor is out to get an employee.[57] A showing of disparate treatment is frequently achieved at arbitration when similarly situated male and female employees are treated differently. In *TYK Refactories Company*,[58] for example, Arbitrator Ronald F. Talarico decided that the employer did not have just cause to discharge the female grievant for an early quit. Arbitrator Talarico found that the grievant completed her assigned duties and then waited in her automobile without leaving the work site. Arbitrator Talarico ruled that the grievant's discharge constituted disparate treatment because similarly situated male employees were not disciplined. Disparate treatment of female employees need not be associated with discipline. Arbitrary termination of female employees for "economic reasons" violated the labor contract according to Arbitrator John E. Gorsuch. The employer, *Silver Slipper Saloon*,[59] terminated three female slot maids for economic reasons and subsequently employed three men to perform the work of the discharged females. In his opinion, Arbitrator Gorsuch said,

> In the instant case the Company stated that the grievant's employment was terminated in order "to cut expenses." However, the Company witnesses admitted that shortly after the severance of the grievants, the Company was employing the same number of cleaning

---

[50] *Sennello v. Reserve Life Insurance Company*, 49 FEP 1159 (11th Cir. 1989).

[51] *Smith v. Wal-Mart Stores No. 471*, 51 FEP 1599 (5th Cir. 1990).

[52] *Jones v. Jones Brothers Construction Company*, 51 FEP 357 (7th Cir. 1989).

[53] *Campbell v. Ingersoll Milling Machine Company*, 51 FEP 1798 (7th Cir. 1990).

[54] *Liao v. Tennessee Valley Authority*, 49 FEP Cases 441 (11th Cir. 1989).

[55] *Walker v. St. Anthony's Medical Center*, 50 FEP 845 (8th Cir. 1989), and *Montana v. First Federal Savings & Loan Assn. of Rochester*, 49 FEP 269 (2nd Cir. 1989).

[56] *King v. University of Wisconsin System*, 52 FEP 809 (7th Cir. 1990).

[57] *State of Michigan, Dept. of Corrections*, LAIG 3139 (Straw, 1982), and *Canadian Public Employees Union*, 4 LAC(3d) 385 (Swinton, 1982).

[58] *TYK Refractories Company*, 96 LA 803 (Talarico, 1991); see also *St. Paul's Towers*, 195 AAA 14 (Lucas, 1974).

[59] *Silver Slipper Saloon*, 56 LA 192 (Gorsuch, 1971).

employees doing the same type of work as the grievants but now with male employees designated as porters. See transcript pages 29-31 and 50. Therefore, it must be concluded that wage expenses were not, in fact, reduced as a result of the severance of the grievants. Consequently, the Company has not met the burden of proof justifying any elimination of an alleged classification of "slot maid."

ABSENTEEISM AND TARDINESS

An attendance policy that intentionally or unintentionally discriminates against an employee on the basis of gender violates Title VII. While a poor attendance record is a legitimate nondiscriminatory reason for discharge, poor attendance is not grounds for discharge when absenteeism is caused by or linked with sexual harassment. In *Ambrose v. U.S. Steel Corporation*[60] the District Court of Northern California determined the employer at fault when a female employee was discharged following her sexual harassment by a male supervisor. The attendance record of *Ambrose* was above par and worked in favor of Ambrose. To be precise, *Ambrose* presented her (a) attendance and (b) good work record. The Court considered these two attendance records and concluded:

Plaintiff must then demonstrate that excessive absenteeism was not the true reason for U.S. Steel's employment decision. Id. at 256. Plaintiff's exhibit 14 was a list of her absences in 1978 and 1979 that had been compiled by Clark. The list shows 19 days absent plus six weeks of sick leave in 1978. In 1979, 11 days are listed. At the same time that Clark recommended that Ambrose be removed from her position, she had been absent eight days in 1979 according to the list. Although the list was shown to be somewhat inaccurate, it does reflect Clark's and Benson's understanding of the number of absences at the time. The list also demonstrates that as of December 10, 1979, when Clark recommended to Benson that plaintiff be fired, plaintiff had been absent far fewer times than she had when Clark had rated her attendance as satisfactory.

Excessive absenteeism and sexual harassment has been examined:

If the employer has cited complainant's excessive absenteeism as a reason for its employment decision, then the complainant may attempt to prove (1) that the facts recited by the employer are not true [Boyd v. James S. Hayes Living Health Care Agency, 44 FEP Cases 332, 671 F.Supp 1155 (1987)], (2) that her attendance at the time of her discharge was no worse than it had previously been, when no adverse action had been taken [*Ambrose v. U.S. Steel Corporation*, 39 FEP Cases 30, N.D. Cal. (1985)], or (3) that similarly absent employees who did not reject sexual advances were not fired [B.L. Schlei & P. Grossman, Employment Discrimination Law, 1291-92 (2nd ed. 1983)]. A fourth item of proof, but one that does not necessarily impugn the employer's motivation would be that the complainant's absenteeism resulted from the harassment.[61]

---

[60] *Ambrose v. U.S. Steel Corporation*, 39 FEP Cases 30, N.D. Cal. (1985).
[61] Barbara Lindemann and David D. Kadue. *Sexual Harassment in Employment Law*. Washington, D.C.: BNA Books, Inc., 1992, 155.

In an analogous sexual harassment case, the complainant may attempt to prove that the excessive absenteeism cited by the employer as the basis for its action was itself the result of sexual harassment, or that the sexual harassment otherwise prevented the complainant from working [*Cline v. General Elec. Capital Auto Lease*, 55 FEP Cases 498, 506 (N.D.Ill. 1991)]. A review of circuit court sexual harassment cases suggests that about a fourth of them have involved increased absenteeism after incidents of harassment. E.g., First Circuit: *Lisett v. University of P.R.*, 864 F.2d 881, 890, 54 FEP Cases 230 (1st Cir. 1988) . . . Third Circuit: *Andrews v. City of Philadelphia*, 895 F.2d 1469, 1474-75, 54 FEP Cases 184 (3d Cir. 1990) . . . Fifth Circuit: *Waltman v. International Paper Company*, 875 F.2d 472, 50 FEP Cases at 182 . . . Sixth Circuit: *Wheeler v. Southland Corp.*, 875 F.2d 1246, 1248, 50 FEP Cases 86, 88 (6th Cir. 1989) . . . Seventh Circuit: *Swanson v. Elmhurst Chrysler-Plymouth*, 882 F.2d 1235, 1237, 50 FEP Cases 86, 88 (6th Cir. 1989) . . . *Eighth Circuit: Barrett v. Omaha Nat'l. Bank*, 726 F.2d 424, 426-27, 35 FEP Cases 593 (8th Cir. 1984) . . . Tenth Circuit: *Hicks v. Gates Rubber Co.*, 833 F.2d 1406, 1410, 45 FEP Cases 608 (10th Cir. 1987).[62]

The evidence presented by the union did not convince Arbitrator Joseph M. Stone that the female grievant faced discrimination on the basis of her gender. The grievant worked twenty years without incident and then developed irritable bowel syndrome (IBS), hypertension, and a sinus condition, causing excessive absenteeism from 1980 until her discharge in January 1983. The *Army, Harry Diamond Laboratories*[63] followed progressive discipline, and Arbitrator Stone concluded excessive absenteeism to be a nonpretextual reason for firing the grievant. And while Arbitrator Stone sustained the discharge, his award instructed the parties to reverse the termination to a thirty-day suspension if the Merit Systems Personnel Board elected to reverse a thirty-day suspension cited by management as a necessary part of its progressive discipline program.

The sex discrimination charge was dismissed in another Department of Defense case, *Army, Anniston Army Depot*.[64] The female grievant charged sex discrimination because women were required to inform their supervisor before going to the restroom in another building, a notification requirement not made for men because they need not leave the building to use the restroom. Arbitrator William D. Ferguson amended the reprimand for AWOL to a reprimand for insubordination. Arbitrator Ferguson reasoned that the grievant was not AWOL because she did not need to get permission to use the restroom. Anniston Army Depot policy and the direct order of her supervisor required the grievant to notify her supervisor before leaving the building. Arbitrator Ferguson concluded that failure to obey agency policy and/or a supervisor's direct order is insubordination.

Arbitrator Robert M. Rybolt would not delete, add to, or change the existing agreement nor was he empowered to grant the union an amendment to the labor

---

[62] *Ibid.* p. 199.

[63] *Army, Harry Diamond Laboratories*, LAIRS 16050 (Stone, 1984); see also *American Airlines, Inc.*, 77-1 ARB 8167 (Turkus, 1977).

[64] *Army, Anniston Army Depot*, LAIRS 13327 (Ferguson, 1981); see also *Servomation Corporation*, 81-1 ARB 8134 (Wren, 1980).

agreement through the arbitration procedure that could not be obtained at the bargaining table. The union argued that Selkirk Metalbestos[65] subjected the male grievant to reverse gender discrimination by not granting him an exemption from the need to submit a doctor's note to cover his absence, thereby causing the grievant to accumulate points under an attendance control program. Arbitrator Rybolt ruled that the employer's decision to exempt a pregnant employee from the need to submit a doctor's note to avoid accumulating attendance control points was an act of compassion that need not be extended to the grievant.

Agreeing with the union, Arbitrator Ronald F. Talarico overturned the discharge of a female grievant who was fired for an early quit. She went to her car 40 minutes before the end of her shift. Arbitrator Talarico reinstated the grievant and made her whole on the basis of unchallenged testimony that she had completed her assigned tasks, that she did not leave company property, and that a similar situated male employee was not disciplined. Arbitrator Talarico ruled that the unequal treatment of similarly situated men and women indicated disparate treatment.[66] Arbitrator Edward D. Pribble found that *Advance Circuits, Inc.*[67] acted unreasonably when it held the female grievant to a 96 percent average attendance standard, but varied the time frame used to determine the average from one employee to another. Arbitrator Pribble ordered that the grievant's record be cleaned and that she be made whole because management granted leaves for a variety of reasons to white male employees and not the female grievant whose reason for a leave request was legitimate. The Employer had amended its absenteeism program and Arbitrator Pribble based his award on management's failure to notify the union that the company had varied from its 96 percent average attendance standard. Management incorrectly counted the grievant's absences and then rejected her petition for a leave of absence. The grievant requested a leave of absence when she was injured in an off-work automobile accident.

WHISTLEBLOWING

Protective whistleblowing occurs when management asks an employee to engage in an action that violates the law and the employee reports management's request, and management then disciplines the employee for turning in the boss. Active whistleblowing takes place when an employee observes a violation of the law, the employee seizing the initiative and disclosing the employer's activities to proper authority.[68] Section 704(a) of Title VII prohibits retaliatory action against any individual or labor organization that opposes or participates in the

---

[65] *Silkirk Metalbestos*, 20 LAIS 1046 (Rybolt, 1992).
[66] *TYK Refractories Company*, 96 LA 803 (Talarico, 1991).
[67] *Advance Circuits, Inc.*, BMS 8905.14 (Pribble, 1989).
[68] Kurt H. Decker. *The Individual Employment Rights Primer*. Amityville, N.Y.: Baywood Publishing Company, 1991, 143.

investigation of unlawful employment practices guarded by Title VII. The antiretaliation provision of Title VII bars retaliation against an employee's relative, potential witnesses, and individuals who oppose another employer's discrimination.[69] Relief from retaliation for whistleblowing is also available under the Civil Rights Act of 1866, as amended, the National Labor Relations Act, the Railway Labor Act, state whistleblowing laws, such as those of New Jersey[70] and California,[71] through employment-at-will standards, and at arbitration.

However, it is a long standing tenet of arbitration that an employee may not claim a whistleblowing exemption in order to avoid discipline for cause or a proper personnel action. Arbitrator William J. Hannan ruled against the union in *Charleroi School District*.[72] The school district terminated the grievant ten days after the union filed her grievance challenging the district's denial of the grievant's promotion to full-time status. The evidence provided by the parties led Arbitrator Hannan to the conclusion that management's denial of promotion to the grievant was based upon normal personnel action. Arbitrator Hannan did not conclude that the promotion denial was grounded upon an irresponsible comment made to the grievant about her gender during the promotion interview. According to Arbitrator Hannan, the grievant's claim that she was terminated for filing the grievance falls under state law and, thus, is not substantively arbitrable under the labor contract.

Circumstantial evidence of retaliation for filing a sex discrimination complaint almost always causes arbitrators to rule in favor of the union. The significance of bare faced retaliation for grievance filing was considered by Arbitrator Isadore B. Helburn in 1978. In finding against *Amoco Chemicals Corporation*,[73] Arbitrator Helburn wrote:

It may thus be said that D__ put the gun to her own head by grieving. It was the grievance rather than discussions initiated by supervision that led to termination. While the Company certainly did no intend to punish D__ for grieving, this was the unwitting outcome of the chain of events. Such a result cannot be tolerated since the implications strike so deeply into the core of the ongoing relationship between Union and Company.

We must note the possibility that the decision to terminate would have been reached had D__ not complained against Vassallo. That possibility is speculative, however, and cannot be used as a basis for sustaining the discharge.

The conclusion to sustain the grievance provides no comfort for the arbitrator. D__'s record is unimpressive despite continued efforts on the Company's part to affect im-

---

[69] 421 FEP Manual 781 (1993). See also Barbara Lindemann and David D. Kadue. *Sexual Harassment in Employment Law*. Washington, D.C.: BNA Books, Inc., 1992, 285-287. An employer may not take reprisal against an employee whose wife filed an EEOC claim, against an employee who testified on behalf of spouse, against an employee for defending a fellow employee, or against a family member of an employee who whistleblows.

[70] *Sandom v. Travelers Mortgage Service*, 54 FEP 1259, 752 F.Supp 1240 (1990).

[71] *Tameny v. Atlantic Richfield Company*, 27 Cal.3d 167, 164 Cal. Rptr. 839 (1980).

[72] *Charleroi School District*, 86 PSEA 3156 (Hannan, 1986).

[73] *Amoco Chemicals Corporation*, 70 LA 504 (Helburn, 1978).

provement. The parties must understand that the award is based solely on procedural deficiencies and is not meant to imply satisfactory performance on D__'s part. Neither is the award intended to constrain the Company from taking future disciplinary action against the grievant, including discharge, if the action is for just cause.

In its agreement with the Seymour Education Association, the *Seymour Board of Education* agreed that "there shall be no reprisals of any kind taken against any teacher by reason of his membership in a professional organization or participation in its activities."[74] The board failed to renew the contract of the girls' softball and basketball coach because of decreased enrollment. After reviewing the record provided by the parties, Arbitrator Lawrence T. Holder, Jr., ruled for the union. Arbitrator Holder based his decision on undisputed union evidence that the grievant was recommended for contract renewal by her athletic director and staff; that the amount of practice time for girls' softball and basketball increased under the grievant's leadership; that the number of games increased from eight to eighteen while the grievant coached; and that the girls acquired new uniforms and equipment as a result of the grievant's efforts. The board abruptly decided not to renew the grievant's contract after she testified at an HEW hearing over the alleged inequality of the girls' sports program in comparison to boys' sports. Arbitrator Holder found the board in violation of the whistleblowing provision of the labor contract, directed that the grievant be made whole, and reinstated the grievant in her coaching position.

PROBATIONARY EMPLOYEES

Status as a probationary employee has little relevance under Title VII.[75] That is, the Title VII right to equal treatment as well as freedom from retaliation for filing a sex discrimination complaint applies to all employees, including those on probation. For example, the District Court of South New York determined that the police department was entitled to a summary judgment when it elected to discharge a probationary female police officer who was arrested for making false statements and obstructing administration.[76] But upon review, the Second Circuit Court dismissed the summary judgment because a jury might find that the police department discharged the probationary female officer for filing rape charges against the male officer.[77]

Unsatisfactory performance is a common reason for the discharge of probationary employees, a standard frequently upheld by arbitrators. On the other hand, gender harassment by a supervisor is grounds for a probationary employee to seek remedy under Title VII. In *Carrero v. New York City Housing Author-*

---

[74] *Seymour Board of Education*, 100 AIS 9 (Holder, 1978).
[75] *Smith v. Texas Dept. of Water Resources*, 41 FEP 1328 (5th Cir. 1986).
[76] *Sorlucco v. New York City Police Department*, 54 FEP 389 (SNY Dist. 1989).
[77] *Sorlucco v. New York City Police Department*, 54 FEP 398 (2nd Cir. 1989).

ity,[78] the Second Circuit affirmed the lower court's reinstatement of a probationary female employee who was denied adequate training and fair evaluations when she refused to submit to her supervisor's sexual demands and filed a harassment complaint.

The lack of a no-discrimination clause in the labor agreement may render a sex discrimination complaint nonarbitrable.[79] But where a no discrimination clause existed, Arbitrator Herbert H. Oestreich ruled that the labor agreement applied to sex discrimination charges filed by a probationary employee.[80] The grievant, a probationary employee, was charged by male co-workers with sex discrimination, a charge which the grievant countered with a sex harassment complaint of her own. In exonerating the employer, Arbitrator Oestreich found that the company had investigated the sex discrimination complaints, found no basis for the claims of either party, and informed all concerned of its findings. In his opinion, Arbitrator Oestreich sustained management's action on the following basis:

> Her foreman's overall performance rating is listed as "unsatisfactory." Her termination notice, given to her the same day, gives the following reasons for releasing her during the probationary period:
> 1. Excessive or unjustified absences or tardiness.
> 2. Inefficient or careless performance of duties, including failure of reasonable standards of workmanship or productivity, and wasting of materials.

Arbitrator Robert W. Smedley also considered a probationary grievant's sex harassment allegation and ruled in favor of management. The employer, *Tooele Army Depot*,[81] provided evidence that it had acted in good faith, despite the grievant's counter arguments, by basing its discharge on the grievant's insubordination, inattention to duty, absence from work, and uncooperativeness.

A probationary fire inspector's complaint of sex discrimination was found to be without merit by Arbitrator Robert D. Steinberg.[82] The *County of Orange* released the grievant when she could not complete the physical portion of her suppression training program due to a lack of upper-body strength. Arbitrator Steinberg examined the evidence and decided that the employer's requirement of upper-body strength was necessary and job relevant, particularly since a reduction in personnel created the need for inspectors to fight fires. In *Tinker AFB*,[83] Arbitrator Elvis C. Stephens ruled that the grievance was arbitrable and then dismissed the case on its merits. Arbitrator Stephens found that the grievant's sexual harassment complaint was based upon a single incident evolving from her breaking up with another employee, a complaint which he dismissed. In his opinion, Arbitrator Stephens detailed the fairness of the performance standards

---

[78] *Carrero v. New York City Housing Authority*, 51 FEP 596 (2nd Cir. 1989).

[79] *MJB Company*, 77 LA 1294 (Burns, 1982).

[80] *Aerojet General Corporation*, 88 LA 786 (Oestreich, 1987).

[81] *DOD, Army, Tooele Army Depot, Utah*, LAIRS 13727 (Smedley, 1981).

[82] *County of Orange*, IAFF 00467 (Steinberg, 1981).

[83] *Tinker AFB, Oklahoma City Air Logistics Center*, 84 FLRR 2-2122 (Stephens, 1983).

developed and applied by the employer. Arbitrator Stephens agreed with the supervisor's testimony that the grievant's termination was justified by inadequate performance.

Deciding what constitutes a probationary employee can be a tricky endeavor. The NLRB has held for many years that discrimination for union activities cannot motivate the layoff of workers. With NLRB standards in mind, Arbitrator Clare B. McDermott ruled that the discharge of a probationary female employee was motivated by poor performance and a poor work record rather than management animus for the grievant's former union activity or gender discrimination.[84] In his discussion, Arbitrator McDermott pointed out that the existence of clear and specific contract language made the grievant a probationary employee, despite her authorized receipt of pension benefits from the company.

When the company fails to investigate a good faith sex discrimination complaint, including those made by probationary employees, management opens itself to a due process allegation from the union. For example, the union prevailed when a probationary employee's discharge was not preceded by a management investigation of the grievant's good faith sex discrimination complaint. Arbitrator Elaine Frost found that the *City of Grand Rapids* violated the no-discrimination clause of the labor contract when it discharged the female probationary employee on the basis of a performance evaluation conducted by a single supervisor with a known bias against women.[85] In her analysis, Arbitrator Frost considered state and federal law as well as the no-discrimination clause negotiated by the parties in their labor agreement. Said Arbitrator Frost:

State and Federal law prohibit sex discrimination in employment. To establish a violation of these laws, direct proof of discrimination – such as an admission that adverse employment action was based on sex – is the best proof. But direct proof of discrimination is not needed. The cases recognize the difficulty of uncovering direct proofs, since discriminatory actions are frequently hidden. The courts have, therefore, permitted an inferential method of establishing civil rights violations which relies heavily on circumstantial evidence. . . . If evidence of discrimination is brought to management's attention, the reasonable response is for it to investigate and, if substantiated, to correct whatever harm was done. Here, there is no evidence that claims of sex discrimination were brought to management's attention before the grievance was filed on November 28, 1985. But, it is also clear that no later than that date, supervision was appraised of the claim. On November 28th the departmental decision had been made to fail Grievant but she had not yet received her final evaluation (dated the next day) and, more importantly, the final departmental action to terminate her probation was not taken until Smith signed the Probation Expiration Notice on December 4, 1985. It appears to the arbitrator that there was ample opportunity for management to investigate and determine whether there was validity to the claims of discrimination. And since those charges were made against the primary evaluator of the Grievant, upon whose judgment his superiors relied, the

---

[84] *Bethlehem Steel Corporation, Burns Harbor Plant*, 91 LA 293 (McDermott, 1988). See also *Hercules, Inc.*, 215 AAA 5 (Marx, 1976).
[85] *City of Grand Rapids*, 86 LA 819 (Frost, 1986).

arbitrator concludes that it was unreasonable not to investigate the claim before taking action of December 4th.

Some employers believe they have the right to discharge probationary employees for any reason, such as how they part their hair. *Bethlehem Steel Corporation*,[86] for example, claimed that it could discharge a female probationary employee for having green hair. Umpire Seymour Strongin was more impressed by union evidence supporting its contention that the female employee with green hair was actually discharged for her lack of physical stature while male employees of the same physical stature were retained. Umpire Strongin reasoned that the employer could not discharge female probationary employees for having green hair unless it would discharge male employees for the same reason.

POOR PERFORMANCE, NEGLIGENCE, AND INCOMPETENCE

The Civil Rights Act of 1964, as amended, seeks to promote the employment of persons based upon their ability instead of their gender. However, Title VII does not require the employment of men or women whose performance is below par. The Supreme Court emphasized in *Duke Power* that Title VII does not command employers to give job opportunities to unqualified workers simply because they are a legally protected class. Neither Congress nor the Supreme Court requires employers to keep negligent or incompetent employees. An employer who can show that employment decisions are based upon reasonable factors other than gender is not in violation of the law. When it comes to poor performance, the courts have evaluated complaints of sex discrimination against the same standards applied to racial bias. The courts are likely to sustain discharge where an employee's negligence, incompetence, and poor performance are corroborated by consistently low performance evaluations, supporting memoranda, and the testimony of supervisors.[87]

Looking at general case histories that do not involved matters of discrimination, arbitrators usually agree that poor work justifies corrective action and that management should consider the nature of the problem before termination. Collectively, arbitrators hold that unsatisfactory performance can result in discharge, suspension,[88] transfer, and/or demotion[89] for carelessness, failure to meet performance standards,[90] and disability. Carelessness results from negligence or wanton disregard for the employer's property or operations. Carelessness may

---

[86] *Bethlehem Steel Corporation*, 73 LA 1207 (Strongin, 1979).

[87] *Williams v. Cerberonics Inc.*, 49 FEP Cases 695, 871 F.2d 452 (1989); 872 F.2d 361 (1989); and *Bryant v. O'Connor*, 51 FEP Cases 187, 848 F.2d 1064 (1988).

[88] *Circle Pines/Lexington Police Department*, BMS 9509.2 (Imes, 1995).

[89] *Data Com, Inc.*, 86-2 ARB 8532 (Woy, 1986); *Altoona Shop and Save*, 12 LAIS 1267 (Hewitt, 1985); and *Parkin Printing and Stationary Company*, 76 LA 1075 (Robinson, 1981).

[90] *Security Pacific Bank*, 100 LA 145 (Forbes, 1992).

also result in a disciplinary discharge based upon the employee's poor attitude, inability or lack of desire to correct mistakes, and the effect of errors on other employees and customers.[91] However, carelessness and failure to meet performance standards are separate issues.

Failure to meet performance standards, unlike carelessness, is treated as a nonculpable disciplinary problem because the employee is not guilty of fault or wrongdoing. Arbitrators regularly allow termination to stand when the discharged employee has failed to meet reasonable performance standards. Arbitral authority, in judging the reasonableness of such discharge action, commonly considers whether co-workers have had to help rectify the discharged employee's errors; the adequacy of the employee's training; the supervision and equipment available for performing the job; the absence of harassment from counseling provided to the grievant; the consistency of the employee's mistakes over a variety of work assignments; and the weight of the performance records or work samples submitted for establishment of the worker's inability to perform.[92] Most arbitrators agree that termination, transfer, or layoff because of disability depends on whether the employer has good reason to believe that the employee cannot perform satisfactorily or without undue hazard to himself or co-workers.[93]

Returning to sex discrimination, the *Social Security Administration, Los Angeles*[94] had just cause to terminate the grievant during her probationary period because she verbally abused her supervisors and co-workers, ranked below average on her probationary period performance appraisal, and proved incompetent as a receptionist. The grievant was unable to avoid discharge by filing an unsubstantiated claim of race and sex discrimination against the Social Security Administration. When taken as a whole, the record submitted by *Hopemen Brothers, Inc.*[95] constituted a preponderance of evidence that the grievant was discharged for unsatisfactory performance, frequent absence, tardiness, being away from her work station, and spending too much time with other employees. Arbitrator Walter A. Fogel concluded that the close monitoring of the grievant's behavior by her supervisor was born out of concern for the grievant's poor performance rather than because of her gender. The grievant's record of unsatisfactory work overwhelmed the union's sex bias challenge despite the testimony of the grievant's supervisor. He openly stated that he believed women should be home making babies instead of working in the shipyard.

---

[91] *Lash Distributors, Inc.*, 74 LA 274 (Darrow, 1980).

[92] *Adel Precision Products Corporation, 8 LA 282 (Cheney, 1947); Western Stove Company, Inc., 12 LA 527 (Aaron, 1949); and Pet Incorporated, 76 LA 292 (Jason, 1981).*

[93] *Des Moines Asphalt and Paving Company, 76 LA 1233 (Evenson, 1981).*

[94] *Social Security Administration, Los Angeles, LAIRS 15500 (Darrow, 1983).*

[95] *Hopemen Brothers, Inc.*, 75 LA 944 (Fogel, 1980); see also *Charleroi School District,* 86 PSEA 3156 (1986).

Arbitrator A. Dale Allen, Jr. split his award in *KDFW TV*.[96] The television station discharged the grievant from her position as a weather anchor because her low viewer ratings made her unsuitable for the position. Arbitrator Allen sustained the discharge because management's right to change on-air personalities in the television industry goes beyond traditional management rights in other industries. That is, the termination of a female grievant to help the station's audience ratings is not evidence of gender bias. Arbitrator Allen granted the grievant one month's salary because she was not provided adequate advance notice of her termination.

While most all labor agreements allow for a probationary employee to be discharged without cause, arbitrators are willing to reinstate probationary employees whose discharge results from gender bias.[97] The grievant's careless safety habits at *Aerojet General Corporation*[98] constituted just cause for her discharge, particularly since the grievant was a probationary employee with poor attendance. Arbitrator Herbert H. Oestreich ruled against the union because the grievant's sex discrimination claim was fully investigated by management and found groundless before she was terminated. According to Arbitrator Oestreich, the union's uncontroverted testimony that the grievant's co-workers disliked working with a women in the janitorial position constituted prima facie evidence of sex discrimination. However, Arbitrator Oestreich dismissed the union's allegation due to convincing evidence that the grievant had been terminated for her careless safety habits rather than her gender.

A statement by the union that some sort of sex discrimination has occurred did not prove that *Pennzoil*[99] violated the antidiscrimination article of the labor contract. Arbitrator William C. Stonehouse, Jr., concluded that *Pennzoil* had just cause to discharge the grievant when she was injured at work because she was too small to perform the lifting required by her job. Arbitrator Storehouse judged that the work-related injury suffered by the grievant would not have been incurred by a person with more physical strength. A female employee who repeatedly violates a safety rule requiring the wearing of safety glasses may be disciplined.

Negligence and carelessness that result in a vehicle accident is just cause for discipline according to Arbitrator Martin F. Scheinman.[100] Management had settled upon a thirty day suspension in the incident, a suspension that Arbitrator Scheinman reduced to five days. The union proved sex bias through evidence that the penalty assessed to the female grievant was greater than the penalty as-

---

[96] *KDFW TV, Inc.*, 94 LA 806 (Allen, 1990). For opposite, see *Monterey Coal Company, Wayne Mine*, 13 INDUS REL REP 18.1 (Wren, 1982); *Standard Brands, Inc.*, 59 LA 596 (Dolnick, 1972); and *Chrysler Corporation*, 71-2 ARB 8659 (Alexander, 1971).

[97] *U.S. Steel Corporation, Trenton Works*, 64 LA 948 (Wits, 1975).

[98] *Aerojet General Corporation*, 88 LA 786 (Oestreich, 1987).

[99] *Pennzoil Company*, 78 LA 1070 (Storehouse, 1982); see also *Olin Corporation*, 73 LA 291 (Knudson, 1979), and *Los Angeles Community College District*, 8 LAI 4715 (Rothstein, 1979).

[100] CR, 20 SCARAB 3-23855 (Scheinman, 1982).

sessed to male grievants under similar circumstances. Arbitrator Scheinman did not order the discipline completely reversed because the grievant was responsible for the accident.

The requirement that men and women be treated the same under similar circumstances also applies to the wearing of protective clothing. In *City of Niagara Falls*,[101] Arbitrator Fred L. Denson found the union's sex discrimination challenge warranted because the city required women in clerical positions to wear protective smocks, but allowed men in clerical positions to go smock free. Arbitrator Denson concluded that management would have remained within the bounds of its antidiscrimination agreement had it issued smocks to both men and women. Management's case would have been stronger had they posted a memorandum stating that smock wearing was contractually mandatory.

LAYOFF AND RECALL

The search of arbitral awards involving layoff and recall of women produced a significant historical view dating to 1945. When World War II ended an immense number of senior female employees who performed traditional male jobs were: laid off and replaced by junior male employees[102] as a result of rearranged work assignments,[103] involuntarily transferred[104] to female-only jobs,[105] demoted to lower-paying jobs,[106] or outright discharged[107] because they were married.[108] Faced with this dilemma, labor arbitrators created several decision making templates. Indeed, some elements of Arbitrator Harry H. Platt's 1945 award in *Re-*

---

[101] *City of Niagara Falls*, 10 LAIS 2096 (Denson, 1983). See also *Saginaw Community Hospital*, LAIG 2577 (Herman, 1980) and *Litton Business Systems, Inc.*, 79-2 ARB 8610 (Stone, 1979).

[102] *Libbey-Owens-Ford Glass Company*, 2 LA 254 (Gilder, 1945); *St. Louis Car Company*, 5 LA 572 (Wardlaw, 1946); *Manion Steel Barrel Company*, 6 LA 1 64 (Wagner, 1947); and *J. L. Anderson Veneer Company*, 8 LA 676 (Guthrie, 1947).

[103] *General Cable Corporation*, 7 LA 691 (Klamon, 1947); *St. Louis Car Company*, 5 LA 572 (Wardlaw, 1946); and *Seattle Department Store Association, Inc.*, 3 LA 150 (Wardlaw, 1946).

[104] *New York Stock Exchange*, 7 LA 602 (Scheiber, 1947).

[105] *California Sanitary Canning Company*, 2 LA 33 (Prasow, 1945); *Procter-Gamble Manufacturing Company*, 1 LA 313 (Prasow, 1945); and *American Can Company*, 3 LA 46 (Scarborough, 1946). Women worked under a separate seniority system in *Pittsburgh Plate Glass Company*, 8 LA 572 (Horvitz, 1947).

[106] *Union Oil Company*, 3 LA 108 (Wardlaw, 1946) and *Cudahy Packing Company*, 7 LA 510 (Fisher, 1947). Demotion was reversed with back pay in *Bethlehem Steel Company*, 6 LA 28 (Selekin, 1946).

[107] *U.S. Rubber Company*, 3 LA 555 (Cheney, 1946) and *Bethlehem Steel Company*, 7 LA 1 63 (Killingsworth, 1947) .

[108] *Tennessee Coal, Iron Railroad Company*, 6 LA 995 (Blumer, 1946).

public Steel Corporation[109] are almost identical to those adopted by the U.S. Supreme Court in a host of interpretations of the Civil Right Act of 1964. Citing a contract clause providing that layoffs shall be determined by length of continuous service where ability to perform the work and physical fitness are relatively equal, Arbitrator Platt wrote:

[f]rom what has been said, I think it logically follows that the layoffs involved here must be considered strictly on an individual basis and not on a group basis. In other words, I do not think that the company has a right to lay off employees with greater seniority than those retained merely because they are women and because the company never employed women before the war. . . . Each of the laid off employees was entitled to retain her job as long as there was work available in the plant in the performance of which her physical capacity and ability were relatively equal to that of the younger employees who were retained.

Placing his template over the facts, Arbitrator Platt sustained the layoffs because the senior women did not have the ability or physical capacity to perform the available work.

Standing in line with his 1946 contemporaries, Arbitrator Charles G. Hampton ruled that qualified women should keep their jobs if they are senior. In reversing the employer's decision to recall junior male employees over senior females, Arbitrator Hampton reasoned that the parties had

set up certain seniority provisions, among which is the following: "When an increase in force is necessary, employees previously laid off will be recalled in order of seniority." This is clearly different language than is used in respect to new jobs and promotions, where it is stated that "the following shall be the determining factors: (1) Length of service; (2) Ability, merit and efficiency; (3) Physical fitness." That it would be more convenient for the company to employ men rather than women is apparent to the arbitrator, but the parties did not make such a stipulation in their agreement of April 1, 1946. Indeed, the agreement says "the provisions of this Contract shall apply to all employees covered by the Agreement without discrimination on account of race, color, sex, national origin or creed. . . ."

The Arbitrator also desires to point out that the company did not discharge these women – it merely refused to recall them from a lay off in line with seniority. Now, if the women are incapable of performing their work, if they are inefficient, or negligent of their duties the company had opportunity, prior to the lay off, to discharge these women for cause, but this was not done.[110]

---

[109] *Republic Steel Corporation*, 1 LA 244 (Platt, 1945); see also *Sinclair Rubber, Inc.*, 1 LA 288 (Gorder, 1946).

[110] *Ohio Steel Foundry Company*, 5 LA 12 (Hampton, 1946). Qualified senior females avoided layoff in *Ingram-Richardson Manufacturing Company of Indiana, Inc.*, 3 LA 482 (Whiting, 1946); *Bethlehem Steel Company*, 7 LA 161 (Killingsworth, 1946); *Chrysler Corporation*, 7 LA 380 (Wolff, 1947); and *Emge & Sons*, 7 LA 544 (Hampton, 1947). Qualified senior females returned with back pay in *A. S. Campbell Company, Inc.*, 2 LA 142 (Capelof, 1946) and *Presto Recording Corporation*, 3 LA 672 (Kaplan, 1946).

While some conflict may have existed between state law and the labor agreement, Arbitrator Hampton believed that the intent of the parties was best achieved by discharging female employees if the Ohio State Inspector so ordered. Females were discharged in other states as a result of protective legislation against women lifting heavy weights,[111] working night shifts,[112] or working where there is a lack of proper restroom facilities.[113]

Today, an employer may layoff and deny recall to any employee, regardless of gender, because of a lack of work, lack of qualifications,[114] necessary reorganization, and in order to comply with a bona fide seniority system.[115] In *U.S. v. Cincinnati, Ohio*,[116] for example, the Sixth Circuit Court agreed with a lower court decision to dissolve an injunction requiring the layoff of senior white male employees rather than junior blacks and females who had kept their jobs because of the injunction. However, without a court order or a legitimate BFOQ, layoff and recall may not be predicated upon biased gender considerations, such as when lack of work is a pretext for sex discrimination.[117] It is unlawful for an employer to layoff a female employee where a claim of sexual harassment by the supervisor is credible,[118] when a "grandfather" clause in the labor contract qualifies a female to perform the work,[119] and when a laid off male employee is not recalled because the employer contravened the job search process in favor of a female employee involved in a romantic relationship with her former supervisor.[120]

Arbitrator Milton Friedman examined public policy allowing the consideration of an employee's "sex in relation to employment in a locker room or toilet facility used only by members of one sex," finding in favor of the *New York City Board of Education*.[121] Arbitrator Friedman was persuaded by the employer's position that the layoff of two senior male physical education teachers was proper while retaining junior female education teachers. The loss of female physical education teachers would have required male physical education teachers in the girls' locker room or involved the extra expense of hiring an aid or

---

The senior female was given a trial period and back pay if she qualified in *Chrysler Corporation*, 8 LA 611 (Wolff, 1947).

[111] *Chrysler Corporation*, 7 LA 386 (Wolff, 1947).

[112] *Pittsburgh Corning Corporation*, 3 LA 364 (Lillibridge, 1946).

[113] *Manion Steel Barrel Company*, 6 LA 164 (Wagner, 1947).

[114] *UE&C Catalytic, Inc.*, 22 LAIS 1075 (Wolf, 1994).

[115] *Altman v. A.T. & T. Technologies, Inc.*, 49 FEP 400 (7th Cir. 1989).

[116] *U. S. v. Cincinnati, Ohio*, 38 FEP 1402 (6th Cir. 1985).

[117] *Dixon v. W.W. Grainger Inc.*, 49 FEP 595 (Mich Ct. App. 1987).

[118] *Gaddy v. Abex Corporation*, 50 FEP 1333 (7th Cir. 1989).

[119] *Rathgeb v. Air Cal, Inc.*, 43 FEP 483 (9th Cir. 1987).

[120] *Davis v. Connecticut General Life Insurance Company*, 53 FEP 1172 (MTenn Dist. 1990).

[121] *New York City Board of Education*, UFT 000204 (Friedman, 1976). See also *Litton Systems, Inc.*, 10 LAI 2376 (Ipavec, 1983); *Proviso Township High School*, 155 AIS 1 (Cook, 1982); and *New Trier Township High School*, 152 AIS 13 (Dolnick, 1982).

assigning extra duties to another female teacher. Arbitrator Friedman based his award in part on the parties' past practice of always having separate male and female physical education teachers, always preparing separate examinations for the male and female gym teachers, always maintaining separate seniority lists for the physical education teachers, and always making teaching appointments from these separate lists.

An employer's request for clarification of an arbitration award calling for the retention of junior female employees and the layoff of senior male employees was denied by Arbitrator M. Zane Lumbley. *B & I Lumber*[122] contented that Arbitrator Lumbley's original award called for

either the layoff of one of two junior employees whose job neither H__ nor M__ is fully qualified to perform (thereby creating a gap in the Employer's operations) or the layoff of a more senior employee (thereby generating another similar grievance).

Arbitrator Lumbley ruled that his authority and jurisdiction was entirely terminated by the completion and delivery of the original award. Had the union joined *B & I Lumber's* request for clarification, Arbitrator Lumbley may have felt compelled to examine the matter.

SEXUAL PREFERENCE

The Civil Rights Act of 1964, as amended, does not address discrimination on the basis of sexual preference. The Title VII ban on gender discrimination does not apply to transsexuals or other individuals who fail to conform to the traditional notion of sex based on anatomical characteristics that distinguish between male and female organisms.[123] It is lawful for an employer to refuse employment to a man applying for a mail room clerical position on the basis of the applicant's effeminate appearance.[124] But while Title VII does not guard sexual preference, it has been concluded under other laws that homosexuals may not be discharged because of their sexual preference.[125]

Discipline and discharge of homosexuals is frequently upheld on grounds other than sexual preference, such as when the homosexual trait affects job performance.[126] For example, the Supreme Court upheld an Oklahoma statute permitting the discharge of a homosexual teacher who advocated social acceptance

---

[122] *B & I Lumber*, 81 LA 282 (Lumbley, 1983); see also *Rath Packing Company*, 11 LAI 603 (Hoffmeister, 1984).

[123] *Ulane v. Eastern Airlines*, 35 FEP 1348, 742 F.2d 1081 (1984). See also *Sommers v. Budget Marketing Inc.*, 27 FEP 1217, 667 F.2d 748 (1982), and *Holloway v. Aurthur Anderson Company*, 16 FEP 689, 566 F.2d 659 (1977).

[124] *Smith v. Liberty Mutual Insurance Company*, 17 FEP 28, 569 F.2d 325 (1978).

[125] *Swift v. USA*, 42 FEP 787, 649 F.Supp 596 (1986).

[126] *Ashton v. Civiletti*, 20 FEP 1601 (DC Dir. 1979); see also *Williamson v. A. G. Edwards & Sons Inc.*, 50 FEP 95, 876 F.2d 69 (1989).

of homosexuality in the classroom.[127] Homosexual teachers have been removed from the classroom for falsified information on their application for employment[128] and for having an affair with a student.[129] In *Singer v. Civil Service Commission*[130] the company did not violate the right to free speech of a homosexual who was discharged for public flaunting of homosexual conduct.

Sometimes the government considers homosexuals to be security risks. The discharge of a homosexual who lost his security clearance for engaging in homosexual behavior overseas need not conform to the merit principles enunciated in the Foreign Service Act.[131] Homosexual harassment of another employee violates Title VII[132] unless the harassment is not severe nor pervasive.[133] A homosexual may not be disciplined for off-duty homosexual activity.[134]

Like the courts, labor arbitrators have given little support to homosexuals who allow their sexual preference to impact job performance, a standard of conduct applicable to all employees. Arbitrator Judith A. LaManna upheld the discharge of a male correctional officer who violated the New York State Penal Code by allowing a minor to observe illegal narcotic activity was conducted.[135] Arbitrator LaManna reasoned that management had the right to question the grievant, a presumed homosexual, about his sexual behavior with the teenage boys involved in the narcotics activity. Arbitrator LaManna wrote:

[t]he Union's suggestion that Grievant was discriminated against because of his presumed sexual preference has no substance. There was no testimony to substantiate an anti-homosexual attitude on the part of either Detective Millor or, more importantly, the Employer. Detective Miller's explanation of the reason for such questioning of Grievant is credible. The age differential of the parties alone would have caused police concern, whether the youths were male or female. In fact, it would have been irresponsible, given those circumstances, if Miller had not made such inquiries in light of the increased current concerns over child molestation.

Arbitrators have sustained the discharge of transsexuals who fail to meet performance standards[136] and homosexuals with a record of excessive absentee-

---

[127] *Oklahoma City Board of Education v. National Gay Task Force*, 37 FEP Cases 505, 470 U.S. 903 (1985).

[128] *Acanfora v. Board of Education of Montgomery County*, 9 FEP 1287, 491 F.2d 498 (1974).

[129] *Naragon v. Wharton*, 35 FEP 748, 737 F.2d 1403 (1984).

[130] *Singer v. Civil Service Commission*, 12 FEP 208, 530 F.2d 247 (1977).

[131] *U.S. Information Agency v. Krc*, 53 FEP 51, 905 F.2d 389 (1990). See also *Doe v. Cheney*, 50 FEP 1307, 885 F.2d 898 (1989), and *Watkins v. Army*, 49 FEP 1763, 875 F.2d 699 (1989).

[132] *Wright v. Methodist Youth Services, Inc.*, 25 FEP 563, 511 F.Supp 307 (1981).

[133] *Morgan v. Massachusetts General Hospital*, 53 FEP 1780, 901 F.2d 186 (1990).

[134] *Norton v. Macy*, 9 FEP 1382, 417 F.2d 1161 (1969).

[135] *New York State Department of Corrections*, 86 LA 793 (LaManna, 1985).

[136] *Iowa State Board of Regents*, DIG 102601 (Harrison, 1978).

ism.[137] By the same token, Arbitrator Joseph R. Rocha, Jr., awarded attorney fees and back pay to a homosexual grievant who was discharged because of his sexual preference and then reinstated when management learned that its action was not carried out in a prompt and timely manner.[138]

Arbitrator George T. Roumell, Jr., agreed with management's assessment that a homosexual who received two written warnings aimed to improve his poor attitude toward work, but continued to be negligent, is being discharged for just cause. Arbitrator Roumell's written opinion offers an important standard against which to examine the union's allegation that the grievant was discharged for his sexual preference.

> S__ has also suggested, at least to the Human Relations Department of the City of Detroit, that he was discharged because of his sexual preference. S__ claims that on January 15, 1984 he accidentally left a survey about AIDS on a counter and that this came to the attention of Town House Manager Paul Richards. S__ concludes that this resulted in his discharge the following day.
>
> If this suggestion were correct, S__'s discharge would be arbitrary and capricious and would not have been made in good faith. See Denver Publishing Co., 52 LA 552, 556 (Gorsuch, 1969). However, S__'s discharge was not motivated because of his sexual preference. W__ is also known by Town House to be a homosexual. Yet, he has worked for Town House for over a year. Furthermore, as already discussed, the reasons asserted by Town House adequately justify S__'s discharge.[139]

Not all arbitrator's agree that a grievant's charge of discrimination on the basis of sexual preference should be subjected to the arbitrary and capricious standard followed by Arbitrator Roumell. Arbitrator Philip P. Tamousch concluded that the union's charge of discrimination on the basis of sexual preference was not arbitrable. The legal memorandum of understanding agreed by the *County of Orange*[140] called for no discrimination against employees by reason of physical handicap, marital status, medical condition, race, religion, color, sex, age, national origin, or ancestry. Arbitrator Tamousch ruled for management because sexual preference was absent from the specific list of reasons covered by the antidiscrimination memorandum negotiated by the parties.

In a case that involved an arbitrability challenge, Arbitrator Thomas P. Gallagher agreed with management's conclusion that the female grievant waived her right to grieve the denial of family health insurance coverage for her adult female "spousal equivalent."[141] Arbitrator Gallagher dismissed the grievance because the labor contract required election of remedy when alleged conduct violates both the contract and the law. The grievant challenged the employer's refusal to contribute toward the dependent's contractual health insurance premiums.

---

[137] *Arizona Portland Cement Company*, 79 LA 128 (Weizenbaum, 1982).

[138] *Customs Service, Boston*, 79 LA 284 (Rocha, 1982).

[139] *Town House Apartments*, 83 LA 538 (Roumell, 1984).

[140] *County of Orange*, 76 LA 1040 (Tamousch, 1981).

[141] *Library Board, City of Minneapolis*, 94 LA 369 (Gallagher, 1989); see also *Michigan Education Association*, 155 AIS 6 (Schwimmer, 1982).

A homosexual whose work is of insufficient quantity and/or quality is subject to progressive discipline and discharge for poor performance.[142] However, a known homosexual with a clean work record, whose behavior does not result in notoriety or public censure, may not be discharged because of sexual preference where his wrong doing is *de minimis*.[143] Employees who attend a "lesbian show" may not be constructively discharged for their behavior or sexual preference so long as the off-duty conduct does not adversely affect the operation of the employer's business.[144]

FACILITIES, GROOMING, AND DRESS CODE

Title VII requires that company facilities, such as restrooms, as well as grooming policy and dress codes treat male and female employees substantially equally.[145] As a practical matter, separate but equal is lawful when it involves sleeping or restrooms.[146] Indeed, an employer who does not provide separate toilet facilities for women can be held to be in violation of Title VII. For example, in *Lynch v. Dean*[147] the Sixth Circuit Court of Appeals in Cincinnati ruled that unsanitary portable toilets had a disparate impact upon female employees. Women as group face greater hazard's from unsanitary portable toilets than men as a group. For example, the unsanitary portable toilets affected the health of women workers while leaving the health of male employees unaffected. By the same token, minimum adjustments in living arrangements aboard a tuna fishing vessel aimed to accommodate female observers on the tuna vessel with an all-male crew are not an unreasonable violation of the male crew member's right to privacy.[148]

Social norms can be cited by an employer to justify substantially equal, but not identical, policies governing the grooming and dress of men and women. Courts have concluded as far back as 1973 that an employer may adopt reasonable grooming and dress requirements in order to conform with the social norms of America's highly competitive business envionment.[149] During this same era, in 1975, the Fifth Circuit Court determined that an employer may adopt minor gender-based differences in grooming, such as short hair for men, but not women, so long as the policy is reasonable and has no more than a negligible effect upon

---

[142] *Internal Revenue Service, Baltimore*, 92 LA 233 (Lang, 1989).

[143] *Customs Service, Highgate Springs*, 77 LA 1113 (Rocha, 1981); see also *Greyhound Lines, Inc.*, 325 AAA 1 (Kaufman, 1985).

[144] *Ralphs Grocery Company*, 77 LA 867 (Kaufman, 1981).

[145] *Ottaviani v. State University of New York at New Paltz*, 50 FEP 251, 679 F.Supp. 288 (1988); see also *Geisler v. Folsom*, 34 FEP Cases 894, 735 F.2d 991 (1984).

[146] *Causey v. Ford Motor Company*, 10 FEP 1493, 516 F.2d 416 (1975).

[147] *Lynch v. Dean, sub. nom., Lynch v. Freeman*, 43 FEP 1120, 817 F.2d 380 (1987).

[148] *Castagnola v. Mosbacher*, 51 FEP 1055, 720 F.Supp. 155 (1989).

[149] *Fagan v. National Cash Register Company*, 5 FEP 1335, 481 F.2d 1115 (1973).

employment opportunities.[150] An employment policy requiring men, but not women, to wear ties[151] is reasonable; and it is reasonable to bar men, but not women, from wearing earrings.[152]

In addition to being reasonable and in conformance with social norms, grooming and dress codes must be administered in an even handed manner. For example, an employer may require all employees to dress conservatively. When this is done, employees who fail to comply with conservative grooming and dress policy may be required to tone down their personal appearance[153] or be discharged following progressive discipline.[154] The requirement that dress codes be enforced evenhandedly applies to uniforms too. A firm that requires women to wear uniforms consisting of five basic color-coordinated items[155] while allowing men to wear appropriate business attire violates Title VII.[156] It is also unlawful gender stereotyping for a hospital to require female employees to wear white or pastel-colored hospital uniforms while male workers are allowed to dress in ordinary street cloths;[157] or for a coat factory to require female sales clerks to wear smocks without applying the same uniform standard to male clerks.[158]

Not all employers seek to tone down employee appearance. The U.S. Supreme Court considered the unwritten appearance code of *Price Waterhouse* and determined that management violated Title VII by denying career advancement to a fully qualified female candidate because she did not dress, walk, talk, or wear her hair "femininely" enough.[159] An employer does not have an unfettered right to require women to wear sexually suggestive attire to work,[160] nor to discipline or demote a woman, such as a cocktail waitress, because she refuses to comply with an unfettered request to wear something "low-cut and slinky" while on the job.[161] On the other hand, a woman's clothing store may fire female employees who fail to wear a revealing swimsuit and cover-up during a swimsuit promotion where the likelihood of unwelcome verbal or physical conduct of a sexual nature from either a co-worker or nonemployees is remote, reasonable business need may exist for an employee to wear an revealing swimsuit.[162]

---

[150] *Knott v. Missouri Pacific Railway*, 11 FEP 1231, 527 F.2d 1249 (1975) and *Willingham v. Macon Telegraph Publishing Company*, 9 FEP 189, 507 F.2d 1084 (1975).

[151] *Fountain v. Safeway Stores*, 15 FEP 96, 555 F.2d 753 (1977).

[152] *DeSantis v. Pacific Telephone and Telegraph Company*, 19 FEP 1493, 608 F.2d 327 (1979).

[153] *Bellissimo v. Westinghouse Electric Corporation*, 37 FEP 1862, 764 F.2d 175 (1985).

[154] *Wislocki-Goin Mears*, 45 FEP Cases 216, 831 F.2d 1374 (1987).

[155] *Carroll v. Talman Federal Savings Loan Assn.*, 20 FEP 764, 604 F.2d 1028 (1979).

[156] The same principle applies to grooming.

[157] *Michigan Department of Civil Rights v. Sparrow Hospital*, 36 FEP 253, Mich CtApp. (1982).

[158] *O'Donnell v. Burlington Coat Factory*, 43 FEP 150, 656 F.Supp. 263 (1987).

[159] *Price Waterhouse v. Hopkins*, 49 FEP 954, US SupCt. (1989).

[160] *EEOC v. Sage Realty Corporation*, 24 FEP 1521, 507 F.Supp. 599 (1981).

[161] *Priest v. Rotary*, 40 FEP 208, 634 F.Supp. 571 (1986).

[162] *EEOC Decision No. 85-9*, 37 FEP 1893, (May 7, 1985).

While Title VII requires that men and women be assigned substantially equal facilities, Arbitrator Lois A. Rappaport found an exception. *Jamaica Hospital*[163] did not violate the labor agreement by failing to provide male employees with new and convenient locker rooms, female locker rooms being new and convenient. Arbitrator Rappaport ruled in favor of management because both male and female locker rooms were provided in order to comply with a Department of Health order requiring that outer garments not be kept in the pathology laboratory area. Arbitrator Rappaport sustained management because the male and female locker rooms were patrolled by the hospital security department; because the union's testimony was given by an employee who had not visited the male locker room in ten years; because the male locker room had been painted recently; and because the hospital was short of locker room space. The union claimed that male employees were discriminated against because they had to report to work early in order to store their coats at the inconvenient locker room. Arbitrator Rappaport found no problem with male employees reporting early because the hospital followed a work rule that allowed male employees to clock in before they stored their coats.

Arbitrator Jonas Silver paralleled *Lynch* when he directed the *Otis Elevator Company*[164] to maintain properly supplied and sanitary restrooms for female employees, male employees having a janitor on duty to keep their restroom sanitary. Arbitrator Silver's findings include a mixture of contractual and legal considerations aimed to provide sanitary lady's restroom facilities.

Apart from its basic position that it is not obligated to fill a vacant position, the Company asserts that while rest room conditions are "not as pristine as before," they have not reached the point of unsafe working conditions nor do they constitute discrimination against female employees. The Arbitrator does not agree.

It is not simply the puddle on the floor or the vomit that may have happened without the Matron on the job and awaited her arrival or even have been cleaned up by an employee before her arrival. It is rather the totality of dirty toilets and sinks, lack of paper, towels and napkins, together with puddles and vomit, that collectively describe a breakdown in elemental sanitary conditions stemming from an absence of the regular attention formerly given these essentials of industrial hygiene. And if it may have been appropriate to term the former conditions as "pristine," the current state of the ladies' rooms is hardly "not as pristine as before," to use the Company's scale of measurement of the decline and fall of the ladies' toilets, a fall that at times defies sitting down.

The testimony of successive witnesses, as heretofore indicated, was sufficiently vivid and unsparing of details to warrant the finding that the ladies' rooms are plain dirty. That which is dirty is a menace to employee health and well being and tantamount to an unsafe working condition in violation of Article VIII, Section 7. When the Company agreed "to provide safe working conditions," it obligated itself not only to assure the physical safety of the work site as such but, equally important, the cleanliness of those facilities functionally indispensable to normal, human needs.

---

[163] *Jamaica Hospital*, 10 LAIS 1132 (Rappaport, 1983).
[164] *Otis Elevator Company, Harrison Plant*, 60 LA 1332 (Silver, 1973).

Moreover, the Arbitrator is empowered to take judicial notice of the requirements of Federal enactments which affect the issue between the parties herein. Thus, the Federal Occupational Health and Safety Act of 1970, declares public policy in part to be: "Section 2(b). The Congress declares it to be its purpose and policy . . . to assure as far as possible every working man and woman in the Nation safe and healthful working conditions and to preserve our human resources (1) by encouraging employers and employees in their efforts to reduce the number of occupational safety and health hazards at their places of employment."

Title VII of the Civil Rights Act of 1964, as amended in 1972, says in part:

Section 703(a). It shall be an unlawful employment practice for an Employer
1. to fail or refuse to hire or to discharge any individual or *otherwise to discriminate against any individual with respect* to his compensation, terms, *conditions, or privileges of employment, because of such individual's* race, color, religion, sex, or national origin; or
2. *to limit,* segregate, or classify *his employees* or applicants for employment *in any way which would* deprive or tend to deprive any individual of employment opportunities *or otherwise adversely affect his status as an employee because of such individual's* race, color, religion, *sex* or national origin. [Emphasis supplied.]

The foregoing Federal laws must be regarded as attaching to the contract provisions which are subordinate thereto. They require that the "safe working conditions" of Article VIII, Section 7 of the Agreement be consistent with national policy to reduce safety and health hazards at the place of employment and that the "no discrimination . . . because of sex" of Section 3, accord with the law's ban on limiting employees in any way which would adversely affect employee status because of sex. As heretofore found the Company's failure to maintain the ladies' rooms in a sanitary state during working hours breached the aforesaid Sections of the Agreement and, in so neglecting, the Company likewise failed to comport with those Federal standards which adhere in those Sections of the Agreement.

Arbitrator Silver rejected a past practice which management cited to justify its unwillingness to maintain sanitary toilet facilities for female employees.

Unless separate dress codes can be justified by genuine health and safety needs,[165] an employer who does not apply dress codes equally to male and female employees is likely to lose at arbitration.[166] Arbitrator Edward E. McDaniel considered the grievance of a male employee who purposefully tested the reasonableness of the *South Park District*[167] appearance requirement by violating the dress code repeatedly. Arbitrator McDaniel split his decision by first sustaining the union's allegation that the unfettered dress code implemented by the district set an unreasonable double standard for male and female employees. The employer had just cause to suspend the grievant since he acted insubordi-

---

[165] *U. S. Steel Corporation, Trenton Works*, 64 LA 948 (Wits, 1975).
[166] *City of Niagara Falls, Housing Authority*, 10 LAIS 2096 (Denson, 1983).
[167] *South Park District*, 75 PSEA 0256 (McDaniel, 1975).

nately, and violated the long standing arbitral principle that employees should do as they are required and then grieve.

The union prevailed in an appearance code grievance involving both hair and clothing that took place in the overseas *Dependent Schools, Okinawa, Japan.*[168] The male grievant charged sex discrimination and a violation of Title VII when the Department of Defense (DOD) required the grievant to change his long hair-style, to pin his hair up, or to wear a wig; furthermore, DOD prohibited the grievant from wearing blue jeans, sandals, or collarless shirts to work. Arbitrator John H. Abernathy's decision favored the union because the parents of the grievant's pupils did not write letters or testify against the grievant's appearance, because the grievant's appearance did not violate any health or safety require-ments, because management was arbitrator, and because the grievant's appear-ance did not create a disruptive work environment.

KINSHIP, FRIENDSHIP, AND NO-NEPOTISM RULES

While it may appear straightforward, determining who is covered by an em-ployer's nepotism rule is frequently problematic.[169] The no-marriage rule, the no-spouse rule, the no-kin rule, the no-friends rule, and the no-fraternization rule are all arguably subsets of the no nepotism rule.[170] In actual practice, however, nepotism restrictions are enforced differently from company to company and from public agency to public agency. Some firms do not allow spouses, kin, or friends to work in the same field office, while others ignore altogether the re-striction on employing relatives. Take federal policy, for example, U.S. Office of Personnel Management policy allows relatives to work for the same agency so long as a public official neither refers nor advocates appointment, employment, promotion, or advancement of a relative in an agency over which he exercises jurisdiction or control.[171] One relative may not report directed to another in the organizational chain of command.

The list of relatives covered by Title V, Part 310, of the Code of Federal Regulation is exhaustive, including the obvious family relationships such as spouse, father, mother, son, daughter, uncle, and aunt, as well as a host of in-laws, step-relatives, and half-blood relations. Depending on facts and circum-stances, the provisions of Part 310 may be affected or superseded by other laws

---

[168] *Dependent Schools, Okinawa, Japan,* LAIRS 19551 (Abernathy, 1989); see also *St. Elizabeth Hospital,* 9 LAI 3842 (Gross, 1980).

[169] Portions of this section can be found in Vern E. Hauck. "Nepotism, Arbitration and Employee Assistance," *Journal of Employee Assistance Research,* Vol. 2, No. 1, Summer 1993, 28.

[170] The no-marriage rule is not specifically considered in this chapter, and the no-friends rule has seldom been addressed by the courts and arbitrators.

[171] Chapter 1, Title 5, Part 310 *Employment of Relatives, Code of Federal Regulation,* revised as of January 1, 1980.

governing employment. Exceptions to Part 310 are made for relatives who are "qualified preference-eligible," meaning that they are eligible for hire or promotion based on personal merit; for relatives hired to meet emergencies posing an immediate threat to life or property; and for some relatives seeking summer or student employment.[172]

Yuhas v. Libbey-Owens Ford Company,[173] a leading case involving nepotism, was decided in 1977. Reversing the District Court, the Seventh Circuit considered the legality of a no-spouse rule, finding the rule justified by business necessity. According to the Court, the employer's nepotism policy in a nearly all male plant did not violate Title VII because the rule improved the work environment, did not penalize women on the basis of a physical characteristic, averted potential conflicts of interest where one spouse is a supervisor, and helped to eliminate bias. The Seventh Circuit deemed the no-spouse rule a rational business policy that did not violate Title VII, even though the business need for the rule was supported more by hypothetical employment concerns than concrete evidence.[174] Importantly, the no-spouse policy adopted by the employer in *Yuhas* did not apply to employees married after being hired.

The Supreme Court has not elected to consider the nepotism rule directly. Nevertheless, the High Court indirectly issued some general support for *Yuhas* in *Furnco v. Waters Construction Company.*[175] In *Furnco* the Supreme Court ruled that companies are not obligated to adopt hiring procedures that maximize employment opportunities for minorities (and women). Viewing *Yuhas* and *Furnco* simultaneously, employers rightfully anticipate problems, such as work assignment bias, and rightfully claim business necessity even though these problems are not ripe. *Yuhas* and *Furnco* open the possibility that fairly administered no-spouse rules will remain in compliance with Title VII despite a sexually discriminatory disparate impact. That is, the no nepotism rule is probably lawful, despite a disparate impact, provided all relatives and spouses (male and female) are refused employment.[176] But, if an exception is made for male employees, failure to make the same exception for women violates Title VII.[177]

Three other Title VII cases may be relevant to no nepotism policy. Citing *Yuhas*, the district and appellate courts in *Espinoza v. Thoma*[178] agreed that the no-

---

[172] Chapter 1, Title 5, Part 338 *Qualification Requirements (General), Code of Federal Regulation*, revised as of January 1, 1980.

[173] *Yuhas v. Libbey-Owens Ford Company*, 16 FEP 891 (7th Cir. 1977).

[174] *Cleveland Board of Education v. La Fleur*, 6 FEP 1253, 414 US 632 (1974) and *Dothard v. Rawlinson*, 15 FEP 10, 433 US 321 (1977).

[175] *Furnco v. Waters Construction Company*, 17 FEP 1062, 438 US 567 (1978).

[176] *Bracamontes v. Amstar Corporation*, 16 FEP 1525 (ED LA Dist. 1976); *Harper v. Trans World Airlines*, 11 FEP 1074 (8th Cir. 1975); and *Sime v. Trustees of California State University and Colleges*, 11 FEP 1104 (9th Cir. 1975).

[177] *Linebaugh v. Auto Leasing Company*, 18 FEP 752 (Ky Dist. 1978); *Tuck v. McGraw-Hill, Inc.*, 13 FEP 778 (SD NY Dist. 1978); and *Sanbonmatsu v. Boyer*, 8 EPD 9704 (NY S.Ct. 1974).

[178] *Espinoza v. Thoma*, 17 FEP 1362 (8th Cir. 1978).

spouse rule is not outlawed by Title VII. In *Thoma*, the woman lived with an employee and gave birth to a child out of wedlock. While not formulated with the live-in mate in mind, the appellate court felt that the no-spouse rule was broad enough to apply to unmarried employees living together. *Meier v. Evansville School Corporation*[179] is an instance where no evidence of intentional discrimination could be provided to show harm from the no-spouse rule. Prior to marriage, the woman and her husband taught in the same public school. After marriage, the woman, without her consent, was transferred to another school. The court could not find a violation of Title VII because the marriage was undertaken with full knowledge of the no-nepotism rule. The husband became department chair;[180] the spouse did not suffer financial loss; and, marriage, not the sex of the woman, led to the wife's transfer. *Meier* opens the possibility that, if spouses hold similar teaching jobs at the same location, transfer of either spouse without consent violates Title VII (sex bias) unless a business need is demonstrated.[181]

The requirement that the employer provide a compelling business need to justify a no-spouse policy that effectively excludes female applicants was considered by the Eighth Circuit Court in *EEOC v. Rath Packing Company*.[182] The Eighth Circuit used essentially the same decision criteria as *Yuhas*, but came to different conclusions. The *Rath* court found that the no-spouse rule in the meatpacking plant violated Title VII because most of the workers were male and none of the business justifications cited by the employer for the nepotism policy could be considered compelling. In *Rath* the employer testified that the no-spouse policy was followed to avoid problems of dual absenteeism, vacation scheduling, supervision of spouses, and employee pressure to hire kin.

Cease and desist orders from the EEOC are not the same as court decisions, but are binding. According to the EEOC, employment information about friends or kin working for an employer is not relevant to the competence of a job applicant. To be precise, the EEOC positions that seeking information about friends or kin is illegal if the request is connected to disparate treatment or has a disparate impact. By the same token, an employer who gives preference to friends or kin of employees violates Title VII if such preference reduces or eliminates opportunities for women. That is, a no-nepotism rule may be illegal if it has an adverse impact on the job opportunities for women.[183] However, an employer is not guilty of sex discrimination by following a no-nepotism policy that bars an employee from voting for a distant relative seeking promotion to

---

[179] *Meier v. Evansville School Corporation*, 16 FEP 1713 (Ind Dist. 1975). See also *Thomas v. Metroflight, Inc.*, 43 FEP 703 (10th Cir. 1987), and *George v. Farmers Electric Cooperative, Inc.*, 32 FEP 1801 (5th Cir. 1983).

[180] *Fitzpatrick v. Duquesne Light Company*, 37 FEP 843 (3rd Cir. 1985).

[181] *Harper v. TWA*, 9 FEP 105, 385 F. Supp 1001.

[182] *EEOC v. Rath Packing Company*, 40 FEP 580 (8th Cir. 1986). See also *Terbovitz v. Fiscal Court of Adair County, Ky.*, 44 FEP 841 (6th Cir. 1987).

[183] 421 FEP Manual 356.

executive director.[184] And, an owner's decision to discharge a female employee involved in a romance with his son did not violate Title VII, even though favoritism toward the son was shown by keeping him on the job.[185] The discharge of a female employee who dated a co-worker was upheld by the Fifth Circuit Court of Appeals because Wal-Mart Stores administered its nonfraternization policy evenhandedly.[186]

The right of employers to construct and amend nepotism policy is supported by arbitrators. And, the application of a no-nepotism rule is more likely to be sustained by arbitrators when the rule clearly lists those family members who shall not be considered for employment.[187] An ambiguous nepotism policy that essentially does not exist cannot be used to justify a failure to follow contractual seniority provisions or to bypass a worker for promotion,[188] particularly when the grievant is qualified.[189] For example, a no-nepotism policy that was too broad was struck down by Arbitrator Edward A. Pereles in *Miami Shores Village*.[190] Arbitrator Pereles faulted the employer because the couple had lived together prior to marriage with no negative impact upon job performance. Arbitrator Pereles felt the employer should have remained flexible in light of the couples' previous work record. However, Arbitrator Pereles sustained the grievant's shift change following marriage even though the company knew of the grievant's live-in arrangement before marriage.

For the most part, couples who meet on the job and subsequently marry are not subject to discharge for nepotism. Arbitrator Raymond R. Roberts considered the application of a no-nepotism rule when the employer discharged a female employee after her marriage to a co-worker.[191] Roberts wrote:

Arbitrators have uniformly held that a No Hire Spouse policy does not apply to employees presently in the work force who might subsequently marry. . . . [Only] one significant factual issue is contested in the present case. That is, the question of whether or not Grievant was on notice that the Company intended to apply its No Spouse rule to existing employees and what the consequences of a violation of that rule would be. The Arbitrator resolves that issue in favor of the Company and finds that Grievant was told in advance of her marriage to M__ that the Company interpreted and intended to apply that rule to existing employees so that one of the employees would be required to resign, or the most junior employee would be terminated.

While the Arbitrator finds that that was true prior to Grievant's marriage, he does not find that that was the case prior to the employment of either Grievant or M___. Quite the

---

[184] *Williams v. Housing Authority of Sanford, Florida*, 49 FEP 1540 (MFla Dist. 1988).

[185] *Platner v. Cash & Thomas Contractors Inc.*, 53 FEP 940 (11th Cir. 1990).

[186] *Smith v. Wal-Mart Stores No. 471*, 51 FEP 1599, 891 F.2d 1177 (1990).

[187] *New Mexico Public Service Company*, 78 LA 883 (Herr, 1982); see also *County of Dauphin*, LAIG 3230 (O'Connell, 1982).

[188] *Twentieth Century Fox Film Corporation*, 87-2 ARB 8520 (Christopher, 1987). See also *Brinks, Ltd.*, 18 LAC(3d) 422 (Saltman, 1985).

[189] *Maryeville Exempted Village Board of Education*, 16 LAIS 3324 (Heekin, 1988).

[190] *Miami Shores Village*, 16 LAIS 4270 (Pereles, 1989).

[191] *Ritchie Industries, Inc.*, 74 LA 650 (Roberts, 1980).

contrary, the original rule as posted and explained to employees, when women were hired into the Bargaining Unit, was clearly only a rule against the original hiring of spouses, which could not be reasonably interpreted as applicable to existing employees who might subsequently marry. . . . Arbitrators have uniformly held that a No Hire Spouse policy does not apply to employees presently in the work force who might subsequently marry. See for example World Airways, Inc., 64 LA 276, 74-2 ARB PARA. 8655.

In his conclusions, Arbitrator Roberts ruled that the employer did not provide adequate evidence that the no-spouse rule was reasonably related to the needs of the business. Put another way, intrusion into the personal lives of employees after hire is not justified by a no-spouse rule.[192]

Furthermore, many arbitrators require that the "just cause" standard frequently enunciated in labor contracts must be satisfied in order to discharge an employee for marriage to a co-worker. In his opinion, Arbitrator Marshall J. Seidman stated that the "test of just cause still must be satisfied. If the application of the rule would do an injustice in the particular case, the Arbitrator not only has the authority, but the obligation, to set aside the discharge where it does not constitute just cause to remove an employee from his employment."[193] Arbitrator Seidman rationalized that the actual record of service, seniority, attendance, and loyalty of the grievant counted against the notion that the worker would become an entirely different worker the moment he married a co-worker. Arbitrators normally hold that a good worker will continue being a good worker both before and after marriage, though a divorce or separation can be disruptive to the employment of an otherwise good employee. The no-spouse rule has also been set aside where the rule is improperly communicated to employees,[194] is not followed consistently,[195] or is unreasonable.[196]

A few arbitrators have allowed discharge for marriage. In I.B.E.W., Local 2[197] Arbitrator James P. O'Grady agreed with management's decision to terminate an office employee who married another member of the organization. Arbitrator O'Grady cited the grievant's full knowledge of the nepotism rule and the fact that the rule had been applied consistently for eighteen years as the basis for his award. Arbitrator Robert L. Gibson concurred with the discharge of an em-

---

[192] World Airways, 64 LA 276 (Steele, 1975); Food Basket Stores, 71 LA 959 (Ross, 1978); Hayes Industries, Inc., 44 LA 820 (Teple, 1965); Sierra Pacific Power Company, 75 ARB 8348 (1975); Dover Corporation, 63 LA 1268 (Williams, 1974).

[193] Columbus, Inc., 83 LA 163 (Seidman, 1984); see also Van Nuys Communications Company, 84 LA 882 (Gentile, 1985).

[194] Western Airlines, 53 LA 1238 (Wyckoff, 1969) and Hayes Industries, Inc., 44 LA 820 (Teple, 1965).

[195] World Airways, 64 LA 276 (Steele, 1975); Food Basket Stores, 71 LA 959 (Ross, 1978).

[196] Hayes Industries, Inc., 44 LA 820 (Teple, 1965).

[197] I.B.E.W., Local 2, 90 LA 383 (O'Grady, 1987). See also State of Michigan, Dept. of Social Services, LAIG 3159 (Rayl, 1982), and Abbie J. Lane Memorial Hospital, 2 LAC(3d) 126 (Christie, 1981).

ployee who married a co-worker despite a plant rule prohibiting the employment of members of the immediate family.[198]   Arbitrator Gibson concluded that neither the contract, state law, nor Title VII of the Federal law were violated because *Kewanee Machinery* did not intend to engage in gender discrimination. That is, Arbitrator Gibson found no convincing evidence supporting the union's claim of disparate treatment. Arbitrator Gibson said:

> From the evidence presented at the hearing in this arbitration case, there does not appear to be any violation of either Federal or State Law prohibiting discrimination because of sex. The policy in this case applied equally to males and females and does not, in itself, indicate in any way that it is intended either directly or indirectly to deprive one of employment, or job opportunities, because of his or her sex.
>
> The more serious question, based on the evidence presented in this instance, is whether or not the Company has uniformly applied this rule to all employees. Insofar as the "no spouse" aspect is concerned it has uniformly applied the rule. The only exceptions in the application and administration of the close relative rule are the three brother combinations in the plant. The last of these commenced approximately 15 years before this case arose. The arbitrator does not believe this sufficient variation or deviation from the policy to warrant a finding that the Company has not uniformly applied the policy and, therefore, discriminated against this Grievant.

Arbitrators have considered grievances involving the transfer of spouses, supporting employers who establish business need.[199]   The *New York City Board of Education*[200] did not violate the labor agreement when it involuntarily transferred the grievant because her husband was promoted to a supervisory position over her. But without proof of business need, transfer (like the discharge of co-workers who marry after employment) is considered improper.[201]

In *Duquesne Light Company*,[202] for example, Arbitrator William J. Hannan found that management improperly transferred a married employee due to its kinship restriction. The couple worked together prior to marriage and continued to work efficiently in the same department for eleven months after the wedding.

---

[198] *Kewanee Machinery*, 64 LA 844 (Gibson, 1975). For opposite, see *Phelps Dodge Magnet Wire Company*, 8 LAI 4402 (Ipavec, 1981); *New Mexico Public Service Company*, 8 LAI 4776 (Cohen, 1981); and *Steadley Company*, 81-1 ARB 8222 (Penfield, 1981).

[199] *Hughes Aircraft Company*, 48 LA 1123 (Beatty, 1967); *Midland Ross Company*, 55 LA 258 (McNaughton, 1970); *New York Shipping Association*, 52 LA 931 (Turkus, 1969); *Roland Industries, Inc.*, 76-1 ARB 8066 (1976). For contrary opinion, see *Robertshaw Controls*, 55 LA 283 (Block, 1970); *Norandix, Inc.*, 71 LA 1168 (Feldman, 1978); and *Mid-America Dairymen*, 79-2 ARB 8525 (1979).

[200] *New York City Board of Education*, UFT 000347 (Altieri, 1980); see also *Boston School Committee*, 138 AIS 5 (Conlon, 1981).

[201] *Temple-Eastex, Inc.*, 9 LA 782 (Taylor, 1977); *Linn County, Iowa*, 78-1 ARB 8057 (1978); *North Central Airlines*, 77-2 ARB 8376 (1977); and *Mason and Hanger*, 64-3 ARB 8985 (1964).

[202] *Duquesne Light Company*, 87 LA 420 (Hannan, 1986); see also *Fitzpatrick v. Duquesne Light Company*, 37 FEP 843 (3rd Cir. 1985).

Arbitrator Hannan agreed that the no-nepotism rule was reasonable, but unenforceable because the restriction was unknown to employees. Even when the no-nepotism rule is known to employees, however, many arbitrators have required the employer to meet the "just cause" requirement of the labor contract before transferring employees who marry co-workers after initial employment.[203] The no-nepotism rule was known to the employees at the *Veterans Affairs Medical Center, Huntington*[204] and Arbitrator Stuart R. Waters ruled that management correctly non-selected the grievant for promotion to Contract Specialist because her selection would have called for the grievant to report directly to her husband and required the husband to sign off on the grievant's work. The couple was required to work in positions wherein the wife did not report directly to the husband.

Unions have consistently reversed the transfer of employees when management ignores contractual seniority rights in favor of no-kin policy.[205] That is, both involuntary transfer[206] and the denial of transfer[207] because of a no-kin policy frequently violate seniority provisions of the labor agreement. Arbitrator Blinn ruled in favor of the union because the grievant was a qualified senior bidder seeking transfer, because the no-kin policy had been inconsistently applied, and because management failed to provide evidence that the grievant's performance would be impaired because his son worked in the same department.[208] Along the same lines, Arbitrator John B. Coyle granted the grievant's transfer request in *Plymouth-Canton Community Schools.*[209] The grievant sought transfer to a custodial position in a school where his step-daughter-in-law was Head Custodian. Arbitrator Coyle reasoned that the clear and specific seniority clause in the labor contact required that the senior qualified bidder be awarded the job-in-point.

Like Arbitrator Coyle, Arbitrator Arnold B. Peterschmidt found in favor of the union in *Safeway Stores, Inc.*[210] The contract contained provisions requiring that transfers involving promotion be determined by seniority and qualifications. Arbitrator Peterschmidt noted (a) that the contract was silent regarding kinship policy; (b) that the no-kin policy was not discussed during negotiation; and (c) that nothing in the seniority clause stopped the grievant from reporting directly to his relative. Contractual silence regarding kinship restrictions, distance be-

---

[203] *North Pocono District*, 86 PSEA 2875 (McCaffree, 1986).

[204] *Veterans Affairs Medical Center, Huntington, Virginia*, 93 FLRR 2-1286 (Waters, 1992).

[205] *Bureau of the Mint, Denver*, LAIRS 14754 (Bardwell, 1982).

[206] *State of Michigan, Social Services*, LAIG 3163; *Lucky Stores, Inc.*, 1673 RSLR A-18 (Blackmar, 1981); and *Food Basket*, 81-2 ARB 8426 and 8533 (Kaufman, 1981).

[207] *SUNY-Oswego, Auxiliary Services*, 15 LAIS 2090 (Denson, 1988).

[208] *Frys Food Stores Inc.*, 87-1 ARB 8273 (Blinn, 1986).

[209] *Plymouth-Canton Community Schools*, 203 AIS 1 (Coyle, 1986); see also *Long Island Jewish Medical Center*, 10 LAIS 1264 (Florey, 1983).

[210] *Safeway Stores, Inc.*, 74 LA 886 (Peterschmidt, 1980).

tween relatives in the chain of command, and senior qualified bidder requirements are all grounds for finding in favor of a union which elects to challenge a no-nepotism rule.[211] For example, Arbitrator Norwood J. Ruiz awarded promotion to foreman even though the grievant would be supervising his brother. The grievant was the only employee qualified to fill the position permanently and the employer's inconsistent application nullified the no-nepotism rule.[212]

Arbitrator John F. Sass considered the right of an employee to transfer and promotion who was cohabiting with another employee in *A. J. Bayless Markets, Inc.*,[213] a matter raised before the courts in *Thoma*. The employer first promoted the grievant to Produce Department Manager and then demoted him on the basis of a no-kin policy. Arbitrator Sass ruled that it was reasonable for the company to apply its no-kin rule to the grievant's situation even though the policy did not specifically refer to cohabiting couples. And since *A. J. Bayless Markets* had the right to demote the grievant from a management position for almost any reason, Arbitrator Sass ruled that the demotion could not be considered a disciplinary action subject to the "just cause" provision of the labor contract. In sum, a specific seniority clause overwhelms a general company policy against kinship.

Arbitrators seldom consider grievances emanating from those refused employment, but arbitrators who have been confronted with grievances from job applicants have consistently indicated that employers can refuse to hire kin of current employees.[214] To be precise, arbitrators almost always find no-nepotism policy reasonable and based upon business necessity when the policy specifically bars the hiring of spouses already married to an employee as well as hiring a son,[215] daughter,[216] or nephew.[217]

In *Euclid Electric and Manufacturing Company*,[218] for example, Arbitrator Samuel S. Kates held that the "rule against having both a husband and wife in the bargaining unit at the same time is in my opinion not an unreasonable one." Arbitrator Kates specifically ruled that the agreement barring sex discrimination was not violated because the company rule in dispute only prohibited the hiring of a spouse married to an employee. Arbitrator Ralph S. Novak considered the no-spouse rule "in compliance with all state and federal laws and regulations

---

[211] *LOC, Washington, DC*, LAIRS 15213 (Bowers, 1983).

[212] *VA Medical Center, New Orleans*, LAIRS 15836 (Ruiz, 1983); see also *Clevepak Corporation*, 11 INDUS REL REP 25.4 (Jewett, 1980).

[213] *A. .J. Bayless Markets, Inc.*, 8 LAIS 100 (Sass, 1981); see also *McKellar General Hospital*, 15 LAC(3d) (Beatty, 1984). For denial of bidding, see *Martin Marietta Chemicals, Cement Division*, 11 INDUS REL REP 20.3 (Dunn, 1980).

[214] *Ritchie Industries, Inc.*, 74 LA 650 (Roberts, 1980), and *World Airways*, 64 LA 276 (Steele, 1975).

[215] *Amgraph Packaging, Inc.*, 89-2 ARB 8334 (Greenbaum, 1989).

[216] *County of Riverside*, 86 LA 903 (Gentile, 1985).

[217] *Florida Power and Light Company*, 90 LA 195 (Sloane, 1987).

[218] *Euclid Electric and Manufacturing*, 45 LA 641 (Kates, 1965).

pertaining to" gender discrimination.[219] In fact, Arbitrator Novak concluded that his award followed the federal call for affirmative action required under Executive Order 11246 and *Alexander v. Gardner-Denver.*[220]

In a little different factual situation, Arbitrator A. L. Springfield decided two disputes between the parties regarding the no-nepotism rule. First, Arbitrator Springfield ruled that a nepotism bar against the employment of married co-workers does not require the discharge of two divorced employees who are living together. Second, Arbitrator Springfield found that the reasonableness of the no-spouse rule is not arbitrable.[221] In another unusual case, a decision to terminate a new hire after the end of her probationary period was reversed by Arbitrator P. M. Williams.[222] *Dover Corporation*, the employer, allowed the grievant's probationary period to laps despite management's knowledge that the grievant was married to an employee on military leave. Arbitrator Williams ruled that the employer's inaction constituted contributory negligence. The grievant notified Dover Corporation that she was married to a co-worker when she was initially hired. Arbitrator Williams did not consider the grievant's renege on a commitment to resign from her job when her husband returned from military duty to be a violation of the labor agreement.

---

[219] *American Machine and Foundry Company*, 68 LA 1309 (Novak, 1977); see also *Studebaker Corporation*, 49 LA 105 (Davey, 1967).

[220] *Alexander v. Gardner-Denver Company*, 415 US 147 (1974).

[221] *Public Service Company of New Mexico*, 70 LA 788 (A. L. Springfield, 1978).

[222] *Dover Corporation*, 63 LA 1268 (Williams, 1974).

Chapter 5

Employment Conditions

Employment conditions deal with alleged gender discrimination faced by workers who already hold a job, are not being disciplined or laid off, and are not challenging hiring bias. Claims of gender discrimination in transfer, promotion, seniority, training, and job assignment are examples of disputes falling into the employment conditions category.

EXTERNAL LAW

The relationship between external law and arbitral practice has been analyzed extensively in Chapter 2. While Title VII outlaws sex discrimination, it is not always clear just what actions are in violation of the statute. This lack of judicial clarity is particularly true in instances where the courts are asked to consider a unique question of law being raised under Title VII for the first time. Nevertheless, under the guise of interpreting Section 301 of the Taft-Hartley Act, the Supreme Court created rules pertaining to the authority of arbitrators.

Briefly, it is generally conceded that the authority of an arbitrator stems from the collective bargaining agreement, and courts should not question arbitrators authorized to interpret the agreement. But when the agreement does not provide guidance or when external law is unclear or conflicts with the agreement, the authority of the arbitrator is less certain and the *Steelworkers Trilogy* provides limited judicial guidance. The *Gardner-Denver*[1] decision by the Supreme Court provides a partial answer to questions raised about the relationship between external law and arbitration.[2] Per *Gardner-Denver*, the arbitrator is required, as called for in *Steelworkers*, to follow the terms of the agreement and not external law. Thus, if there is conflict between the contract and external law, the arbi-

---

[1] *Alexander v. Gardner-Denver*, 7 FEP 81, 415 U.S. 987 (1971).
[2] *Strozier v. General Motors Corporation*, 24 FEP 1370, 635 F.2d 424 (1981).

trator, according to the Supreme Court, must follow the agreement. But where the contract is silent or the contract requires following external law, the arbitrator can, apparently, turn to the external law. Arbitrators, in all probability, are more frequently influenced by law than is acknowledged, an inevitable outcome because most arbitrators are lawyers and others arbitrators who are not lawyers undergo legal training.[3]

The scope of external law considered by the courts when a sex discrimination challenge is hoisted ranges beyond Title VII. The Seventh Circuit Court of Appeals in Chicago considered the relationship between Title VII and state protective legislation in *Le Beau v. Libby-Owens-Ford Company*.[4] Citing the EEOC's 1965 guidelines on sex discrimination, the Chicago Court ruled that state protective laws may serve as a basis for BFOQ exemptions from Title VII. It was reasonable and prudent for Libby-Owens-Ford to comply with state law and continue its practice of exempting female employees from overtime work. In a different case, also in Illinois, the employer did not violate pregnancy bias statutes by refusing to place a pregnant employee on weight lifting restrictions while nonpregnant employees were not subjected to lifting restrictions. Evidence presented to the District Court of Northern Illinois verified that the lifting restrictions were placed upon the nonpregnant employees by medical doctors. The pregnant employees' contract made the performance of weight lifting duties optional and the court reasoned that evidence retrieved from personnel files did not support the claim that lifting restrictions had a disparate impact upon pregnant women.[5]

The U.S. Supreme Court considered the right of pregnant employees to unemployment compensation benefits in *Wimberly v. Labor & Industrial Relations Commission of Missouri*.[6] The High Court ruled that a pregnant employee who voluntarily terminates employment for reasons not attributable to work is not covered by federal statutes that forbid states from denying unemployment compensation to persons who leave work because of pregnancy. The Missouri policy was aimed at workers who leave work voluntarily and, thus, did not single out pregnant women for unfavorable treatment. Similarly, a three week minimum earning requirement established by the Equal Rights Amendment to the Massachusetts Constitution did not discriminate against three women taking maternity leave. No sex bias was found because the Massachusetts law was administered in a uniform fashion, and treated all workers who leave work for an extended period the same.[7] A Minnesota Court awarded unemployment com-

---

[3] Vern E. Hauck, "The Efficacy of Arbitrating Discrimination Complaints," *Labor Law Journal*, Vol. 35, No. 3, March 1984, p. 175.

[4] *Le Beau v. Libbey-Owens-Ford Company*, 33 FEP 1700, 727 F.2d 141 (1984).

[5] *Gregory v. State of Illinois*, 51 FEP 652, DC Northern Illinois (1989).

[6] *Wimberly v. Labor, Industrial Relations Commission of Missouri*, 42 FEP 1261, 479 U.S. 511 (1987).

[7] *Buchanan v. Director, Employment Security Division*, 36 FEP 1884, Mass SupJudCt (1984).

pensation benefits to a female former meat cutter who left work due to sexual harassment.[8]

The relationship between the sex discrimination law and the labor agreement was considered by Arbitrator William F. Dolson in 1971 when *American Air Filter Company*[9] denied overtime to the grievant based upon her gender, justifying the denial of overtime upon Kentucky Revised Statutes (KRS) Number 337.880.[10] Here is what Arbitrator Dolson said:

There has been much discussion in the arbitration field concerning the proper role of an arbitrator in a case where relevant statutes and governmental regulations are brought to his attention. That are at least three major schools of thought. There are arbitrators who confine themselves strictly to contract language and leave the parties to the proper courts or administrative tribunals for interpretation or enforcement of statutes and governmental regulations. See Meltzer, "Ruminations About Ideology, Law, and Labor Arbitration," in *The Arbitrator, The NLRB, and The Courts*, p. 1 (BNA, 1967). Other arbitrators are of the opinion that contracts include all law applicable thereto, therefore the law (constitutional, statue, and common) is applicable to each collective bargaining agreement. See Howlett, *The Arbitrator, The NLRB, and The Courts*, p. 67 (BNA, 1967). Then there are arbitrators who take the middle ground. They hold the view that no arbitrator should render an opinion which, if followed should require an employer (or union) to breach a statute, and that arbitrators may apply the law if it is clear and not ambiguous. See Mittenthal, "The role of Law in Arbitration," *Developments in American and Foreign Arbitration*, p. 42 (BNA, 1968).

In determining what are "applicable laws," it is the belief of the Arbitrator that Title VII has to be considered along with KRS 337-080. The Arbitrator recognizes that there have been arbitration awards in which arbitrators have held that the resolution of a question of sex discrimination and conflicting Federal and state laws are not properly within the jurisdiction of the arbitrator. See *United Air Lines*, 48 LA 727 (Kahn, 1967), the *Ingraham Co.*, 48 LA 884 (Yagoda, 1966), and *Pitman-Moore Div.*, 49 LA 709 (Seinsheimer, 1967). It should be noted, however, that in none of these cases was there included broad language similar to that contained in arbitration clause of Paragraph 564. Moreover, other arbitrators have recognized that it is a function of the arbitrator to apply Title VII even if it is in derogation of state statutory law. See *Avco Corp.*, 54 LA 165, 70-1 ARB, Par. 8400 (Turkus, 1970) and *Simoniz Co.*, 70-1 ARB, Par. 8024 (Howlett, 1970). Nor has any national policy developed since the enactment of Title VII which would remove cases involving civil rights from the jurisdiction of arbitrators. In a recent case, *Dewey v. Reynolds Metal Company*, 429 F.2d 324, 2 FEP Cases 681 (6th Cir. 1970), the Court said that: "Nor do we find any national policy for ousting arbitrators of jurisdiction to finally determine grievances initiated by employees, based on alleged violation of their civil rights (p. 332, 429 F.2d, 2 FEP Cases 692)." After carefully consid-

---

[8] *McNabb v. Cub Foods*, 43 FEP Cases 1517, Minn SupCt (1984).

[9] *American Air Filter Company, Famco Division*, 57 LA 549 (Dolson, 1971).

[10] At the time of the award the Kentucky Revised Statutes Number 337-080 provided that "[n]o female shall be permitted to work in any laundry, bakery, factory, workshop, store or mercantile, manufacturing or mechanical establishment, hotel restaurant, telephone exchange or telegraph ofice more than sixty hours in one week, nor more than ten hours in any one day."

ering the Agreement and the above decisions, the Arbitrator concludes that he has the authority to resolve the question of sex discrimination and conflicting Federal and state laws.

The defense of compliance with the Kentucky Revised Statutes, particularly KRS 337-080, is not available to the Company. Title VII of the Civil Rights Act requires equal standing of the sexes in all matters of employment, including the assignment of overtime. Therefore, the Company, by denying the Grievant overtime work on August 31, 1970 and September 1, 1970 because of her sex, acted improperly and such denial constituted a violation of the Agreement.

The balance between state law and the contract was decided by the parties before the grievant filed her sex discrimination charge in *New York City Tech.*[11] In their labor contract the parties established a Duplicate Proceedings Section that forbade the processing of a discrimination grievance under both the labor contract and any court or governmental agency at the same time. And even though the union argued that the grievance included contractual violations of other articles besides the discrimination clause, Arbitrator George Nicolau ruled for management. The violations cited by the union were not separate from the sex discrimination charge, and the female grievant filed her gender bias claim while the arbitration hearing was in recess.

The State University of New York won a judgment involving external law in *Staten Island, Higher Education Office.*[12] While Arbitrator Robert L. Stutz disagreed with management's conclusion that affirmative action decisions were not subject to arbitral review, the Arbitrator did rule in management's favor. The discrimination clause placed the grievant's complaint within the arbitrator's jurisdiction. Management won, however, because the university remained within the bounds of due process, was not arbitrary, followed the same evaluation procedure for all persons in the grievant's classification, and no mistreatment of workload, office space, or secretarial help could be shown to hinder the grievant's inability to meet reasonable standards. Arbitrator Arthur Stark agreed with management's assessment that maternity leave could not be counted for time worked toward tenure. The employer, *Mathematics Department, CUNY*[13] properly denied tenure to the grievant because she worked less than a full year toward tenure, and took maternity leave during a substantial portion of another year. Thus, the grievant actually worked less than two years of the necessary three years needed for a three year tenure requirement. Importantly, the University did not violate the grievant's right to due process which the University guarded by following its own bylaw requirements for denying tenure.[14] A due process violation may have cause Arbitrator Stark to decided for the Union.

---

[11] *New York City Tech*, CUNY 000247 (Nicolau, 1975).

[12] *Staten Island, Higher Education Office*, CUNY 000245 (Stutz, 1975); see also *Proviso Township High School District 209 Board of Education*, 155 AIS 1 (Cook, 1982).

[13] *City, Mathematics Department*, CUNY 000135 (Stark, 1974).

[14] *Queens, German and Comparative Literature Department*, CUNY 000120 (Scheiber, 1972).

Arbitrator George H. Hildebrand awarded for the union in *Niagara County Community College*,[15] even though the female college instructor's term contract stated "there will be no right of appeal" in the event of nonrenewal of a term appointment. Arbitrator Hildebrand reasoned that the meaning of the term appointmentwas blurred by its context. That is, "all that the exclusion actually provides is that where there is no taint of discrimination, then the College may let a term appointment run out its natural course without incurring thereby an obligation either to reappoint or to defend its action." Arbitrator Hildebrand ruled that the grievant's right to nondiscriminatory treatment under state law as well as specific contract language barring sex discrimination superseded the no appeal clause of the grievant's term contract. The record provided by the union included correspondence between the male faculty which showed in writing that they intended to preclude the reappointment of the grievant and her ability to grieve the action, because of her gender and her outspoken feminist life-style. To be precise, sex bias was found by Arbitrator Hildebrand because the grievant's job was purposefully amended so that she would not qualify, because no fair and reasonable standard of expectation for the grievant's job was established, because the employer claimed the issue was not arbitrable rather than providing evidence of the grievant's poor performance, and because a man would not be discharged for holding the same feminist life-style views as the grievant.

Arbitrators have upheld federal regulations and/or the labor agreement where employees are require to select one of two or more alternative forums for the filing of a sex discrimination charge. For example, Arbitrator Edgar A. Jones, Jr.[16] and Arbitrator Ira F. Jaffe[17] denied arbitration because the employee filed a grievance and sought relief from sex discrimination in an alternative federal forum. Indeed, management may require an employee to utilize an alternative forum which has been established in compliance with Title IX to resolve a sex bias claim.[18] But where relief in an alternative forum was not any issue, Arbitrator Richard Mittenthal considered the effect of a federal consent decree which corrected the underrepresentation of women in the position of Spare Parts Man.[19] Arbitrator Mittenthal concluded that management properly bypassed the male grievant in favor of a female selectee with relatively equal qualifications in order to comply with a consent decree issued by the federal forum.

The *Cheecktowaga Central School Board of Education*[20] did not violate the labor agreement nor the Civil Rights Act of 1964 by refusing the use of sick leave bank time to cover the breast feeding of a newborn. Arbitrator Joseph

---

[15] *Niagara County Community College*, 81 AIS 17 (Hildebrand, 1976).

[16] *Air Force, Space Division, Los Angeles*, LAIRS 17290 (Jones, 1986).

[17] *Social Security Administration, Office of Hearings and Appeals*, LAIRS 16193 (Jaffe, 1984).

[18] *New London, Board of Education*, 83 AIS 17 (Post, 1976).

[19] *LTV Steel Company, Indiana Harbor Works*, 15 LAIS 3756 (Mittenthal, 1987).

[20] *Cheektowaga Central School Board of Education*, 80 LA 225 (Shister, 1982).

Shister ruled in favor of management because the labor contract allowed for the use of the sick leave bank when an employee is incapacitated by severe sickness or injury, the need to breast feed not being a severe sickness or injury.

Management may consider and follow employment policy that seeks to comply with federal affirmative action guidelines.[21] But in an unusual case, the right of disabled veterans to promotion in accordance with 38 USC 2014 was weighed against the rights of women and minorities seeking promotion in compliance with a Department of Labor affirmative action plan. Arbitrator Charles B. Craver ruled that veteran's rights need not be balanced against the statutory rights of women and minorities when making promotion decisions. That is, the right of veterans to promotion is a reward for the sacrifice of military service and is superior under a bona fide affirmative action plan.[22]

PERFORMANCE APPRAISAL AND MERIT SYSTEMS

Title VII allows an employer to apply different standards of compensation for employees based upon a bona fide seniority system, merit system, or system that measures the quantity or quality of production. However, performance appraisal or merit systems that misjudge employees because of gender bias or which function as a pretextual cover for sex discrimination violate the law. For example, Price Waterhouse violated Title VII, disparate treatment, where negative sexist views and stereotyped comments about women caused the company to lower the evaluation of a female whose candidacy for partnership was placed on hold.[23] Similarly, a law firm improperly denied partnership to a female associate where she was evaluated negatively for being too involved with women's issues, targeted for sexist comments showing differential treatment, and reproached for her actions while a male member was not disciplined for his statement that women are parttime attorneys.[24] An employer does not violate the law by commenting on a women's performance evaluation form that she is a mother not interested in long term employment when the mother tells the supervisor herself about her short term work objective, the supervisor merely making a written confirmation of the women's preference for short term employment.[25]

In *Wrangler v. Hawaiian Electric Company* the court found Title VII sex discrimination because management gave negative performance evaluation scores to the female worker and then turned down her request for help and instruction.[26] Prima facie evidence of sex discrimination was also found by the Sixth Circuit

---

[21] *Hernando County District School Board*, DIG 101167 (Davidson,1975).

[22] *DOL, Washington, DC*, LAIRS 19178 (Craver, 1989).

[23] *Hopkins v. Price Waterhouse*, 52 FEP 1275, (DC DC. 1990); 44 FEP 825 (DC Cir. 1987); and 49 FEP 954 (US SupCt. 1989).

[24] *Ezold v. Wolf, Block, Schorr, Solis-Cohen*, 54 FEP 808 (DC Pa. 1990).

[25] *Key v. Gillette Company*, 50 FEP 1613 (DC Mass. 1982).

[26] *Wangler v. Hawaiian Electric Company*, 53 FEP 943 (DC Hawaii, 1990).

Court in *Mills v. Ford Motor Company*.[27] The female worker was discharged due to biased performance evaluations. Time sheets and supporting testimony from subordinates verified that the grievant's production level equaled that of other male supervisors and she used fewer hours to attain this level. The housekeeping and safety problems of Mills were no worse than those of her male peers. Evidence of sex discrimination exists where written performance evaluations drop from good to poor after a female employee requests promotion, the poor evaluations resulting in her discharge.[28] And, an employer may not escape a sex discrimination charge by applying the same system of vague standards for performance evaluation to all employees.[29] To avoid violating civil rights law, performance appraisal or merit systems should seek to establish quantifiable rating elements, apply those elements uniformly, and train supervisors in performance evaluation.[30]

The Utah District Court dismissed sex harassment charges alleging that a female supervisor engaged in a pattern of unfair performance evaluations for women. The plaintiffs testified that they had not been sexually harassed and their claim that an incompetent male employee was retained while they were terminated could not be proven.[31] The Second Circuit Court found sexual harassment when a female employee's refusal to provide sexual favors resulted in inadequate training and an unfair performance evaluation.[32] It is not sex discrimination when an employer elects to delay performance evaluation of a women on sick leave, provided the sick leave delay policy is applied uniformly to all employees. The Fifth Circuit Court of Appeals did not consider it relevant or material that the women's pay increase was postponed.[33]

In 1972 Arbitrator Thomas G.S. Christensen found neither race nor sex discrimination when *New York City Tech, Social Science Department*[34] elected to forgo the reappointment of a black female grievant who was not informed about her unsatisfactory performance evaluations. Arbitrator Christensen first stated that performance evaluation reports should tell plainly whether an employee's ranking is satisfactory or unsatisfactory. He noted that failure to follow proper performance observation procedures would void a nonreappointment decision by *New York City Tech*. Indeed in 1975, Arbitrator George Nicolau found himself without authority to examine the performance evaluations of a grievant seeking reappointment to the *CUNY, Psychology Department, York*[35] because the matter involved a question of academic judgment. After examining and finding no pro-

---

[27] *Mills v. Ford Motor Company*, 41 FEP 1397 (6th Cir. 1986).

[28] *EEOC v. United States Steel Corporation*, 37 FEP 1232, 758 F.2D 1462 (1985).

[29] *Martinez v. El Paso County*, 32 FEP 747, 710 F.2d 1102 (1983).

[30] *Goldman v. Marsh*, 54 FEP 1689 (DC EArk. 1983).

[31] *Hanson v. American Express Company*, 53 FEP 1193 (DC Utah, 1986).

[32] *Carrero v. New York City Housing Authority*, 51 FEP 596 (2nd Cir. 1989).

[33] *Jones v. Flagship International, Sky Chiefs*, 41 FEP 358 (5th Cir. 1986).

[34] *New York City Tech, Socal Science Department*, CUNY 000071 (Christensen, 1972).

[35] *CUNY, Psychology Department, York,* CUNY 000249 (Nicolau, 1975).

cedural errors in the administration of the grievance process, Arbitrator Nicolau ruled in favor of the University.

In a different case that also involved the City University of New York, Arbitrator Christensen concluded that the *New York City Board of Higher Education*[36] did not discriminate on the basis of gender when it discharged the female grievant for her poor performance evaluations. Management acted within its contractual obligation because "two of the last three evaluations" stated the grievant performed unsatisfactorily. The union argued that the Board improperly discharged the grievant on the basis of critical comments written into the performance evaluations, rather than referring directly to the unsatisfactory benchmark. Arbitrator Christensen dismissed the union's challenge because the labor contract was new to the parties and some leniency to management was necessary under the circumstances. The Arbitrator warned that future disregard of the need to refer directly to the unsatisfactory benchmark as well as the need to advise the employee about performance deficiencies would result in a decision favorable to the union.

The *Iowa State Board of Regents*[37] did not discriminate because of gender by granting the grievant a terminal year, forgoing the grievant's tenure request. In reaching his award, Arbitrator Allen J. Harrison cited evidence that the grievant's colleagues and superiors gave her the benefit of the doubt. They had expressed strong reservations about her permanent employment at the library, gave ample notice that she should not expect to receive an additional probationary period, and did not engage in behavior that would support the grievant's gender discrimination complaint.

In *Letterkenny Army Depot*[38] the grievant charged disparate treatment when her performance appraisal ranked her "fully successful" instead of "exceptional," a charge that Arbitrator John M. Hamrick denied. According to Arbitrator Hamrick, the employer's union failed to provide ample evidence to prove its disparate treatment contention. Further, management's failure to respond to the union's grievance in a timely manner did not warrant an automatic decision in favor of the grievant. Arbitrator Hamrick concluded that the automatic remedy language in the labor contract could not apply in this grievance, because the automatic remedy clause conflicted with applicable laws, rules, and regulations. Arbitrator Hamrick ruled that performance appraisal rankings are something an employee must earn, not something to be obtained through an automatic remedy clause. The employer's procedural error under the labor contract was considered to be *de minimis* by Arbitrator Hamrick.

---

[36] *New York City Board of Higher Education*, 32 AIS 5 (Christensen, 1972); see also *City, Mathematics Department, CUNY,* CUNY 000135 (Stark, 1974).

[37] *Iowa State Board of Regents*, DIG 102601 (Harrison, 1978).

[38] *Letterkenny Army Depot, Pennsylvania*, 92 FLRR 2-1747 (Hamrick, 1992).

EQUAL PAY

The Equal Pay Act of 1963 (EPA) and Title VII make it illegal for an employer to pay different wages or other forms of remuneration to employees of the opposite sex for equal work. The Bennett Amendment[39] to Title VII was aimed to ensure consistency between the two laws; but despite it all, the relationship between EPA and Title VII remains unclear.[40]   In most cases an employee's claim of unequal pay for equal work, the comparable worth matter, is handled the same under both laws, particularly when both laws have jurisdiction and the employee files a complaint under both statutes.[41]   For example, an employee denied a promotion may recover for wage discrimination under EPA and seek additional recovery under Title VII for denial of promotion opportunities.[42] Even so, many courts hold that a violation of EPA is also a violation of Title VII, but the reverse is not true.[43]   A wage discrimination claim under Title VII frequently requires the employee to prove intentional discrimination, neither the disparate impact nor the disparate treatment concept being embodied in EPA.[44] One other important point, Title VII outlaws several forms of wage discrimination not covered by EPA – such as age and national origin.

Three terms, *skill, effort, and responsibility*, are key to understanding the application of EPA. This law requires that employers avoid gender-based wage differentials when employees perform work that requires equal skill, effort and responsibility and that is performed under similar working conditions.[45]   The Eighth Circuit Court says that skill refers to experience, training, education, and ability that are necessary to perform the job-in-point.   Neither an employee's unnecessary skill nor a high level of efficiency justifies an EPA pay differential claim.[46]   In *Briggs v. Anderson,*[47] for example, the job requirement called effort was reduced so that an employer properly paid a woman less than her male

---

[39] 421 FEP Manual 401-402.

[40] EPA is part of the Fair Labor Standards Act (FLSA) and became law before Title VII. EPA covers executives, administrators, and professional employees as well as the same employees covered by FLSA.

[41] *Korte v. Diemer*, 53 FEP 936 (6th Cir. 1990); *EEOC v. White and Sone Enterprises*, 50 FEP 1076 (11th Cir. 1989); and *Ottaviani v. State Univ. of New York at New Paltz*, 51 FEP 330 (2nd Cir. 1989).

[42] *County of Washington v. Gunther*, 25 FEP 1521, 452 US 161 (1981); see also *Schnellbaecher v. Baskin Clothing Company*, 50 FEP 1846 (7th Cir. 1989).

[43] *Forsberg v. Pacific Northwest Bell Telephone Company*, 54 FEP 1873 (9th Cir. 1988); *Korte v. Diemer*, 53 FEP 936 (6th Cir. 1990); and *Fallon v. State of Illinois*, 50 FEP 954 (7th Cir. 1989).

[44] *Fallon v. State of Illinois*, 50 FEP 954 (7th Cir. 1989).

[45] *Corning Glass Works v. Brennan*, 9 FEP 919, US SupCt, 1974; see also *Schwartz v. Florida Board of Regents*, 58 FEP 373 (11th Cir. 1991).

[46] *Pelier v. City of Fargo*, 12 FEP 945, 533 F.2d 374 (1976); see also *Gray v. University of Arkansas*, 50 FEP 1112 (8th Cir. 1989).

[47] *Briggs v. Anderson*, 40 FEP 883 (8th Cir. 1986).

predecessor. According to the Fifth Circuit, effort involves physical or mental exertion needed to the perform a job. As long as the amount of effort is the same, pay differentials are not justified by different kinds of effort. But, pay differentials are okay when physical or mental exertion is sporadically performed, when additional tasks take extra effort,[48] consume significant time, or are of economic value to the employer.[49] Responsibility differs from effort and involves the degree of accountability required to perform the job. Minor differences in responsibility do not justify higher wages for one gender over another, but supervisory requirements, heavier patient load, and greater danger are responsibilities that justify wage differentials.[50] Similar working conditions allude to surroundings and hazards, such as exposure to toxic materials, possible job injury, or undesirable physical surroundings. A wage differential based upon work shift assignment is not justified on the grounds of working conditions.[51]

The EPA call for equal pay for equal work does not mean that work assignments must be identical,[52] nor does equal pay for equal work mean that work assignments be merely comparable.[53] Rather, EPA applies whenever the skill, effort, and responsibility required for work assignments under similar working conditions are "substantially equal." The courts have determined that EPA applies whether or not the employer formally assigns substantially equal work. EPA is violated so long as the employer knowingly allows employees to perform substantially equal work without equal pay.[54] Minor differences in required skill, effort and responsibility between jobs do not make the equal pay standard inapplicable,[55] nor will the statute be voided by different job classifications, titles, and descriptions when the elements of the actual work performed are substantially equal.[56]

There are four exceptions to which an employer may point in order to avoid an EPA challenge. First wage differentials based upon seniority are legitimate. To be precise, a salary disparity that favors males but is based on seniority is proper,

---

[48] *Princeton City Schools District Board of Education*, 22 LAIS 3677 (Stanley, 1994).

[49] *Hodgson v. Brookhaven General Hospital*, 9 FEP 579, 436 F.2d 719 (1970); *Brennan v. Owensboro-Davies County Hospital*, 11 FEP 600, 523 F.2d 1013 (1975); *Usery v. Columbia University*, 15 FEP 1333, 568 F.2d 953 (1977).

[50] *Johnson v. Crossville Nursing Home*, 17 FEP 567, USDC NAla (1978); see also 29 CFR 1620.17.

[51] *Corning Glass Works v. Brennan*, 9 FEP Cases 919, US SupCt, 1974 and *Usery v. Columbia University*, 15 FEP 1333, 568 F.2d 953 (1977).

[52] *EEOC v. Maricopa County College District*, 35 FEP 234, 736 F.2d 510 (1984).

[53] *Thompson v. Sawyer*, 28 FEP 1614, 678 F.2d 257 (1982).

[54] 29 CFR 1620.13 and 29 CFR 1620.14

[55] *Clymore v. Far-Mar-Co.*, 31 FEP 1840, 549 F. Supp. 438 (1982); see also, Eighth Circuit, 709 F.2d 499 (1983).

[56] *Epstein v. Department of Treasury*, 35 FEP 677, 739 F.2d 274 (1984); see also *Brewster v. Barnes*, 46 FEP 1758, (4th Cir. 1986).

even when the seniority system is informal.[57]   Second, a bona fide merit system justifies wage differences that may emerge between opposite sexes.[58] However, the courts have been picky about what constitutes a bona fide merit system. A merit system that does not provide for advancement,[59] wage rewards,[60] or systematic employee evaluation is likely to violate EPA.[61] Third, differences in pay are legal so long as such differences are based upon the quality or quantity of production, it being okay to pay an employee more who produces more under a piece rate system. By the same token, a piece rate system that pays women less in order to equalize total compensation is unlawful if there is no qualitative difference in the work produced.[62]

Fourth, justification for an employer's wage differential may fall into a catch all category called "factor other than sex."   The wide range of considerations falling into this category grant the employer latitude to continue many systems of pay that are rooted in business need. For example, objective job evaluation and pay classification systems that produce a wage differential regardless of the employee's sex do not violate EPA.[63] This fourth category applies when an employer bases pay differentials upon starting salaries,[64] profitability,[65] market rate,[66] corrective remedy,[67] state law,[68] retention,[69] and/or red circle rates.[70] A collective bargaining agreement is not a factor other than sex, a labor agreement that perpetuates prior wage discrimination being in violation of EPA.[71] Indeed, a

---

[57] *EEOC v. Whitin Machine Works*, 35 FEP 583, 699 F.2d 688 (1983); *EEOC v. Cleveland State University*, 28 FEP 1782, USDC NOhio (1982).

[58] *Willner v. University of Kansas*, 52 FEP 515 (10th Cir. 1988).

[59] *Morgado v. Birmingham-Jefferson County Civil Defense Corporation*, 32 FEP 12, 706 F.2d 1184 (1983), cert. denied, 464 B.S. 1045.

[60] *Grayboff v. Pendelton*, 36 FEP 350, USDC NGa. (1984).

[61] *Maxwell v. Tucson*, 42 FEP 205 (9th Cir. 1986); *Schwartz v. Florida Board of Regents*, 58 FEP (11th Cir. 1991); *Bence v. Detroit Health Corporation*, 32 FEP 434, 712 F.2d 1024, cert. denied 465 U.S. 1025; and *King v. University of Wisconsin System*, 52 FEP 809 (7th Cir. 1990).

[62] *Laffey v. Northwest Airlines*, 35 FEP 508, 740 F.2d 1071 (1984).

[63] *Aldrich v. Randolph Central School District*, No. 91-7566, 5/5/92 (2nd Cir. 1992).

[64] *Glenn v. General Motors*, 46 FEP 1331 (11th Cir. 1988); *Kouba v. Allstate Insurance Company*, 30 FEP 57, 691 F.2d 873 (1982).

[65] *EEOC v. Affiliated Foods*, 34 FEP 943, USDC WMo. (1984); *Hodgson v. Robert Hall Clothes*, 11 FEP 1271, 473 F.2d 589 (1973), cert. denied 11 FEP 1310, 414 U.S. 866 (1973).

[66] *Thompson v. Sawyer*, 28 FEP 1614, 678 F.2d 257 (1982); *Spaulding v. University of Washington*, 35 FEP 217, 740 F.2d 686 (1984); *Dept. of Labor v. Georgia St. College*, 43 FEP 1525 (11th Cir. 1985); Hatton v. Hunt, 57 FEP 1486, USDC WTn. (1991).

[67] *Ende v. Board of Regents of Regency University*, 37 FEP 575, 757 F.2d 176 (1985).

[68] *Beall v. Curtis*, 37 FEP 644, USDC MGa. (1985); aff'd. 40 FEP 984 (11th Cir. 1985).

[69] *Winkes v. Brown University*, 36 FEP 120, 747 F.2d 792 (1984).

[70] *Covington v. Southern Illinois University*, 43 FEP 839 (7th Cir. 1987), cert. denied, 44 FEP 1672.

[71] *Anderson v. University of Northern Iowa*, 39 FEP 1379, 779 F.2d 441 (1985).

union that contributes to pay differentials by signing a labor contract which perpetuates past wage discrimination faces EPA charges right along with management.[72]   While they are exempt from EPA, seniority systems, merit systems, other systems that base wage differentials upon the quality or quantity of production, and "factors other than sex" are subject to the requirements of Title VII.[73]

Comparisons of skill, effort, responsibility, or working conditions must be made between work assignments at the same establishment. As a result, employees who work at the same physical location must be paid in accordance with EPA; employees at different locations must be paid equal wages for substantially equal work if they serve the same administrative head.[74] For example, federal employees work for the same administrative head, and the civil service is required to pay all employees equally for substantially equal work regardless of their physical location.[75] But where a woman works for a federal contractor in offices that are located hundreds of miles from where a man works, EPA does not apply. Besides being located hundreds of miles apart, the offices of the federal contractor were operationally distinct, independently managed, and under separate budgets for different customers.[76] EPA does not preclude different pay scales under these circumstances.

In 1984 the Court of Appeals in Washington, D.C. ruled that Northwest Airlines violated EPA by paying male pursers more than female flight attendants, granting males a cleaning allowance, and allowing males more favorable layover accommodations than females. The nominal supervisory assignment given to male pursers did not exempt Northwest Airlines from an EPA violation.[77] Similarly, the use of different sewing machines by female bindery workers who performed substantially equal tasks as male bindery workers does not exempt the employer from EPA coverage.[78] According to the Third Circuit, Wheaton Glass Company violated EPA by basing a 10 percent pay differential favorable to men upon the occasional assignment of other duties not asked of women. The Third Circuit found that not all male employees were asked to perform occasional extra assignments, and women were both willing and able to perform the additional duties.[79]

---

[72] *Laffey v. Northwest Airlines*, 13 FEP 1068, 567 F.2d 429 (1976).

[73] 421:402 FEP Manual. The relationship between EPA and Title VII remains unclear even though the Bennett Amendment to Title VII sought to create consistency between the statutes.

[74] 29 CFR 1620.9

[75] *Grumbines v. U.S.*, 34 FEP 847, 586 F.Supp. 1144 (1984).

[76] *Foster v. Areata Associates*, 38 FEP 1850, 772 F.2d 1453 (1985).

[77] *Laffey v. Northwest Airlines*, 35 FEP 508, 740 F.2d 1071 (1984); cert. denied, 469 U.S. 1181.

[78] *Thompson v. Sawyer*, 28 FEP 1614, 678 F.2d257 (1982).

[79] *Schultz v. Wheaton Glass Company*, 9 FEP 502, 421 F.2d 259 (1970); cert. denied, 398 U.S. 905).

Overall job content is the focus of judicial inquiry under EPA. And where this overall focus finds real differences in physical effort, skill, duties, or responsibility, employers may correctly pay men and women differently.[80] Male employees at Affiliated Foods were justifiably paid higher wages than women because they were required to lift and carry heavier items.[81] The New York Telephone Company was justified in making a pay differential favorable to male technical instructors over female clerical instructors where the men had many years of training in their field and the women had little or no training.[82] Increased responsibility and stress of coaching a revenue generating sport at the College of William and Mary justified paying a male college coach more than female coaches.[83] It is against the law for an employer to lower an employee's wages to achieve compliance with EPA.[84]

The definition of wages covered by EPA is broad, almost any form of compensation for employment being considered wages.[85] Medical, hospital, accident, and life insurance, retirement plans,[86] and annual leave are benefits subject to the provisions of EPA.[87] Profit sharing,[88] gain sharing, expense accounts, bonuses, uniform cleaning allowances, hotel accommodations, use of company car,[89] use of company telephone service,[90] use of food service staff to cater the company picnic,[91] unemployment benefits,[92] and gasoline allowances are also included within EPA's broad definition of wages.[93]

---

[80] *Sheehan v. Purolator Inc.*, 49 FEP 1000 (2nd Cir. 1988).

[81] *EEOC v. Affiliated Foods*, 34 FEP 943, USDC WMo (1984).

[82] *Waterman v. New York Telephone Company*, 36 FEP 41, USDC SNY (1984).

[83] *Jacobs v. College of William and Mary*, USDC EVa (1980).

[84] 29 USC 206(d)(1).

[85] *Newport News Shipbuilding & Dry Dock Company v. EEOC*, 32 FEP 1 (US SupCt. 1983); see also *EEOC v. Atlanta Gas Light Company*, 36 FEP 1671, 751 F.2d 1188 (1985), and *EEOC v. Texas Industries*, 40 FEP 118 (5th Cir. 1986).

[86] *Arizona Governing Committee v. Norris*, 32 FEP 233 (US SupCt. 1983); *Probe v. State Teachers' Retirement System*, 40 FEP 102 (9th Cir. 1986); *Spirt v. TIAA-CREF*, 34 FEP 1510, 735 F.2d 23 (1984); *Chastang v. Flynn & Emrich Company*, 12 FEP 1533, 541 F.2d 1040 (1976); *Rosen v. Public Service Electric & Gas Company*, 5 FEP 709, 477 F.2d 90 (1973); *Bartmes v. Drewrys U.S.A.*, 3 FEP 795, 444 F.2d 1186 (1971); and *Mixson v. Southern Bell Telephone & Telegraph Company*, 4 FEP 27, USDC NGa. (1971).

[87] *Cleveland Bd. of Education v. LaFleur*, 6 FEP 1253, 414 U.S. 632 (1974); *Levin v. Delta Air Lines*, 34 FEP 1192, 730 F.2d 994 (1984); *California Federal Savings & Loan v. Guerra*, 42 FEP 1073 (US SupCt. 1987); *Harness v. Hartz Mountain Corporation*, 50 FEP 376 (6th Cir. 1989). These cases consider annual leave benefits.

[88] *Chastang v. Flynn & Emrich Company*, 12 FEP 1533, 541 F.2d 1040 (1976).

[89] *Sheehan v. Purolator Inc.*, 49 FEP 1000 (2nd Cir. 1988).

[90] *Anaconda Aluminum Company*, 62 LA 1049 (Warns, 1974).

[91] *Columbus Board of Education*, DIG 102757, GA 000119 (Miller, 1975).

[92] *Wimberly v. Labor and Industrial Commission of Missouri*, 42 FEP 1261 (US SupCt. 1987); *Austin v. Berryman*, No. 91-1750, 1/28/92 (4th Cir. 1992).

[93] 421:404 FEP Manual.

Once again, the basic policy established by EPA is that an employer may not pay unequal wages for equal work, and fringe benefits offered voluntarily must also be without gender bias.[94] In practice, however, there are a number of noteworthy court and arbitration decisions which add flexibility to the equal pay for equal work standard. In 1990, for example, the Fourth Circuit Court of Appeals ruled that employers may not use gender-based actuarial studies to allocate fringe benefits to spouses or family members of one gender and not the other.[95] However, an otherwise illegal head of household rule does not violate EPA when the rule provides the greatest coverage for employees with the greatest need at the lowest cost.[96] And while differences in cost alone cannot justify an employment policy that provides one gender with fringe benefits and not the other,[97] it is lawful for an employee pension plan to have a disproportionate impact on one gender where the retirees total pension benefit is based on actual life span.[98] Because it is not considered a wage, it is acceptable for a restaurant to reimburse kitchen workers (mostly male) and not counter workers (mostly female) for the cost of uniform cleaning when the employer and not the employee is the primary beneficiary of the reimbursement practice.[99] In *Burnett & Sons*[100] Arbitrator David A. Concepcion ruled the union's grievance nonarbitrable on procedural grounds since the grievant waited over one year after performing the work to claim the same pay for truck driver work as her male co-workers.

COMPARABLE WORTH AND EQUAL PAY

Comparable work and comparable worth differ even though the terms are frequently merged during conversation. On one hand, the comparable work concept applies to different jobs which require the performance of similar enough functions and skills to justify equal pay for all employees asked to undertake the task. EPA is a legitimate basis from which to challenge discriminatory wage practices falling within the scope of comparable work. On the other hand, the comparable worth argument is founded upon the premise that wages should be based upon the value of the work to the employer rather than substantially equal work. Title VII is a legitimate basis from which to raise a comparable worth challenge, EPA not being as helpful as Title VII for gaining relief against an

---

[94] *Hison v. King & Spalding*, 34 FEP 1406 (US SupCt. 1984).
[95] *Dole v. Shenandoah Baptist Church*, 54 FEP 501 (4th Cir. 1990); also see *EEOC v. Fremont Christian School*, 39 FEP 1815, 781 F.2d 1362 (1986).
[96] *EEOC v. J. C. Penny Company* 46 FEP 815 (6th Cir. 1988); also see *Colby v. J. C. Penny Company*, 55 FEP 266 (7th Cir. 1991).
[97] 29 CFR 1620.11
[98] *City of Los Angeles v. Manhart*, 17 FEP 395, 435 U.S. 702 (1978).
[99] *Donovan v. KFC Services*, 30 FEP 1846, USDC ENY (1982); see also *Laffey v. Northwest Airlines*, 35 FEP 508, 740 F.2d 1071 (1984); cert. denied, 469 U.S. 1181.
[100] *Burnett & Sons*, 21 LAIS 1107 (Concepcion, 1994).

employment situation which involves a potential violation of the comparable worth doctrine.[101]

Proving comparable worth is difficult because (a) an employee must show that management intentionally pays females less than males, and (b) no substantial business justification exists for the practice. Another method of proving comparable worth is for an employee to show that management is perpetuating past discrimination by setting present wage scales on outdated discriminatory wage structures which segregated women into lower paying jobs.[102] In *UAW v. State of Michigan*[103] the Cincinnati Court of Appeals ruled that the state is not liable under Title VII for wage disparities where studies fail to show that gender was considered in setting marketplace pay rates that favor males. But, there are lawful circumstances where men and women are paid differently despite doing the same work. Following prevailing market wage rates may shield an employer from a violation of Title VII even when comparable worth, not equal pay, exists between men and women.[104] In *Power v. Barry County, Michigan*, for example, prison matrons were unable to sustain a comparable worth challenge, even though female prison matrons were paid less than male correction officers. The District Court of Western Michigan ruled that the female prison guard's theory of comparable worth was without proof of intentional discrimination by the state of Michigan.[105]

The equal pay for equal work concept is regularly considered by arbitrators.[106] Arbitrator Arthur B. Jacobs ruled that the *Regents of California University*[107] did not violate the labor agreement by granting greater salary increases to jobs occupied primarily by males. Arbitrator Jacobs concluded that management's use of business community standards and state government statistical data to calculate pay raises was proper. The method of calculating pay raises resulted in a majority of women receiving pay increases of only 6 percent while higher increases were granted to males. Arbitrator Jacobs found the employer's proof convincing that women were not discriminated against because the pay increases were granted on the basis of work performed. Said Arbitrator Jacobs, "under these

---

[101] *County of Washington v. Gunther*, 25 FEP 1521, 452 U.S. 161 (1981).

[102] *Electrical Workers, IUE v. Westinghouse Electric Corporation*, 23 FEP 588, 631 F.2d 1094 (1980).

[103] *UAW v. State of Michigan*, 50 FEP 1560 (6th Cir. 1989).

[104] *State, County Municipal Employees v. Washington*, 38 FEP 1353, 770 F.2d 1401 (1985); see also *Spaulding v. University of Washington*, 35 FEP 217, 740 F.2d 686 (1984).

[105] *Power v. Barry County, Michigan*, 29 FEP 559, USDC WMich. (1982).

[106] *Wisconsin Education Association Council*, 83 LA 703 (Dash, 1984); *Warwick School Committee*, 137 AIS 3 (Bornstein, 1981); *Howmet Corporation*, 192 AAA 5 (Forsythe, 1974); *Indiana School District No. 24*, 5 PPA 22.5 (Boyer, 1977); *Centerline Public Schools*, 7 PPA 16.15 (Roumell, 1978); *Bangor School District*, 78 PSEA 0696 (Dunn, 1978); *Snohomish County*, 6 LAI 242 (Boedecker, 1979).

[107] *Regents of California University*, 57 AIS 8 (Jacobs, 1974).

conditions, nothing can be read into the [staff policy] and the [contract] which requires equal pay for unequal work only because the pay categories differ in their gender composition."

Equal pay for equal work is also at issue when male basketball coaches are paid more than female basketball coaches. Arbitrator Jonas Aarons found that *Camden County College* [325][108] did not violate the labor agreement by paying the men's basketball coach more than his female counterpart. The jobs differed in the number of hours worked, the number of games played, the number of unpaid assistants, and the duties involved. In a somewhat different set of circumstances involving basketball coaches' pay, Arbitrator Richard L. Kanner ruled in favor of management even though the duties of each coach were equal at the time the arbitrator rendered his award.[109] The facts of the case showed that when the contract was agreed the duties of the two coaches were substantially different. Arbitrator Kanner found that the parties had locked themselves into the labor agreement until the next round of negotiations and, therefore, no sex discrimination occurred. Arbitrator Seymour Strongin ruled in favor of management, upholding a contractual difference in extracurricular pay for coaches of men's and women's softball. Arbitrator Strongin noted that the specific understanding on wages emerged from the same contract that contained the antidiscrimination clause and, therefore, the two provisions were in harmony rather than contradictory.[110]

Not all arbitrators have ruled in favor of management when the union challenges pay differences for coaches of boys' and girls' sports. Arbitrator S. Herbert Unterberger split his award in *Wallingford Swarthmore District*.[111] Arbitrator Unterberger set aside management's argument that equal pay for equal work laws do not apply because the coaches for the boys' and girls' basketball teams were both male. Instead, the arbitrator elected to based his decision on evidence and documentation of the four criteria established by the parties for determining salary, criteria of time, skill, effort, and responsibility. In the end, Arbitrator Unterberger awarded 85 percent of the pay rate for boys' basketball as the pay for the coach of the girls' team and granted the union's request of 65 percent for the boys' basketball coach.

The equal pay for equal work standard favored the union in *Washoe County School District*.[112] Although the coaches had been aware of the wage difference between male and female coaches in the school district for nineteen months, Arbitrator Arnold O. Anderson ruled against the employer's procedural arbitrability challenge because the issue raised by the union was one of a continuing nature. Next, Arbitrator Anderson paralleled EPA criteria by establishing that equal pay was to be given whenever coaching assignments are equal in relation to "skill,

---

[108] *Camden County College*, 71 AIS 1 (Aarons, 1975).
[109] *Carrollton School District*, DIG 104020, GA 000216 (Kanner, 1978).
[110] *Arlington County School Board*, DIG 102729, GA 000116 (Strongin, 1976).
[111] *Wallingford Swarthmore District*, 76 PSEA 0634 (Unterberger, 1976).
[112] *Washoe County School District*, 67 AIS 12 (Anderson, 1975).

effort, and responsibility." Then following his own decision template, Arbitrator Anderson first ruled that the workload for female coaches who taught girls' tennis and golf was the same as the workload for male coaches in charge of the boys' tennis and golf team. The evidence provided by the parties showed that the number of students in girls' and boys' tennis and golf was the same, the number of matches was the same, and the same rules governed both sports. But despite these similarities, Arbitrator Anderson ruled that the district properly paid the male coaches of boys' track and field more than female coaches of girls' track and field. The workload for boys' track and field differed substantially from the workload for girls' track and field, making the male appointments more demanding in terms of skill, effort, and responsibility. There were more students on the boys' track and field team than the girls' team, the matches differed, the boys competed in more events, and the boys had more matches.

Turning to basketball, the *Garfield Board of Education* was found to be in violation of the antidiscrimination clause of the labor agreement and was directed by Arbitrator Gladys Gershenfeld to pay the female coaches of girls' basketball the same wage as males coaching boys' basketball.[113] The work schedule of the coaches was equal, the number of student athletes supervised was equal, the demands of the job substantially equal, and all basketball coaches faced similar emotional stress and pressure. The employer claimed that an interpretation of the labor agreement was not possible because both parties had ratified the contract and, therefore, stand in *pari delicto*, or in equal fault with regard to violation of Title IX, state law, and EPA. Arbitrator Gershenfeld ruled for management and required the parties to comply with Title IX, state law, and EPA as part of their labor agreement.

Many labor contracts require that senior men be paid more than junior women, and vice versa. And under EPA seniority is a legitimate basis for wage differences between men and women, a standard followed by Arbitrator William J. Berquist when he decided in favor of the *City of Eveleth*.[114]

As is clear, this grievance does not involve a situation where the position with its functions and responsibilities and the holder thereof, Mr. Mejasich, were within the bargaining unit under the recognition clause. If it did, then, in the opinion of this Arbitrator, on the basis of either the application of past practice of the salary rate to the position over a period of many years or on the basis on an agreement to rate applicable to the position by virtue of Section I of Article IV captioned "Vacations and Sickleave," this Arbitrator would have determined and ruled that the proper monthly salary rate to be paid the Grievant for the performance of the job or position in dispute is the monthly salary rate paid to the previous incumbent at the time of his retirement on May 31, 1984.

In the opinion of this Arbitrator, the record does not substantiate a finding that the City discriminated against the Grievant on the basis of sex, and therefore, there is no violation of Section B of Article I of the Contract. The City compared at least two positions of

---

[113] *Garfield Board of Education*, 4 PSAA 774120, 90 AIS 8 (Gershenfeld, 1977).
[114] *City of Eveleth*, 87 LA 343 (Berquist, 1985); see also *House of Corrections, County of Hillsborough*, 12 LAI 355 (McCausland, 1983).

similar nature with similar functions and job responsibilities of that of the Grievant and the monthly salary rates applied to the two comparable jobs were substantially the same as the monthly salary rate applied to the position and job of the Grievant. In addition, the fact that Mr. Mejasich was paid more than the Grievant, as presently in the position, does not in and of itself constitute evidence or proof of discrimination against the Grievant on the basis of sex. The creation of the position which was occupied by Mr. Mejasich prior to his retirement was a job that was created and in existence for a substantial period of time under a separate legal entity – the Public Utilities Commission and was governed by the Commission and not the City. There is adequate reason, exemplified by the record, for the difference in the monthly salary rate other than "on the basis of sex."

According to Arbitrator James W. Woy, factors other than gender were considered by *Data Com, Inc.*[115] when management elected to remove the grievant from a working leader position. The decrease of the grievant's pay below that of a male counterpart did not constitute sex discrimination because five other male working leaders were also demoted and management removed all six workers in an effort to reduce costs. An unknown honest error by management ten years earlier which resulted in male custodians receiving a third-shift differential not granted to second shift female custodians did not constitute sex discrimination nor did the mistake establish a binding past practice. Arbitrator Paul F. Probest agreed that management properly corrected the error by lowering male custodial pay to that of female custodians.[116]

Overtime pay is a form of compensation that must be distributed in accordance with contractual agreement, and without regard to gender. *Phillips Consumer Electronics Company*[117] did not engage in sex discrimination when it sought employees from several departments to work overtime in the shipping department. Arbitrator Dennis R. Nolan examined the record and found that the grievant's sex discrimination complaint was without merit because denial of the grievant's overtime petition was not intentional and because other women were selected to work overtime. The *Overhead Door Company*[118] violated the labor contract when it denied overtime to senior women because the work involved regular lifting of fifty-two-pound loads, work requirement that was once in compliance with the post World War II wave of so-called women's protective legislation. According to Arbitrator Edward P. Archer, the ability of the three female grievants to perform the work was not considered; rather, the qualified grievants were denied the overtime work simply because of their gender. One of the grievants weighed less than one hundred pounds and was unable to perform the

---

[115] *Data Com, Inc.*, 86-2 ARB 8532 (Woy, 1986).

[116] *Westmoreland County Community College*, 86 PSEA 3055 (Probest, 1986); see also *Central Bucks District*, 76 PSEA 0490 (Short, 1976), and *Gresham, Oregon, Grade School District 4*, 5 PSAA 785136 (Snow, 1978).

[117] *Philips Consumer Electronics Company*, 91 LA 1040 (Nolan, 1988); *PCL Packaging, Ltd.*, 11 LAC(3d) 333 (O'Shea, 1983); *Ferrerro Corporation*, 8 LAI 2094 (Walter, 1980).

[118] *Overhead Door Company*, 8 LAIS 123 (Archer, 1981).

overtime work-in-point, and Arbitrator Archer denied this woman her overtime grievance. However, the other two senior female union members were heavier, stronger, qualified, and able to perform the overtime assignment. Since he could not determine which of the two women would have elected to perform the overtime, Arbitrator Archer awarded eight hours overtime pay to be split between the two qualified grievants.

PROMOTION

The rule was decided over two decades ago and it is still followed today. It is a violation of Title VII as well as the employee's unwritten employment contract to discriminate on the basis of gender when deciding promotion.[119] An employer who unintentionally discriminates may still violate the Title VII promotion rights of women if women suffer from the discriminatory consequences of the employer's actions or policies. When disparate impact occurs the courts may elect to remedy the effect of an employer's illegal discrimination against women collectively by ordering that women be promoted over equally qualified men. Employers who choose between equally qualified male and female applicants for promotion find the courts taking a dim view of subjective judgment and outdated methods of evaluation.[120] The employer's promotion criteria must objectively evaluate each applicant's tenure, job knowledge, and experience.[121] Proof of disparate impact is often decided on the basis of statistical evidence[122] and employers are exonerated if their percentage of minority employees is proportional to the geographical labor market[123] and labor force.[124]

The court is likely to find a violation of the law, disparate impact and/or disparate treatment, where past employment practices continue to exclude a disproportionate percentage of the same gender from promotion.[125] For example, evidence of sex bias exists where the company follows a promotion from within policy and there is a gross disparity between the percentage of women in lower-level positions and the percentage of women in upper-level positions.[126] The court may conclude that Title VII has been violated if: a disproportionate percentage of women are kept from gaining the necessary experience for promo-

[119] *Hison v. King Spalding*, 34 FEP 1406 (US SupCt, 1984).
[120] *Albemarle Paper Company v. Moody*, 10 FEP 1181, 422 U.S. 405 (1975).
[121] *Rich v. Martin Marietta Corporation*, 11 FEP 211, 533 F.2d 333 (1975).
[122] *Sprogis v. United Air Lines*, 3 FEP 621, 444 F.2d 1194 (1971).
[123] *Hazelwood School District v. U.S.*, 15 FEP 1, 433 U.S. 299 (1977) and *Vuyanich v. Republic National Bank*, 24 FEP 128, 505 F.Supp 224 (1980).
[124] *Rich v. Martin Marietta Corporation*, 11 FEP 211, 533 F.2d 333 (1975).
[125] *Edwards v. Occidental Chemical Corporation*, 51 FEP 1602 (9th Cir. 1990).
[126] *Shidaker v. Tisch*, 45 FEP 494 (7th Cir. 1987).

tion;[127] the standards for promotion used by foremen are subjective;[128] or the employer manipulates work assignments detrimentally so that output figures inhibit the promotion of protected women.[129] On the other hand, an employer may elect to make promotion decisions on the basis of job-relevant physical attributes regardless of qualifications so long as the age and beauty criteria are applied equally to men and women.[130] This standards appears culturally arbitrary, American men not being deliberately beautiful.

The court is likely to find a disparate treatment violation of Title VII where the employer's rationale for rejecting a female applicant includes projected inconvenience, annoyance, extra expense,[131] or lack of toughness.[132] The court might conclude that disparate treatment has occurred if: the employer's decision to promote a male supervisor is based on the belief that employees will feel uncomfortable working with a woman supervisor;[133] a woman is required to have administrative skills not required of males seeking promotion;[134] the standards for making promotion recommendations used by foremen are subjective;[135] the employer allows co-workers who have sexually harassed the female candidate to participate in the decision to promote the harassed woman, the criteria for promotion being subjective;[136] the employer uses an employee's unlawful act as an intentional pretext to discriminate against either sex when deciding promotions;[137] or, the employer's failure to promote either gender can be statistically regarded as disparate treatment, even though no disparate impact occurs.[138] Title VII does not bar an employer from promoting a paramour over male employees when females are equally discriminated against.[139] And, the preference right of veterans established by the Vietnam Era Veterans' Readjustment Assistance Act of 1974,[140] granted as a reward for military service to the United States of America, supersedes the promotion right of women and minorities under Title VII.[141]

---

[127] *Palmer v. Baker*, 52 FEP 1458 (5th Cir. 1990). See also *Petitti v. New England Telephone & Telegraph Company*, 54 FEP 142 (1st Cir. 1990); *Pitre v. Western Electric Company*, 51 FEP 656, (10th Cir. 1988); and *Klapac v. McCormick*, 640 F.2d 1361 (1977).

[128] *Rowe v. General Motors Corporation*, 4 FEP 445, 457 F.2d 348 (1972).

[129] *Taylor v. Safeway Stores, Inc.*, 11 FEP 449, 524 F.2d 263 (1975).

[130] *Malarkey v. Texaco*, 34 FEP 1823, 704 F.2d 674 (1983).

[131] *Griggs v. Duke Power Company*, 3 FEP 175, 401 U.S. 424 (1971).

[132] *Thomas v. Cooper Industries*, 39 FEP 1826, USDC WNc (1986).

[133] *Hagans v. Andrus*, 25 FEP 502, 651 F.2d 622 (1981).

[134] *Willis v. Watson Chapel School District*, 52 FEP 903 (8th Cir. 1990).

[135] *Rowe v. General Motors Corporation*, 4 FEP 445, 457 F.2d 348 (1972).

[136] *Waltman v. International Paper Company*, 50 FEP 179 (5th Cir. 1989).

[137] *McDonnell Douglas Corporation v. Green*, 5 FEP 965, 411 U.S. 792 (1973).

[138] *Furnco Construction Corporation v. Waters*, 17 FEP 1062, 438 U.S. 567 (1978).

[139] *DeCintio v. Westchester County Medical Center*, 42 FEP 921 (2nd Cir. 1986).

[140] 38 U.S.C. 2014.

[141] *DOL, Washington, DC*, LAIRS 19i78 (Craver, 1989).

In one corner, Title VII does not require an employer to promote an unqualified employee.[142] Indeed, the promotion of an unqualified male over a qualified female violates Title VII.[143] And when a qualified female has inferior qualifications to a qualified male, the male may be selected for promotion.[144] It is not a violation of Title VII to promote either the man or the woman when either candidate is "head and shoulders" better.[145] But, a candidate must be unquestionably "head and shoulders" better.[146] Turning to the middle ground, it has been lawful for an employer to select either the man or the woman when the qualifications for promotion of both candidates are substantially equal.[147] So unless the court has enforced a quota to overcome disparate impact, the employer need not give promotion preference to women when the man and the woman are equally qualified. A state may consider gender in order to fulfill affirmative action objectives where the two candidates for promotion are nearly equal.[148] Similarly, the Air Force correctly promoted candidates from outside the base in order to gain so-called new blood, the motivation for promotions not being gender driven.[149]

Except where a BFOQ is shown, like the business need for an actress, the employer's evaluation of qualification for promotion must be made without regard to gender. In reality, however, promotion decisions are based upon both objective and subjective factors that may be cited by either the employer or the employee to substantiate their individual position in a gender discrimination complaint. In 1989 the Supreme Court looked into the matter of mixed motive disputes, the circumstance where an employer's promotion decision is motivated by both permissible and nonpermissible factors.[150] In *Price Waterhouse v. Hopkins* the woman was denied promotion because she did not dress, walk, or talk "femininely enough," all nonpermissible factors that counted against the candidate's promotion request. *Price Waterhouse* agreed that the non-permissible factors had impacted its decision; however, the company asserted that the female's rejection was mostly due to her lack of interpersonal skills and abrasive personality traits. The High Court ruled that in mixed motive cases where a promotion decision is based upon both permissible and nonpermissible factors an employer must show by a preponderance of the evidence, 51 percent, that "it would have made the same decision even if it had not allowed gender to play

---

[142] *Griggs v. Duke Power Company*, 3 FEP 175, 401 U.S. 424 (1971).

[143] *Farber v. Massillon Board of Education*, 54 FEP 1063, (6th Cir. 1990).

[144] *Grano v. Development Department, Columbus*, 31 FEP 1, 699 F.2d 836 (1983).

[145] *Ramey v. Bowsher*, 53 FEP 1757 (DC Cir. 1990).

[146] *Rossy v. Roche Products Inc.*, 50 FEP 822 (1st Cir. 1989).

[147] *Texas Department of Community Affairs v. Burdine*, 25 FEP 113, 450 U.S. 248 (1981); see also *Hale v. Cuahoga County Welfare Department*, 51 FEP 1264 (6th Cir. 1989).

[148] *Conlin v. Blanchard*, 51 FEP 707 (6th Cir. 1989).

[149] *Risher v. Aldridge*, 51 FEP 956 (5th Cir. 1989).

[150] *Price Waterhouse v. Hopkins*, 49 FEP 954, US SupCt (1989).

such a role." On remand the lower court found that *Price Waterhouse* utilized a preponderance of nonpermissible factors when it denied partnership to Hopkins.[151]

Arbitrator Robert J. Mueller was confronted with a *Price Waterhouse* type situation in *Veterans Administration Medical Center, Tomah*.[152] The union claimed that the female grievant's immediate supervisor made remarks fraught with gender bias which influenced two members of the interview panel to vote against the grievant's promotion. The union testified that the grievant's immediate supervisor prepared job standards and job evaluations which resulted in discrimination against the grievant because of her gender. The employer stated that the immediate supervisor was not the selecting officer, that an engineer with strong electrical knowledge was needed on the job, and that electrical engineering experience was desirable. Arbitrator Mueller found in favor of management because the employee selected for promotion scored highest on the Civil Service list, had nine years of experience in the electrical field, and had strong electrical knowledge. Arbitrator Jack A. Warshaw elected to discount allegedly sexist remarks made by the grievant's supervisor as hearsay in *National Homes Corporation*.[153] The female grievant was not upgraded when the male occupant of the position above her was upgraded. Management stated that its decision to upgrade the nonunion worker was based upon his thirty-one years' experience and fear that the senior worker would quit. Arbitrator Warshaw concluded that the union did not shoulder its burden of proving gender discrimination. Furthermore, the duties of the female grievant were not significantly changed following the upgrade given to the senior male.

Sometimes employees request a leave of absence in order to attend a promotion interview. Just such a request was made in *City of New York, Police Department*[154] and management denied the grievant's petition. Arbitrator Carlin Meyer awarded in favor of the employer because the labor agreement left leave of absence decisions to the discretion of the agency head. The record provided by the parties convinced Arbitrator Meyer that management acted reasonably, applied police department policy regarding the granting of leave in a uniform and consistent manner for all employees, and the union failed to proved ample evidence to sustain its charge of gender discrimination.

Promotion to associate professor and tenure go hand in hand at many American universities. In 1990 the Supreme Court established that universities are educational institutions subject to Title VII and must reveal confidential tenure review materials to the EEOC when the commission is called upon to investigate

[151] *Price Waterhouse v. Hopkins*, 54 FEP 750, DC Cir (1989).

[152] *Veterans Administration Medical Center, Tomah*, LAIRS 15216 (Mueller, 1983).

[153] *National Homes Corporation*, 9 LAIS 1150 (Warshaw, 1982). The admissibility of evidence regarding sex discrimination was considered in *Windsor Board of Education*, 3 LAC(3d) 426 (Gorsky, 1982).

[154] *City of New York, Police Department*, 20 LAIS 3242 (Meyer, 1992).

a gender bias charge involving tenure.[155]   The majority of gender bias complaints involving denial of tenure have fallen under the disparate treatment doctrine,[156] and the rule of law is that women must be judged against the same criteria as men when the tenure decision is made. It is a violation of Title VII to deny promotion and tenure to a women if a man with the identical ability, experience, qualifications, and record of performance is given tenure.[157]   So long as they remain gender neutral, universities may establish promotion priorities, set academic potential and achievement requirements, and rely upon the good faith judgment of peer review committees and other reviewing authorities.[158]   Arbitrator Robert F. Barlow directed *Northeastern University*[159] to revise and repeat its review process when a female assistant professor was denied tenure and promotion, adequate evidence of gender discrimination not being provided by the grievant.

Arbitrators have consistently denied promotions to women who are unqualified either physically and/or because they lack experience[160] or training.[161]   Arbitrator B. R. Skelton agreed that management did not engage in sex bias when it selected a male instead of the female grievant for promotion. The grievant was one of thirty-six applicants and one of three finalists for promotion. But, the grievant was not selected for promotion because the two male finalists had five times the amount of hands on experience as the grievant. Arbitrator Skelton held that management properly disregarded the grievant's outside carpentry experience, which was performed without agency instruction, off agency time, and the grievant had not been accountable to anyone for the finished product.[162]

In *WFMJ-Television*[163] and *Missouri Utilities Company,*[164] for example, the employers' promotion standards were found reasonable. In both awards the arbitrator agreed that an unqualified female could not gain a promotion solely because of her gender, despite the union's disparate treatment claim. Similarly,

---

[155] *University of Pennsylvania v. EEOC,* 51 FEP 1118 (US SupCt 1990). Arbitrator Milton Friedman refused to order witness to testify concerning confidential university promotion review committee matters, *CUNY, Staten Island,* 47 AIS 1, CUNY 000013 (Friedman, 1973).

[156] *Carlile v. South Routt School District,* 35 FEP 689, 739 F.2d 1496 (1984).

[157] *Gutzwsiller v. Fenik,* 48 FEP 395 (6th Cir. 1988).

[158] *Zahorik v. Cornell University,* 34 FEP 165, 729 F.2d 85 (1984); see also *Ottaviani v. State University of New York at New Paltz,* 51 FEP 330 (2nd Cir. 1989).

[159] *Northeastern University,* 82 AIS 21 (Barlow, 1976).

[160] *DOD, Army Corps of Engineers, New Orleans,* LAIRS 13458 (Foster, 1981); see also *ITT-Continental Baking Company,* 8 LAI 2831 (Springfield, 1981), and *Kelly AFB, Texas,* 95 FLRR 2-1010 (Massey, 1994).

[161] *Southwestern Electric Power Company,* 77 LA 553 (Bothwell, 1981); see also *Sola Basic Industries,* 78-1 ARB 8090 (Owen, 1978).

[162] *Veterans Administration Medical Center, Gainesville,* LAIRS 16328 (Skelton, 1984); see also, *State of Michigan, Department of Transportation,* LAIG 3120 (Huston, 1982).

[163] *WFMJ-Television,* 75 LA 400 (Ipavec, 1980).

[164] *Missouri Utilities Company,* 68 LA 379 (Erbs, 1977).

female employees have been denied promotion when: they are unqualified and statistical evidence does not support the claim of disparate impact;[165] the unqualified female applicant is argumentative so that productivity is disrupted;[166] and the sex discrimination grievance filed by the Union consists of a claim between two female applicants seeking promotion.[167] In a situation between a man and a woman, the *U.S. International Trade Commission*[168] agreed with the contention of the union that the International Trade Commission it had engaged in a general pattern of employment discrimination against women in the work force. Notwithstanding, Arbitrator Jones found that the International Trade Commission properly bypassed the female grievant for promotion because she lacked essential qualifications relative to those of the successful male applicant.

Arbitrators have considered disparate impact charges and required the promotion of (a) qualified women[169] and (b) women who are incorrectly declared unqualified by their employers.[170] Arbitrators have also required promotion of qualified females under Title VII when the employer's only evaluation consisted of a subjective interview.[171] Arbitrators and courts have ruled that too much reliance on subjective interviews may serve as the basis for both disparate impact and/or disparate treatment findings.[172] For example, Arbitrator W. Thomas Mulhall decided that the only male member of an all-female unit was properly denied promotion. The union failed to provide data on the number of male applicants for the unit promotion, failed to overcome testimony that the selecting officer made the promotion decision without knowledge of the grievant's gender, and failed to prove disparate treatment.[173]

Arbitrator Roland H. Strasshofer, Jr., split his award when confronted with a disparate treatment challenge. The *Veterans Administration Medical Center, Cleveland*[174] was directed to post a notice stating its willingness to comply with the labor agreement. However, Arbitrator Strasshofer denied the female grievant a promotion because she was properly considered before outside candidates. There were a number of women in high- and medium-ranked positions at the Medical Center, and the grievant's record documented deficiencies in work

---

[165] *AIRCO, Inc.*, 67 LA 453 (Ables, 1976).

[166] *Stayton Canning Company*, 75 LA 2 (Axon, 1980).

[167] *WLS Stamping Company*, 66 LA 584 (Emerson, 1976).

[168] *ITC, Washington, DC*, 78 LA 1 (Jones, 1981).

[169] *Consolidated Natural Gas Service*, 64 LA 37 (Sembower, 1974); see also *County of Santa Clara*, 71 LA 290 (Koven, 1978).

[170] *Braniff Airways, Inc.*, 66 LA 421 (Lieberman, 1976).

[171] *Honeywell, Inc.*, 61 LA 1021 (Doppelt, 1973).

[172] *Hughes Helicopter Company*, 288 AAA 1 (Richman, 1982).

[173] *DOD, Army Armor Center, Fort Knox*, LAIRS 13555 (Mulhall, 1981).

[174] *Veterans Administration Medical Center, Cleveland*, LAIRS 16339 (Strasshofer, 1984).

quality. At *Veterans Administration Medical Center, Newington,*[175] Arbitrator Robert Whitman did not find ample evidence of gender discrimination. The arbitrator found that the grievant was denied advanced training as a result of her supervisor's negative feelings toward her. Arbitrator Whitman considered the supervisor's failed attempt to terminate the grievant evidence of ill feelings. Arbitrator Whitman directed that management ensure that the female grievant be given advanced training the same as other employees and that the grievant be promoted within one year.

Arbitrator Bernard H. Cantor split his award in *Internal Revenue Service, Atlanta*[176] because the service improperly: omitted the grievant's name from the best qualified promotion list; lowered the grievants scores on several performance appraisal elements; and failed to consider that the grievant's performance appraisal evaluated her for performance above her job classification level. On the other side, however, Arbitrator Cantor found no evidence of sex discrimination. In a different case, the *City of Fort Worth*[177] improperly awarded the captain position to the third-highest candidate because she was female. Said Arbitrator Harold E. Moore, the law requires sufficient proof to support variance from the standard policy that management select the top candidate for promotion to captain regardless of gender. That is, Arbitrator Moore ruled that applicable law called for gender not to be considered as a factor when qualifying employees for promotion to captain. Arbitrator Moore ruled in favor of the union and awarded the captaincy to the top-ranked male candidate.

JOB POSTING, SENIORITY, AND PROMOTION

Seniority[178] and job-posting rights[179] are frequently entwined with promotion, and are by far the most common basis for challenging promotion decisions. Disparate treatment challenges have also been entwined with termination,[180] suspension,[181] academic freedom,[182] and unfairness.[183] Arbitrators consistently agree in

---

[175] *Veterans Administration Medical Center, Newington,* LAIRS 12428 (Whitman, 1979).

[176] *Internal Revenue Service, Atlanta, Georgia,* 92 FLRR 201613 (Cantor, 1992).

[177] *City of Fort Worth,* 92-2 ARB 8466 (Moore, 1992).

[178] *Teamsters v. U.S.,* 14 FEP Cases 1514, 431 U.S. 324 (1977).

[179] *Olin Corporation,* 79-2 ARB 8460 (1979); *Brown County Medical Health Center,* 68 LA 1363 (Lee, 1977); and *County Sanitation Districts,* 67 LA 833 (Roberts, 1976).

[180] *TYK Refractories Company,* 96 LA 803 (Talarico, 1991) and *HHS, Public Health Service, Food and Drug Administration,* LAIRS 17249 (Sands, 1986).

[181] *CR,* 20 SCARAB 3-23855 (Scheinman, 1982).

[182] *Merriville Board of School Trustees,* 86 AIS 2 (Dolnick, 1976).

[183] *Safeway Stores, Inc.,* 60 LA 670 (Williams, 1973); *Anaconda Aluminum Company,* 62 LA 1049 (Warns, 1974); *St. Paul's Towers,* 195 AAA 14 (Lucas, 1974); *3 M Company,* 8 LAI 778 (Grabb, 1980).

all these cases that unqualified female candidates need not be promoted even if they have bona fide seniority rights or other contractual guarantees.[184]   Denial of bona fide seniority and job-posting rights by *U.S. Steel Corporation*[185] was upheld by Arbitrator Milton Friedman, for example.   The contract required that promotion be based on ability to perform the work, physical fitness, and continuous service.   Arbitrator Friedman agree with management's assessment that the female grievant lacked the physical strength to perform the job, other women having passed the physical strength requirement during the job's contractual trial period.

Seniority and job-posting rights are not accorded deference when gender is an important social factor associated with the job.[186]   For example, both senior female and senior male employees have been denied promotions to janitorial or supervisory positions in locker rooms for the opposite gender.[187]   Arbitrator James C. Duff found for management by adopting the business necessity exemption enunciated by the courts.   The *Board of Education of Erie*[188] correctly barred a senior male employee from girls' physical education instructor because, in this case, the male's seniority rights were subordinate to the employer's broad educational goals.   Arbitrator Duff concluded that management could properly consider gender as a prerequisite qualification for positions where the sex of the employee has a factual nexus with the ability to perform the full range of instructional duties required by the job.

Arbitrators have ruled that experience and training requirements for promotion take priority over female employee seniority rights as long as the employer's standards are job related and reasonably applied to all employees.[189]   Arbitrator William L. Richard found that the company acted in accordance with the labor agreement by not promoting the female grievant to journeyman sooner.   The grievant claimed that she was not placed on job assignments necessary to fulfill promotion requirements.   But undisputed testimony showed that the apprenticeship program was amended by the parties and Arbitrator Richard reasoned that past practice regarding seniority did not apply to the new program.   Arbitrator Richard held that the company was not required to promote an apprentice who was not qualified and that the union failed to meet its burden of proof concerning gender bias.[190]   Arbitrator Thomas J. Erbs paralleled *Duke Power* in an award

---

[184] *Reynolds Metals Company*, 76-2 ARB 8454 (1976).

[185] *U.S. Steel Corporation*, 65 LA 626 (Friedman, 1975).

[186] Social factors have been considered significant by the Supreme Court, *Dothard v. Rawlinson*, 15 FEP Cases 10, 433 U. S. 321 (1977).

[187] *Columbus Board of Education*, 305 AIS 8 (Duff, 1994). See also *Canajoharie Central School District*, 21 LAIS 3387 (Goldsmith, 1993).

[188] *Board of Education of Erie, Pennsylvania*, 70 LA 567 (Duff, 1978).

[189] *Missouri Utilities Company*, 68 LA 379 (Erbs, 1977); *County Sanitation Districts*, 67 LA 833 (Roberts, 1976); and *Reynolds Metals Company*, 76-2 ARB 8454 (1976).

[190] *Toledo Edison Company*, 94 LA 905 (Richard, 1990).

favorable to *Illinois Bell Telephone*.[191] Arbitrator Erbs upheld a selection rate that favored men for promotion because the selection rate was based on a valid business necessity as well as backed by a lawful objective test. There were no women in the pool of applicants at *Illinois Bell Telephone* with the necessary training and experience for promotion by the telephone company.

Inappropriate reasons for denying women their seniority and job-posting rights frequently center on outdated stereotypes and employment practices that systematically exclude women. For example, an employer cannot refuse to promote women based on an assumption that women are less capable of doing physical work, that customers prefer male over female employees, or that work has traditionally been performed by men.[192] Even before *Weber v. Kaiser Aluminum & Chemical Corporation*,[193] arbitrators allowed employers to systematically exclude men and women from promotions in order to achieve a balanced nursing staff equal to male-female patient ratios.[194] But where basic statistics show that all, or nearly all, otherwise qualified women have been denied access to promotional prerequisite experience and training opportunities, arbitrators have imitated the courts and required that the grievants be promoted or be given an extended trial period.[195] Arbitrator John H. Dorsey ruled in favor of the union's gender discrimination claim because the female grievant was denied contractually required training and career development, denied promotion because of hiring freezes while five males were promoted despite the freezes, and subjected to unreasonable and unexplained delays in the processing of her promotion request.[196] Arbitrator Dorsey granted retroactive promotion, with back pay, for two and one-half years. One outdated exception to this rule is safety related. The medical hazard of lead poisoning once justified the denial of job-posting rights for women of childbearing age because of possible physical damage to an unconceived fetus.[197] Employers claim that the hazard of physical malformed children to bar women from working near potential lead poisoning.

Several awards involved the promotion of equally qualified female candidates, similar to *Burdine*. Arbitrator William P. Daniel sustained management's decision to promote an equally qualified black woman over her male senior. The *Ann Arbor Board of Education*[198] concluded that the successful applicant was more qualified for the coordinator position because her race (black) and gender fit

[191] *Illinois Bell Telephone Company*, 76 LA 432 (Erbs, 1981).
[192] *Brown-Jordan Corporation*, 64 LA 972 (Woodward, 1975).
[193] *Weber v. Kaiser Aluminum & Chemical Corporation*, 20 FEP 1, 443 U.S. 193 (1979).
[194] *Brown County Medical Health Center*, 68 LA 1363 (Lee, 1977).
[195] *Braniff Airways, Inc.*, 66 LA 421 (Lieberman, 1976); for opposite, see *Hoboken Board of Education*, 58 AIS 15 (Unterberger, 1974).
[196] *CSA, Washington, DC*, 62 LA 1307 (Dorsey, 1974); see also *Cranston Print Works*, 241 AAA 2 (Horowitz, 1978) and *Pacific Gas and Electric Company*, 73-2 ARB 8604 (Eaton, 1974).
[197] *Olin Corporation*, 79-2 ARB 8460 (1979).
[198] *Ann Arbor Board of Education*, 41 AIS 10 (Daniel, 1973).

student and district interest in obtaining a coordinator who matched the recommendations of the Humanness in Education Report. Arbitrator Daniel found no reverse discrimination. In *County of Santa Clara*,[199] Arbitrator Adolph M. Koven agreed that it was proper for the employer to promote deputy sheriff matrons to deputy sheriff without promoting their equally qualified male counterparts. The employer's objective was to overcome a past practice of preferential treatment given to men.

However, in *Consolidated Natural Gas Service*[200] Arbitrator John F. Sembower determined that the employer erred by granting preferential treatment by promoting a male applicant over an equally qualified senior female applicant. The employer's position was based on a rigid definition of the term "equally qualified." Rejecting the employer's position, Arbitrator Sembower stated that the classic *Shelley* rule applied so that the female applicant need not be literally equal to her junior male. The appropriate *Shelley* standard for allowing seniority to prevail is that the senior applicant need be only roughly or approximately equal, whereas to get promoted the junior applicant must be head-and-shoulders better qualified. Arbitrator John A. Bailey concluded in favor of the employer when the junior male bidder's proven leadership skills and considerable experience in the warehouse made him head-and-shoulders better qualified for promotion.[201] The senior female bidder who was bypassed had neither proven leadership skills nor work experience in the warehouse. Superior educational background does not automatically meet the requirements of the *Shelley* rule, particularly when the superior elements of the junior candidate's background are superfluous to the job opening at hand.[202] That is, the criteria followed by management must be job relevant, and the head and shoulders rule must be clearly applicable. Otherwise superflous criteria cannot be followed and used as a bar to the employment of a senior qualified women worker.

Another aspect of *Burdine* concerns the allocation and assignment of proof.[203] Utilizing the Supreme Court's articulation standard enunciated in *Burdine*, Arbitrator John H. Abernathy found in favor of *GSA, Auburn*.[204] The female grievant was passed over in favor of a male candidate for promotion to contract specialist. Arbitrator Abernathy ruled that the agency properly articulated via clear evidence that the male candidate was more qualified because of his education and experience. In *NLRB*[205] Arbitrator Robert G. Williams sustained the grievance in part because management failed to articulate objective factors in its

---

[199] *County of Santa Clara*, 71 LA 290 (Koven, 1978).

[200] *Consolidated Natural Gas Service*, 64 LA 37 (Sembower, 1974).

[201] *TU Electric, Generating Division*, 97 LA 1177 (Bailey, 1991); see also *City of St. Paul, Public Housing Agency*, BMS 9107.5 (Johnson, 1991).

[202] *EEOC, Atlanta*, LAIRS 17568 (Jones, 1986).

[203] The allocation of proof under *Burdine* for disparate treatment cases is detailed in Chapter 3.

[204] *GSA, Auburn*, 86 FLRR 2-1694 (Abernathy, 1985).

[205] *NLRB*, 91 FLRR 2-1378 (Williams, 1991).

selection process. Writing his opinion for the losing party, Arbitrator Williams stated that the burden of proof falls upon the grievant in disparate treatment complaints. In his written opinion, Arbitrator Williams recommended that in the future the agency develop and articulate its objective reasons for promotion. *NLRB* was told that its failure to provide objective reasons for its selection would, in the future, lead to the forced appointment of grievants to the position of supervisory attorney. Arbitrator Williams agreed with the union's contention that the alleged objective factors considered by management in its selection process were poorly implemented.

TRANSFER

Unless a valid business necessity exists, an employee transfer system that intentionally or unintentionally discriminates on the basis of gender is illegal. For example, the business need for a female in a position aimed to aid rape victims constituted a BFOQ justifying the involuntary transfer of a female worker by the *University of Pennsylvania*.[206] The employer correctly rejected the woman's request for transfer from headquarters to the field in *Sheehan v. Purolator, Inc.*[207] The employer testified that the plaintiff's transfer petition was motivated by dissatisfaction with salary rather than a desire to avoid gender bias. The Second Circuit Court found the employer's testimony credible because the woman's ex-supervisor had recommended her for promotion, salaries at her headquarters job were higher than salaries in the field, and transfers to the field rare.

A female employee could not avoid transfer by claiming gender discrimination when the record provided by the employer showed that tardiness and insubordination motivated the transfer decision. The *City University of New York*[208] supported its decision to transfer the black female employee with a series of pre-transfer memorandums warning the plaintiff about her tardiness. And the University provided the court with written tardiness reprimands sent to male employees as evidence that its tardiness program was without gender bias. An employer may transfer an employee who suffers from job fatigue and burnout, as evidenced by errors and low productivity.[209] A single comment by a supervisor that he was sorry that he had another female police officer does not render a transfer illegal.[210] It was not tenable to retain the female police officer in her new department because she was unable to take the criticism or counseling needed for her to improve to a satisfactory level of job performance, nor was

---

[206] *Moteles v. University of Pennsylvania*, 34 FEP 424, 730 F.2d 913 (1984).

[207] *Sheehan v. Purolator, Inc.*, 49 FEP 1000 (2nd Cir. 1988).

[208] *Ritzie v. City University of New York*, 49 FEP 647 (DC SNY, 1989).

[209] *Paul v. Federal National Mortgage Association*, 49 FEP 360 (DC Washington DC, 1988).

[210] Routine statements of bias against of women can support a Title VII violation, *Goodwin v. St. Louis County Circuit Court*, 34 FEP 347, 729 F.2d 541 (1984).

there evidence that the grievant would ever realistically be able to work without close supervision.[211]

The courts have found sex discrimination where the reasons given by the employer for transfer are not credible. The Eighth Circuit Court ruled that the lower court erred when it relied upon the inconsistent and contradictory explanations from the *U.S. Postal Service* (USPS)[212] to dismiss a sex discrimination challenge. The USPS failed to transfer the female letter carrier to a clerical job because her work needed improvement, though she was an excellent employee. The USPS testified that she had never been out of consideration for the transfer, but had never been considered for the job. The USPS supervisor could not recall why there were problems with the female letter carrier's work that would preclude transfer. Statistical evidence, the existence of separate career ladders for women, and a change in transfer policy in response to a female's request for transfer from the corrections division to road patrol all supported a finding of gender discrimination in *Kent County Deputy Sheriff's Association v. Kent County*.[213] The courts have been unwilling to dismiss *de minimis* violations of Title VII where the employer's "small violation" of the law resulted in injury or denial of transfer for women.[214] But, there are circumstances that are *de minimis*.[215]

Arbitrator William J. Hannan concluded that *Charleroi School District's*[216] technical error of not telling the employee why the transfer was necessary was *de minimis* and only deserved an admonition. The employer denied the request of a substitute teacher for a change from temporary to full-time employee, and transferred another employee into the grievant's position after the time limit for reappointment lapsed. Finding no evidence of gender discrimination by management, Arbitrator Hannan concluded that the grievance was not arbitrable. The union testified that the unilateral right to make lateral transfers was vested in management. Arbitrator Hannan ruled that the issues of retaliation for the union's grievance and the district's untimely filling of the vacancy are not contract grievances, and fall outside his jurisdictional power as established by the labor agreement between the parties.

---

[211] *Prudhomme v. Police Department*, 54 FEP 1204 (La. Court of Appeals, 1990).

[212] *Edwards v. U. S. Postal Service*, 53 FEP 729 (8th Cir. 1990).

[213] *Kent County Deputy Sheriff's Association v. Kent County*, 44 FEP 857 (6th Cir. 1987).

[214] *Cox v. American Cast Iron Pipe Company*, 40 FEP 678 (11th Cir. 1986).

[215] *City of Aurora*, 96 LA 1196 (Snider, 1990). See also, *Norristown School District*, 14 LAIS 4169 (Stoltenberg, 1987); *Veterans Administration Medical Center, Columbia*, LAIRS 17075 (Garnholz, 1985); *Georgia-Pacific Corporation*, 10 LAI 331 (Bell, 1982); *Hayes International Corporation*, 79 LA 1151 (Valtin, 1982); and *Beaunit Corporation*, 74-1 ARB 8284 (Kennedy, 1974).

[216] *Charleroi School District*, 86 PSEA 3097 (Hannan, 1986); see also *Charleroi School District*, 86 PSEA 3133 (1986).

The *Stockton Unified School District*[217] did not violate contract provisions prohibiting gender discrimination when it transferred a woman from counselor to teacher. The union based its challenge upon the affirmative action and fair employment clauses of the labor agreement, citing the District for arbitrarily and capriciously worsening the male female ratio of employees assigned to counselor positions. In his opinion Arbitrator Paul A. Cassady noted that the union overlooked the fact that the transfer of a male instead of a female from the counselor position would also worsen the ratio between male and female teachers in the classroom. Arbitrator Cassady declined to substitute his judgment for management's by reallocating the District's financial budget so that the female grievant could retain her counselor duties. Arbitrator David M. Keefe made his award in favor of the *River Rouge Board of Education's*[218] transfer of the black-female grievant, dismissing the union's claim of antiunion bias and sex discrimination. Arbitrator Keefe found that the grievant had previously filed a grievance but so had a majority of other teachers. The Arbitrator rejected the grievant's gender discrimination challenge because most teachers in the District were black and female. Arbitrator Keefe refused to hear the complaint of another grievant who failed to attend the hearing. Arbitrator Keefe refused to award attorney fees because the grievant's attorney duplicated union representation.

The involuntary transfer of a female teacher to a new school by the *Hernando County District School Board*[219] complied with four criteria set out in the contract by the parties. Certification, years of service in the building, the best educational program, and the individual's qualifications were all considered by the District, though all four factors were not necessarily weighed equally. Arbitrator Leonard H. Davidson concluded that the District's subjective determination of the four criteria required a level of judgment best left to management. Arbitrator Davidson saw no contact violation resulting from the District's admission that its decision was motivated in part by the desire to comply with federal affirmative action guidelines. On one other interesting point, Arbitrator Davidson found the "demeanor" of the witnesses at the hearing to be relevant. The witnesses showed no "bias or rancor" toward other employees as a result of the affirmative action plan.

When a conflict rose between the labor agreement and a gender discrimination consent decree. Arbitrator Thomas P. Gallagher ruled in favor of the union. To be exact, the union correctly asserted that the seniority and antidiscrimination clauses of the labor contract supersede the consent decree. In reaching his conclusion, Arbitrator Gallagher noted that the male grievant was transferred from the only job in the work area that was open to both men and women so that a female could fill the position. Arbitrator Gallagher stated:

---

[217] *Stockton Unified School District*, 76 AIS 6 (Cassady, 1976).
[218] *River Rouge Board of Education*, DIG 103292 GA 000194 B10-D4 (Keefe, 1975). See also, *Penn Delco School District*, 91 PSEA 0078 (Skonier, 1991).
[219] *Hernando County District School Board*, DIG 101167 GA 000045 F5-G5 (Davidson, 1975).

[o]n balance, I consider the gradual, but eventually total, loss of access by male employees to some positions to be more burdensome discrimination than the loss of merely a more frequent opportunity to bid for those positions by female employees. In other words, the loss to male employees under one result – entire access to any positions – would be greater than the loss to female employees under the other result – an increased frequency in access to those positions as males are reassigned out of them.[220]

In another case won by the union, Arbitrator Frank C. Carroll dealt with the transfer of a male physical education teacher away from girl's physical education duties and into a position requiring him to teach boys only. The *Erie School District*[221] violated the gender discrimination clause of the labor contract because the only reason given by the district for the transfer was management's concern for a female teaching boy's physical education, the same standard not being applied to male teaching girl's physical education. The union said the only justification for the transfer was a change in student enrollment levels within the district. Arbitrator Carroll found it ironic that the district allowed either gender to teach girl's physical education, but only men could teach boy's physical education. Because the school district based its decision to force the grievant's transfer solely upon male gender, Arbitrator Carroll directed that the grievant be transferred back to the coeducational physical education classes he had successfully taught for two years. Apparently, two years of on the job success was considered adquate evidence of the ability of the grievant to perform. Arbitrator Carroll did not address the reverse situation wherein female teachers were barred from teaching boy's physical education classes.

TESTING, TRIAL PERIODS, AND PROMOTION

The declining use of employment tests in the past thirty years is often attributed to the Civil Rights Act of 1964.[222] Many employers consider test valida-

---

[220] *State of Minnesota, Department of Corrections*, 88 LA 535 (Gallagher, 1987). See also *Alpha Beta Company*, 12 LAIS 1134 (Gentile, 1985); *South Washington County School District 833*, 12 LAI 253 (Karlins, 1984); *Wayne County Labor Relations Board*, 79-2 ARB 8415 (Roumell, 1979); *Woodhaven Board of Education*, DIG 103340 (Adler, 1977); and *Upper Merion District*, 75 PSEA 0164 (Rock, 1975).

[221] *Erie School District*, 91 PSEA 0053 (Carroll, 1991). See also *Racine Unified School District*, 93-2 ARB 3562 (Flaten, 1993); *Western School District*, 94 LA 681 (Kanner, 1990); *Denver School District 1*, 8 PSAA 818046 (Ipavec, 1981); *Erie School District*, 78 PSEA 0601 (Duff, 1978); *Stockton Unified School District*, 33 C PER 75 (Henderson, 1977); *McKeesport School District*, 76 PSEA 0817 (Stonehouse, 1976); *Stockton Unified School District*, 76 AIS 6 (Cassady, 1976); *United Telephone Company*, 66 LA 1 (Foster, 1976); and *Kettle Moraine Area Schools*, DIG 102668 (Christenson, 1975).

[222] National Industrial Conference Board, "Personnel Practices in Factory and Office: Manufacturing," *Studies in Personnel Policy*, No. 194, 1964, 14-15; American Society of Personnel Administrators, *The Personnel Executive's Job*. Englewood Cliffs, N.J.: Prentice-Hall, ASPA, 1977.

tion requirements to be too expensive and time consuming. In a few cases, employers actually follow test-free hiring and promotion practices because test free practices are subtle and less subject to scrutiny by legislatures, courts, and labor arbitrators.[223] But while many archaic testing procedures have been voluntarily abandoned or legally banned,[224] the importance of broadly defined testing for hiring, promotion and counseling workers has never been in serious doubt.[225] The congressional record shows that Section 703(h) of Title VII was not enacted to protect minorities from the abusive testing programs.[226] Instead, Section 703(h) was enacted to protect and encourage employers to continue the use of professionally developed ability tests for selection and promotion.[227] The concern of the statutes is not whether employers may use tests because the law says they may. Rather, the paramount concern of the law is to identify the specific circumstances for appropriate employment testing, circumstances in which all applicants have an equal employment opportunity. Indeed, it was the intent of the legislature that employment testing programs should continue where they could be certified as valid predictors of job success, regardless of whether the test was to be used for hiring or promotion purposes.

The leading Supreme Court interpretation of the law regarding testing is *Duke Power*, which prohibits intentional and unintentional discrimination. An employer may use a test to decide promotions so long as the test does not have an adverse effect upon a group of employees protected by Title VII. And, the test must be job related and justified by business necessity.[228] Among other things, *Duke Power* establishes a Title VII violation when job promotion requirements call for a high school diploma and passing test scores that are not relevant to job success. The High Court said that tests must be geared to job descriptions, properly validated, and periodically checked for reliability. A valid test must be grounded in empirical data that correlates important elements of work behavior

---

[223] Sheldon Zadek and Mary L. Tenopyr, "Issues in Selection, Testing and the Law," in *Discrimination in Employment, Fourth Edition* by William P. Murphy, Julius G. Getman and James E. Jones. Washington, DC: Bureau of National Affairs, Inc., 1979, 130.

[224] *Motoral, Inc. v. Illinois FEPC*, 34 Ill. 2d 266, 215 N.E. 2d (1966).

[225] Physical examinations, personal references, interviews, application blanks, biographical inventories, intelligence tests, psychological tests, motor skill tests, work samples, trial periods, performance appraisal inventories, and assessment centers are all relevant testing methods valuable for predicting job success and failure.

[226] 42 U.S.C. 2000E, Section 703(h).

[227] Irving Kovarsky. *Discrimination in Employment*. Iowa City: Center for Labor and Management, University of Iowa, 1976, 74.

[228] *Wards Cove Packing Company v. Antonio*, 49 FEP 1519 (US SupCt. 1989); *Watson v. Fort Worth Bank and Trust Company*, 47 FEP 102 (US SupCt. 1988); *Albemarle Paper Company v. Moody*, 10 FEP 255, 1181, 422 U. S. 405 (1975); and *Robinson v. Lorillard Corporation*, 3 FEP 653, 444 F.2d 791 (1971). The Civil Rights Act of 1991 lessened the business necessity burden set out by *Wards Cove*, 42 U.S.C. 2000e-2(k).

to the job for which the employee is being considered.[229] Compliance with the Uniform Guidelines on Employee Selection Procedures (UGESP) will aid employers seeking to avoid unlawful testing, the UGESP not being legally binding.[230]

A test violates Title VII if it is overly subjective,[231] validated for whites only, or not validated for the actual job for which the candidate is being considered.[232] A woman may not be denied promotion on the basis of a non job-related test. It is also unlawful to deny promotion to a woman on the basis that other women have been treated favorably.[233] That is, an employer's testing program may be free of disparate impact and still violate the disparate treatment standard of Title VII. The court have found tests lawful for determining promotion where sufficient correlation exists between test scores and job performance,[234] where the test was constructed on the basis of a detailed consideration of the job tasks,[235] where the test was justified by critical safety considerations,[236] and where no woman has ever been barred from the job by her score.[237] An employee must show both disparate impact and disparate treatment in order to successfully challenge a test on constitutional grounds, the same standard being less certain under most labor contracts.[238]

Arbitrator Louis A. Toepfer found violation of the labor agreement where the male candidates for an open lieutenant position took it upon themselves to form groups and prepare for the qualifying examination, the female grievant not being asked to be a member of male study group. The *State of Vermont, Department of Public Safety*[239] did not create the study groups preparing for the oral examination; in fact, the study groups were formed by individual officers. Arbitrator

---

[229] *Watson v. Fort Worth Bank and Trust Company*, 47 FEP 102 (US SupCt. 1988); see also *Brito v. Zia Company*, 5 FEP 1207, 478 F.2d 1200 (1973).

[230] *Clady v. City of Los Angeles*, 38 FEP 1575, 770 F.2d 1421 (1985); see also 421 FEP Manual 135-138. UGESP apply to tests, interviews, reviews of education, work samples, physical requirements, and performance evaluations. Cases involving compliance with UGESP include *Albemarle Paper Company v. Moody*, 10 FEP 1181, 422 U. S. 405 (1975). *Connecticut v. Teal*, 29 FEP 1, 457 U. S. 440 (1982); *Police Officers for Legal Rights v. City of Columbus*, 54 FEP 276, 6th Cir. (1990); *Gillespie v. Wisconsin Department of Health & Social Services*, 35 FEP 1487, 7th Cir. (1985); *Douglas v. Hampton*, 10 FEP 91, 512 F.2d 976 (1975); *Guardians Association v. Civil Service Commission*, 23 FEP 909, 630 F.2d 79 (1980); and *U.S. v. Georgia Power Company*, 5 FEP 587, 474 F.2d 906 (1973).

[231] *Culp v. General American Trans. Corp.*, 11 FEP 1308, U.S. Dist. NOhio (1974).

[232] *Albemarle Paper Company v. Moody*, 10 FEP 1181, 422 U.S. 405 (1975).

[233] *Connecticut v. Teal*, 29 FEP 1, 457 U.S. 440 (1982).

[234] *Bernard v. Gulf Oil Corporation*, 51 FEP 1126 (5th Cir. 1989).

[235] *Berkman v. New York*, 43 FEP 318 (2nd Cir. 1978).

[236] *Roby v. St. Louis Southwestern Railway Company*, 39 FEP 129, 775 F.2d 959 (1985).

[237] *EEOC v. Sears Roebuck Company*, 45 FEP 1257 (7th Cir. 1988).

[238] *Washington v. Davis*, 12 FEP 1415, 426 U. S. 229 (1976).

[239] *State of Vermont, Department of Public Safety*, 100 LA 370 (Toepfer, 1993).

Toepfer ruled that the presentation made by a member of the oral examination panel did not constitute sex discrimination on the basis of disparate treatment because the presentation was made as a favor to one of the candidates and was not intended to exclude the grievant.

Arbitrator Charles E. Swenson found that management need not provide a trial period (a trial period is a form of test) for two senior female Police Department Clerks at the *City of St. Cloud*.[240] The union contended that the senior female grievants were discriminated against when a junior male was transferred and promoted to a higher classification instead of allowing the grievants a trial period. Arbitrator Swenson agreed with management's assessment that the grievants were "simply upset because they were not selected." He cited the union for failure to provide adequate supporting evidence of gender discrimination. Arbitrator Robert L. Gibson concluded that *ICI Americas, Inc.*[241] did not discriminate against a female employee who was denied promotion to switchman because she failed a practical skill test. Arbitrator Gibson dismissed the union's claim that the grievant was unable to qualify for promotion because she had not received the same training as her male counterparts.

Arbitrator Thomas L. Hewitt sustained the demotion of the grievants to part-time work after they failed to achieve a satisfactory level of performance during a reasonable trial period. The grievants had received proper training, normal assistance from experienced employees, and were unable to lift and stack heavy packages at the normal rate of speed. Arbitrator Hewitt ruled in management's favor because the slow speed of the grievants caused untimely delivery of products to customers.[242] The *County of Orange*[243] convinced Arbitrator Robert D. Steinberg that its decision to amend the practical test requirements for fire inspector was business related. To be specific, a reduction in force created a need for inspectors to be fire suppression qualified so they could fight fires. The female grievant lacked upper body strength, which made it impossible for her to pass the job simulation test and become fire suppression qualified. Management's decision to change the test was not evidence of gender discrimination.

Arbitrator Arnold A. Karlins disagreed with the union's gender discrimination charge in *Northwestern Bell Telephone Company*.[244] In supporting manage-

---

[240] *City of St. Cloud*, BMS 9006.5 (Swenson, 1990); see also *Basic Vegetable Products, Inc.*, 64 LA 620 (Gould, 1975).

[241] *ICI Americas, Inc.*, 93 LA 408 (Gibson, 1989); see also *Day and Zimmerman, Inc.*, 7 LAI 677 (Weisbrod, 1980) and *McGill Manufacturing Company, Inc.*, 200 AAA 4 (Gibson, 1975).

[242] *Altoona Shop and Save*, 12 LAIS 1267 (Hewitt, 1985); see also *Continental Telephone Company of the South*, 83-2 ARB 8593 (Maxwell, 1983).

[243] *County of Orange*, LAIG 2882 (Steinberg, 1981); see also *PCL Packaging, Ltd.*, 11 LAC(3d) 333 (O'Shea, 1983).

[244] *Northwestern Bell Telephone Company*, 75 LA 148 (Karlins, 1980); see also *Jesco Lubricants Company*, 62 LA 1294 (Allen, 1974), and *Reynolds Metals Company*, 66 LA 1276 (Volz, 1976).

ment's right to require candidates for pole climbing training to pass a physical ability test, Arbitrator Karlins said:

The Chairman of this panel has carefully studied the award of arbitrator Fred Holly in South Central Bell Telephone Company vs. Communication Workers of America, decided February 1, 1980, and referred to by both parties in their briefs. In that case, the issue was not whether use of the PATB is discriminatory, but rather whether the Company acted arbitrability in limiting consideration for pole climbing training to those who scored 12 on the PATB. Arbitrator Holly held that Paragraph 12.02C of the agreement required consideration of "other necessary qualifications" (other than seniority). The pertinent language was " . . . seniority shall govern if other necessary qualifications of the individuals are substantially equal." He held that the failure to consider them was arbitrary action and that the Company was arbitrary in disqualifying those who did not achieve the minimum score of 12. He also found, however, that the PATB had been properly evaluated and is useful in predicting success in pole climbing training. He stated that the fact that "its use as a sole determinant is arbitrary within the meaning of 12.02C of the Agreement does not mean that the Company is automatically deprived of its use" and that "it can be used as a valuable selection aid along with other necessary qualifications."

Arbitrator Karlins noted that management correctly used the minimum score of 12 on the PATB test to qualify employees for training. Success in pole-climbing training at *Northwestern Bell Telephone* was contingent upon other factors such as education, prior training, and job experience.

Arbitrator Michael Fischetti split his award in *Office of Rules and Regulations, Customs Service, Department of Treasury*[245] because the union failed to provide adequate evidence on the availability of women for promotion to GS-14 attorney. And, management raters were unable to duplicate their ratings on a rerate trial, indicating the promotion test was based upon subjective factors. Arbitrator Fischetti found that the grievant's service as a part-time employee worked against her at promotion time. And since it was clear that the grievant would have been promoted had the rating program procedures been properly followed, Arbitrator Fischetti directed management to remedy the grievant by granting priority consideration for the next job opening at GS-14. Similarly, *Champion International Corporation*[246] was required by Arbitrator James L. Reynolds to grant the female grievant the next available opening in the Electrical and Instrumentation apprenticeship program. *Champion International Corporation* violated the labor agreement by requiring the grievant to take the Bennett Test, which she failed to pass at a qualifying level in June 1992, rather than honoring the grievant's 1991 passing score on the General Aptitude Test Battery (GATB). The union provided uncontroverted testimony that the parties had agreed that passing GATB test score would stand for five years, even after the conversion to

---

[245] *Office of Rules and Regulations, Customs Service, Department of Treasury*, 93 FLRR 2-1362 (Fischetti, 1993).
[246] *Champion International Corporation*, BMS 9411.2 (Reynolds, 1994).

the Bennett Test. Arbitrator Reynolds wrote that gender discrimination was not proved because the union's challenge was based upon a comparison with other female employees and there was insufficient evidence to support the contention that the grievant was treated unfairly compared to similarly situated workers.

The *Norfolk Naval Shipyard, Virginia*[247] violated that labor contract as well as merit system principles when it awarded a vacant supervisory police officer position to a female. Noting that applicable laws and merit system guidelines required management to make promotions on the basis of knowledge, skills, and abilities as well as avoiding employment discrimination, Arbitrator Dennis R. Nolan directed management to vacate the appointment. In his award, Arbitrator Nolan found that the successful candidate had been awarded the vacant position in order "to advance the department's need of women in management." The female appointee did not have the requisite experience, had misrepresented her educational achievements, and was given special coaching in preparation for the qualifying test by another officer. Arbitrator Nolan concluded that the employer's reliance on the successful candidate's sex as a tie breaker as well as special coaching constituted violation of sex discrimination regulations and the merit system principles of "equal opportunity" as well as "fair and equitable treatment." Arbitrator Richard L. Kanner found reverse discrimination and ruled that the *Michigan Department of Public Health*[248] violated the labor agreement when by awarding the industrial hygienist vacancy to a white female who scored much lower on the qualifying test than a white male candidate who was passed over. Arbitrator Kanner ordered management to vacate its decision.

Now about trial periods. The union claimed sex discrimination and prevailed in *Braniff Airways, Inc.*[249] where a contract provision called for hiring, transfer, and promotion decisions to be made without regard to gender. Here is what Arbitrator Irwin M. Lieberman had to say about the grievant's contractual trial period:

The most disturbing aspect of this history is the almost total lack of criticism or specific help to this employee during her entire seventy-five days by her supervisor. One can only wonder why. In fact, the testimony indicates that on at least two occasions she was observed by supervision having difficulty and was not given instruction or help. In the same vein, it is impossible to credit the conclusions reached that she had difficulty in handling mechanical equipment when she was qualified to handle, by test, three out of four pieces of the equipment in question.

Perhaps the most surprising element in the history of this employee's qualification period is her induction interview with the manager. Mr. Retzlaff's statements, indicated above, were hardly conducive to encouraging a newly arrived female to succeed. To be

---

[247] *Norfolk Naval Shipyard, Virginia*, LAIRS 21342 (Nolan, 1993).

[248] *Michigan Department of Public Health*, 101 LA 713 (Kanner, 1993).

[249] *Braniff Airways, Inc.*, 66 LA 421 (Lieberman, 1976); see also *Anheuser-Busch, Inc.*, 81-1 ARB 8058 (Seitz, 1980); *Bordo Citrus Products Cooperative*, 74-1 ARB 8165 (Nachring, 1974); *Veterans Administration Medical Center, Newington*, LAIRS 12428 (Whitman, 1979); and *Safeway Stores, Inc.*, 60 LA 670 (Williams, 1973).

told that a female is out of her mind to work in the job was, at most charitable, bad judgment. It is noted that the Company does not have any physical standards for the position.

Arbitrator Lieberman concluded that the gender discrimination suffered by the grievant was most likely due, in large part, to unconscious bias on the part of male employees. The female grievant was restricted from gaining the adequate experience, training, and work opportunity necessary to succeed during her trial period. Arbitrator Lieberman gave considerable weight to the undisputed and unchallenged fact that no female employee had ever been able to remain in the position sought by the grievant, though several had tried.

JOB CLASSIFICATION, WORK ASSIGNMENT, AND EQUAL PAY

It is a violation of Title VII to classify jobs or to separate employees by gender. Keeping separate male and female seniority lists, segregating work assignments and job classifications by gender, limiting women to the lowest paying jobs, and allowing men but not women to transfer shifts constitutes gender discrimination.[250] In 1984, for example, Northwest Airlines violated Title VII because management intentionally separated jobs by gender and paid women less than men for the same work.[251] The Court of Appeals in Washington, DC discounted the Airline's sincere belief that the job classifications it had intentionally separated into male and female work were really different. It is also a violation of Title VII to demote or assign an inferior job title to a worker based on gender while maintaining the same salary level.[252]

There are two defenses that an employer may follow in order to win a Title VII case involving work assignments and/or job classification. The appropriate affirmative defense for a disparate treatment challenge is that sex is a BFOQ, and the correct defense for a disparate impact suit is business necessity.[253] Taking the disparate treatment challenge first, the courts have decided that a woman must provide evidence of a heavier workload than similarly situated men, as well as a salary different than the men's, in order to sustain a Title VII job classification and work assignment disparity.[254] Proof of a salary disparity attributable to sex discrimination under Title VII can occur where a female customer representative is refused a higher paid full-time job classification and the job is filled by men only. However, in the same case, the Eleventh Circuit Court required that proof of an EPA violation must be shown by establishing that the female worker was performing substantially the same work assignment as the men, but the

---

[250] *Mitchell v. Mid-Continent Spring Company*, 17 FEP 1594, 583 F.2d 275 (1978).

[251] *Laffey v. Northwest Airlines*, 35 FEP 508, 740 F.2d 1071 (1984).

[252] *Cox v. American Cast Iron Pipe Company*, 40 FEP 678 (11th Cir. 1986).

[253] *Pan American World Airways Inc.*, 53 FEP 707 (11th Cir. 1990).

[254] *King v. Board of Regents, University of Wisconsin System*, 52 FEP 809 (7th Cir. 1990); see also *Roberts v. College of the Desert*, 53 FEP 1493 (9th Cir. 1988).

women was paid less money than the man despite performing essentially the same work.[255]

In a different case, the employer did not violate disparate treatment theory by firing a secretary for her refusal to wash coffee cups and make fresh coffee. The Ninth Circuit Court exonerated management from the secretary's gender discrimination complaint because the job classification included the duty of preparing conference rooms for meetings. Making fresh coffee and washing coffee cups was a valid part of the work assignment given to that particular secretary.[256] In *Parker v. Secretary, Housing and Urban Development*[257] the employee was unable to prove disparate treatment by showing that she was assigned to higher-grade work, denied a home visit job assignment, and arguing that gender discrimination impacted her work performance.

Fertility is not the same as pregnancy. Fetal protection policies aimed to protect nonpregnant fertile female employees from lead exposure amounts to overt sex discrimination because infertility is not a BFOQ, nor is retention of fertility a business necessity.[258] On the other hand, fetal protection policies that result in work assignments that remove pregnant women from exposure to lead poisoning are justified by business necessity, and set forth a BFOQ.[259] *Delta Air Lines, Inc.*[260] properly removed all pregnant flight attendants from flight status because it was impossible to tell in advanced which pregnant flight attendant would suffer from fatigue, nausea, or a spontaneous on the job involuntary abortion.

An interviewer commits gender bias by making statements and asking questions that are not related to an established BFOQ. In *Barbano v. Madison County*[261] the interviewer stated that he would not consider some women for a top management directorship, questioned a female candidate as to whether she would get pregnant, asked whether her husband would mind her running "around the country with other men," and stated he would not let his wife do it. In an unusual case, the Eighth Circuit ruled that the employer did not discriminate on the basis of gender when a female news anchor was reassigned to reporter because she was too old, too unattractive, not deferential enough to men, and a viewers' program survey reaction to her was negative.[262] In this case, being considered beautiful by the viewing public was a legitimate job requirement.

---

[255] *Waters v. Turner, Wood & Smith Insurance Agency Inc.*, 50 FEP 327 (11th Cir. 1989).

[256] *Pendleton v. East Los Angeles Community Union*, 15 FEP 1370 (9th Cir. 1976).

[257] *Parker v. Secretary, Housing and Urban Development*, 51 FEP 910 (DC Cir. 1989).

[258] *Grant v. General Motors Corporation*, 53 FEP 688 (6th Cir. 1990); see also *Auto Workers v. Johnson Controls, Inc.*, 50 FEP 1627 (7th Cir. 1989).

[259] *Auto Workers v. Johnson Controls, Inc.*, 50 FEP 1627 (7th Cir. 1989).

[260] *Levin v. Delta Air Lines, Inc.*, 34 FEP 1192, 730 F.2d 994 (1984).

[261] *Barbano v. Madison County*, 54 FEP 1288 (2nd Cir. 1990). Arbitrators have also considered the bias of supervisors that women not do some kinds of work, *FMC Corporation*, 70 LA 683 (Johannes, 1978).

[262] *Craft v. Metromedia, Inc.*, 38 FEP 404, 766 F.2d 1205 (1985).

Providing a valid business need for separate male and female job classification and work assignments is more difficult under the disparate impact theory because the employer must defend against unintentional discrimination.[263] It has been unlawful for over twenty-five years, for example, for an employer to adopt a new employment scheme to correct illegal male female job separations if the new scheme turns out to perpetuate historically biased work assignments.[264] In a different vein, it is lawful for an employer to assign female guards to all parts of the prison except male maximum security. The privacy rights of male inmates is of low importance and the pat search conducted by female guards is of short duration and minimum obtrusiveness.[265] The inmates' right to privacy is sufficiently accommodated by instructing female guards not to frisk male prisoner genital areas.[266]

One common grievance raised by male union members is that male employees are required to perform work assignments from which women are excluded. Arbitrator Neil M. Gundermann considered a male grievant's complaint that his reassignment to work in a black neighborhood constituted sex discrimination, finding for management. The *Social Security Administration, Milwaukee*[267] testified that white females were uncomfortable in black neighborhoods. The grievant asserted that he was discriminated against when management first justified his assignment to the black neighborhood on the basis of seniority, the woman being senior. And then when he was senior, the employer changed the rule. The new rule justified the grievant's assignment to the black neighborhood on the need for each employee to be familiar with the territory covered by co-workers, allowing backup in the event of trouble. Arbitrator Gundermann ruled that the need for backup help was a valid business safety reason for the grievant's work assignment. The safety concern meant that management was not obligated to bargain with the union over the job classification and work assignment policy change.

It was proper for the *State of Michigan, Department of Corrections*[268] to excuse female Officers from taking urine samples from males. Arbitrator Malcom G. House concluded that requiring female officers to perform this assignment exceeded "society's accepted standards of decency." The privacy of male clients, the need to avoid sexual harassment of female officers, and the ability of the male Officers to perform other work duties as well as take urine samples bal-

---

[263] *Palmer v. State Department*, 43 FEP 452 (DC Cir. 1987).

[264] *Palmer v. Baker*, 52 FEP 1458 (DC Cir. 1990); see also *EEOC Decision, June 30, 1969*, 1 FEP 914.

[265] *Timm v. Gunter*, 54 FEP 317 (8th Cir. 1990).

[266] *Smith v. Fairman*, 31 FEP 412, 678 F.2d 52 (1982); see also *Madyun v. Franzen*, 31 FEP 817, 704 F.2d 954 (1983).

[267] *HHS, Social Security Administration, Milwaukee*, LAIRS 18465 (Gundermann, 1987).

[268] *State of Michigan, Department of Corrections*, 13 LAIS 3248 (House, 1985); see also *County of Bucks, Department of Corrections*, LAIG 4559 (Symonette, 1991).

anced in favor of management. In another industry, Arbitrator Michael D. Rappaport sustained management's policy decision that only male nurse's aides should be required to perform catheterizations on male patients, female nurses aids being relieved of former male catheterization duties. Arbitrator Rappaport found a legitimate distinction between the type of work assignments that should be given to male and female nurse's aides, a physical distinction between men and women that constituted a reasonable business need to vary male and female work assignments. First, it is medically easier to give catheterizations to male patients. And because of the medical difficulty involved with catheterizations of women patients, Arbitrator Rappaport agreed with management's decision that female nurse's aids should not do catheterizations. Second, the male nurse's aides had always been asked to catheterize male patients. Finally, the work load of the male grievant was not altered by the exclusion of female nurse's aides from all catheterization duties.[269]

A male *Crown Zellerbach Corporation*[270] employee grieved management's decision to exclude women from work on the corrugater takeoff. Arbitrator Herbert N. Bernhardt dismissed the union's gender discrimination charge which asked that the senior male grievant should not be assigned a task that would normally be assigned to a junior female, the union citing past practice. In his analysis, Arbitrator Bernhardt stated that the superior training and experience of the senior male worker was adequate grounds upon which to make the work assignment. The arbitral record included a complaint by the union over a 1973 agreement between Crown Zellerbach and the EEOC, an agreement to which the union was not party. Arbitrator Bernhardt said:

[f]rankly it seems to me that the Union's basic complaint is that Management did not consult with them before implementing its agreement with E.E.O.C. This complaint is well founded, but unfortunately it is stale. The changes which the Union complains of occurred in 1973. It is now 1982.

Clearly, both Management and the Union had to comply with the law. The procedure by which the law was to be implemented, however, was a proper subject of negotiations. Inasmuch as implementation of the agreement with E.E.O.C. affected the terms and conditions covered by the Collective Agreement the Union was entitled to be consulted.

That, however, is water under the bridge. The only remaining question is whether the method chosen by Management violates the Collective Agreement. What management did was to hire men and women from 1973 on an equal basis and require them to do all work tasks, but to exempt the three women hired before 1973 from work tasks from which they were previously exempted. No other changes in any other procedure or provision of the Agreement were made at the time.

From one point of view it might be noted that the Grievant is at least as well off as he would have been absent the changes. That is, all employees hired since 1973 must do the corrugator work whether they are males or females and they will be assigned to that work

---

[269] *Gardena Memorial Hospital*, 76 LA 256 (Rappaport, 1981); see also *Saginaw Community Hospital*, LAIG 2867 (Dempsey, 1981).
[270] *Crown Zellerbach Corporation*, 79 LA 170 (Bernhardt, 1982).

before it is assigned to the Grievant. Still, what is sauce for the goose is sauce for the gander, and the Grievant is entitled not to be the victim of sexual discrimination, every bit as much as the new female. . . . It is at this point, however, that equality of ability comes in. The three more senior women have never been trained to do the corrugator work, which the grievant was trained to do when he was hired.

In a different twist of facts, Arbitrator John P. Windmuller barred the male grievant from acquiring his shift preference due to production requirements. The male custodian was precluded from bidding on the first shift work assignment because over 450 female employees were assigned to the first shift. There was a need for a female custodian on the first shift to service the women's restroom without closing the facility. Arbitrator Windmuller cited the convenience of such a large number of female workers who needed access to the bathroom. Arbitrator Windmuller also supported management's concern for the possibility of an antidiscrimination complaint from the first-shift women. According to Arbitrator Windmuller, the first shift women would have grounds for a sex discrimination grievance if they were denied access to the restroom, an inconvenience to which first-shift men were not subject.[271] A legitimate BFOQ exists to bar workers from job classifications, such as janitor, equipment manager, and physical education teacher, where a portion of the work must be performed in a locker room where the opposite gender is frequently nude.[272]

.Arbitrator Roy L. Vickrey disagreed with the union's belief that the duties of the female union president were changed as a result of gender discrimination and antiunion animus.[273] Arbitrator Vickrey decided that the union contract gave management the right to make unilateral changes in the grievant's duties and job description, provided no improper motive existed. In this case, no improper motive was found. The union witnesses testified that the change in duties were minor, the union president was granted time off to perform union duties, and the chair of the committee which reorganized job duties was female. Indeed, the existence of a sound business motive, such as four times the experience, is adequate justification for management to bypass a junior black female when awarding a roster clerk work assignment.[274]

The union raised a disparate treatment challenge against *WFMJ – Television*[275] when the employer hired a male engineer instead of assigning a female to the engineering classification. Defining discrimination "as treating one different

---

[271] *NCR Corporation, E and M*, 9 LAIS 1191 (Windmuller, 1982).

[272] *FMC Corporation*, 70 LA 110 (Sinister, 1978); *Wayne State University*, 38 AIS 1 (Walt, 1972); *Lafayette School Corporation*, 96 AIS 5 (Elkin, 1977); and *BloomField Hills Schools*, 67 AIS 1 (Gross, 1975).

[273] *Veterans Administration Medical Center, Leavenworth*, 84-2 ARB 8486 (Vickrey, 1984); see also, *Trane Company*, 7 LAI 655 (Odom, 1980).

[274] *Dalton Steamship Company*, 80 LA 928 (Caraway, 1983).

[275] *WFMJ – Television*, 75 LA 400 (Ipavec, 1980); see also *Snap-On Tools Corporation*, 7 LAI 1112 (Butler, 1980). Disparate treatment was considered in *Quaker Oats Company*, 76-1 ARB 8048 (Gibson, 1975).

from another" and being cognizant of the danger that the grievant might use her gender to gain an undeserved work assignment, Arbitrator Charles F. Ipavec ruled in favor of the employer. The exclusive right to judge the competence and acceptability of employees vested in management was balanced against the anti-discrimination clause of the labor agreement. The female grievant did not prove disparate treatment just because she was denied the job and then asked to assist the newly hired engineer. The assistance provided by the grievant related to the operation and manipulation of electronic equipment which was only a simple part of the overall duties assigned to the engineering classification. Had the grievant assisted the new engineer with the more complex technical aspects of his job, such as electronic repair and maintenance, she might have gained an award in her favor. The management rights clause of the labor agreement has been relied upon to justify the adoption of a reclassification scheme aimed to eliminate past gender discrimination,[276] comply with the Fair Labor Standards Act,[277] avoid the layoff of junior female workers,[278] and assign the head coaching job for girls' volleyball to a female teacher with superior qualifications.[279]

Byron Area Schools[280] established a BFOQ that barred women from a student counseling position. Arbitrator Richard L. Kanner agreed with the assessment of management that a male guidance counselor was more appropriate for the job because many young male students were unwilling to discuss personal problems, such as sex and drug use, with female counselors. Arbitrator Charles L. Mullin, Jr., did not find sex discrimination when the *New Kensington District's*[281] choice for a coaching job was based upon qualifications. During the process the District Superintendent recruited the female grievant for the position until it was learned that she was pregnant. Arbitrator Mullin ruled that the Superintendent may have been guilty of gender discrimination, but the ultimate choice of coach was made by the school board rather than the Superintendent. While the Superintendent may have considered the pregnancy, the school board did not consider the grievant's pregnant condition. In another coaching grievance, *Smithfield School Committee*,[282] Arbitrator Patrick A. Liguori found no gender discrimina-

---

[276] *County of Santa Clara*, 71 LA 290 (Koven, 1978).

[277] *Howmet Corporation*, 63 LA 179 (Forsythe, 1974).

[278] *Morton-Norwich Products, Inc.*, 62 LA 1241 (Gross, 1974).

[279] *Adams County School District 14*, 66 LA 180 (Hayes, 1976); see also *Los Angeles Community College District*, 8 LAI 4715 (Rothstein, 1979), and *Gloversville Central School District*, 92 AIS 15 (Williams, 1977).

[280] *Byron Area Schools*, 81 AIS 21 (Kanner, 1976).

[281] *New Kensington District*, 79 PSEA 1557 (Mullin, 1979). For other school job classification awards favoring management, see *Houghton Lake Community Schools*, 134 AIS 1 (Frey, 1980); *St. Albans City Board of School Commissioners*, 141 AIS 4 (McCrory, 1981); *Bellows Free Academy Board of Trustees*, 147 AIS 11 (Randles, 1981); and *Proviso Township High School District 209*, 155 AIS 1 (Cook, 1982).

[282] *Smithfield School Committee*, DIG 102269 (Liguori, 1977). For another split decision see *Greater Baltimore Medical Center*, 4 PSAA 77407 (Strongin, 1976).

tion but ordered the coaching position vacant and refilled in accordance with the affirmative action plan of the school district. The Committee violated its own affirmative action plan by not having the grievant's resume before making the coaching assignment, it being unreasonable for an employer to consider an application for a coaching position without all the necessary facts in hand.

While Arbitrator John W. McConnell did not find gender discrimination, he did find technical reasons to rule in favor of the union in *Fall River School Committee*.[283] The female grievant had six years in the school system and a master's degree while the male teacher awarded the biology-chemistry teaching position had a bachelor's degree and a few weeks' teaching experience. The School Committee articulated that its failure to appoint the grievant to the position was based upon her inability to control her students. Arbitrator McConnell placed the grievant in the position on the basis of specific contract language that read "in filling vacancies preference will be given, in the case of comparable qualifications, to teachers already employed by the Committee." Teachers who were already on the payroll were given an employment advance over new hires.

Arbitrator Aaron S. Wolff found both technical violations of the seniority clause and sex discrimination at *U.S. Steel Corporation*.[284] The company violated the seniority clause of the labor agreement by assigning janitorial duties to a senior female rather than a junior male employee. And, gender discrimination existed on two fronts. The company stated no valid business need to follow its policy of assigning night janitorial work to women only. Management testified that it feared for two other female janitors if a junior male was the only other person in the building at night. Arbitrator Wolff ruled that the grievant could agree to be a temporary victim of gender discrimination. Said Arbitrator Wolff: "[w]hile it may be that at the time of her transfer into the Area 3 Pool, grievant agreed in effect to be discriminated against on account of sex by filling the job as Janitor while there were junior male employees in her seniority unit, there is no legal or contractual basis for holding her to a promise from which she now desires to be liberated." An employer many not just say that the work in point is too strenuous for females; instead, BFOQs must be reasonable and be based upon a valid business need. Arbitrator William E. Rentfro explained that his finding for the union was justified by the expanding role of female workers in society, the Civil Rights Act of 1964, and the seniority clause of the labor agreement. The qualified senior female got the job ahead of the man.[285]

---

[283] *Fall River School Committee*, 79 AIS 5 (McConnell, 1976); see also *Western Michigan University*, 80-1 ARB 8219 (Roumell, 1980) and *CRA, Inc.*, 8 LAI 205 (Neas, 1980).

[284] *U.S. Steel Corporation, Fairfield Works*, 58 LA 860 (Wolff, 1972); see also *Sunnyside Home for the Aged*, 21 LAC(3d) 85 (Pickier, 1985), and *Warwick School Committee*, 137 AIS 3 (Bornstein, 1981).

[285] *Home Provisions Company, Inc.*, 58 LA 288 (Rentfro, 1972). See also *Cincinnati Reds, Inc.*, 56 LA 748 (Kales, 1971); *Glass Container Corporation*, 57 LA 997 (Dworkin, 1971); and *City of Winnipeg*, 22 LAC(3d) 332 (Freedman, 1985).

SENIORITY AND REFERRAL SYSTEMS

In general, the legislation and court interpretations of seniority and referral systems applicable to race discrimination apply to gender discrimination.[286] For example, Section 703(h) applies to all groups and individuals covered by Title VII. Section 703(h) authorizes an employer to establish different terms, conditions, or privileges of employment that are the consequence of a bona fide seniority system, provided, the differences "are not the result of an intention to discriminate."[287] Furthermore, the definition of a seniority system,[288] time limits to filing a complaint,[289] criteria for determining a bona fide seniority system,[290] and remedies for victims of biased seniority systems[291] are the same regardless of protected class. It is legitimate for a bona fide seniority or referral system to be the basis for wage differentials.[292]

A difference in the seniority rights between protected classes often involves the BFOQ exemption to Title VII.[293] When a BFOQ is established for a job, a separate seniority list based on gender may be followed.[294] For example, the need for a female actress, being female to participate in women's professional sports,[295] and the business need to rehabilitate female prisoners[296] constitute valid BFOQs which legally result in separate lines of seniority for men and women. The courts have decided not to allow BFOQs to accommodate stereo-

---

[286] For a full discussion of fundamental seniority and referral system law see Vern E. Hauck, *Arbitrating Race, Religion, and National Origin Discrimination Grievances.* Westport, Conn.: Greenwood Press, 1997, Chapter 4.

[287] *Altman v. AT&T Technologies, Inc.*, 49 FEP 400 (7th Cir. 1989).

[288] A seniority system is virtually any practice that gives preference to workers employed longer, see *Allen v. Prince George's County*, 38 FEP 1220, 737 F.2d 1299 (1984) and *California Brewers Association v. Bryant*, 22 FEP 1, 444 U.S. 598 (1980).

[289] *United Airlines v. Evans*, 14 FEP 1510, 431 U.S. 553 (1977).

[290] *Bernard v. Gulf Oil Corporation*, 51 FEP 1126 (5th Cir. 1989); *Pullman-Standard v. Swint*, 28 FEP 1073, 456 U.S. 273 (1982); and *Teamsters v. U. S.*, 14 FEP Cases 1514, 431 U.S. 324 (1977). Examples of senior system not bona fide are *U. S. v. Georgia Power Company*, 30 FEP 1305, 695 F.2d 890 (1983); *Wattleton v. Boilermakers Local 1509*, 29 FEP 1389, (7th Cir. 1982); and *Sears v. Atchison, Topeka & Santa Fe Railroad*, 25 FEP 337, 645 F.2d 1365 (1981).

[291] *Firefighters Local No. 1784 v. Stotts*, 34 FEP 1702 (1984); *Wygant v. Jackson Board of Education*, 40 FEP 1321 (1986); *Franks v. Bowman Transportation Company*, 12 FEP 549, 424 U. S. 747 (1976); *Romasanta v. United Air Lines*, 32 FEP 1545, 717 F.2d 1140 (1983); and *EEOC v. Rath Packing Company*, 40 FEP 580 (8th Cir. 1986).

[292] *EEOC v. Whitin Machine Works*, 35 FEP 583, 699 F.2d 688 (1983).

[293] The BFOQ exemption for gender, religion, and national origin does not apply to race or color.

[294] Arbitrators have also considered seniority listing, *New Trier Township High Schools Number 203*, 152 AIS 13 (Dolnick, 1982).

[295] *Graves v. Women's Professional Rodeo Assn.*, 53 FEP 460, (8th Cir. 1990).

[296] *Torres v. Wisconsin Department of Health and Social Services*, 48 FEP 270, (7th Cir. 1988).

typed customer preference for working with males,[297] gender requirements for airline flight attendants,[298] non job related height and weight requirements,[299] and unreasonable weight lifting requirements.[300] On the other hand, in 1971 Arbitrator David C. Altrock relied upon the antidiscrimination clause of the contract to order the parties to negotiate a method eliminating separate seniority and lines of progression for men and women. The past practice of gender discrimination had resulted in women being cut out of training opportunities and not being promoted into management slots.[301]

Conflict between the labor agreement and a remedial action program required of the employer by the Office of Federal Contract Compliance (OFCC) was considered by Arbitrator Theodore K. High. The employer, *Babcock and Wilcox Company,*[302] operated three plants in Lancaster, Ohio. And because of past gender discrimination, the OFCC insisted upon a program for filling job vacancies that violated the parties' collective bargaining agreement. That is, the company was required to "voluntarily" fill job vacancies with qualified junior females. In his written opinion, Arbitrator High stated:

The real question for consideration in this case is whether, in fact, the supervening Federal law, or at least the fiat of the officials carrying out the policies of the Office of Federal Contract Compliance, invalidate the provisions of the seniority article of the Labor Agreement, at least as to the members of the "affected class."

While I am unfamiliar with an arbitration award directly on the point, some arbitrator awards have held that it is not sufficient to simply look at an Agreement where questions of discrimination are involved, but that the Agreement must be considered in the context of the applicable law. Thus, the court in *Continental Materials Corp. v. Gaddis Mining Co.,* 306 F.2d 952, (962) held at page 954 as follows:

"It is well settled that the jurisdiction to make awards is derived from the agreement of submission to be interpreted in accordance with the general principles of contract law, *Wright Lumber Co. v. Herron,* 10 Cir., 199 F.2d 446, and that, in the absence of express reservation, the parties are presumed to agree that everything, both as to law and fact, necessary to the ultimate decision is included in the authority of the arbitrator."

I am very sympathetic to the frustration felt by the Union in this case. It felt that it had an agreement on questions of seniority for the employees it represented and now it finds the agreement frustrated by a remedial action program. There is no evidence before me

---

[297] *Fernandez v. Wynn Oil Company,* 26 FEP 815, 653 F.2d 1273 (1981).

[298] *Diaz v. Pan American World Airways, Inc.,* 3 FEP 337, 442 F.2d 385 (1971).

[299] *Dothard v. Rowlinson,* 15 FEP 10, 443 U. S. 321 (1977).

[300] *Weeks v. Southern Bell,* 4 FEP 1255, 467 F.2d 95 (1972). Assigning overtime has also been considered; see *Ferro Corporation,* 8 LAI 2094 (Walter, 1980).

[301] *South Pittsburgh Water Company,* 56 LA 1242 (Altrock, 1971). See also *Cranston Print Works,* 241 AAA 2 (Horowitz, 1978); *ACT Industries,* 234 AAA 12 (Warns, 1978); *State of Rhode Island,* 5 PSAA 77537 (Rubenstein, 1977); and *Valley Kitchens, Inc.,* 72-2 ARB 8711 (Draper, 1973).

[302] *Babcock and Wilcox Company, Diamond Power Specialty Co. Division,* 66 LA 729 (High, 1976); see also *Lykes Brothers Steamship Company,* 79-2 ARB 8563 (Turkus, 1979) and *PCL Packaging, Ltd.,* 11 LAC(3d) 333 (O'Shea, 1983).

that the seniority provision found in Article XI of the Agreement was intended to discriminate against anyone. Nevertheless, where an "affected class" has been found and remedies have been fashioned to meet the problem of the affected class, those remedies have been held paramount to the provisions of the labor agreement, even though that may drastically alter the terms of the labor agreement. See e.g., *U. S. v. Virginia Electric & Power Company*, 3 FEP Cases 529, 3 EPD 8207 (DC EVa. 1971).

In view of the foregoing, I am forced to the conclusion that the remedial action program required of the Company by the Federal Government and which caused the job assignments which gave rise to this grievance represented an intrusion by Federal law into the contractual relationship between the Union and the Company and, to the extent inconsistent with the seniority provisions of the Agreement, supervened its provisions. It follows that there is no basis in the Contract for sustaining the instant grievance and for depriving the Employees named in the "Issue" portion of this Award of the jobs that were awarded as the result of the contested bids.

The contractual relationship between seniority and job assignment is often presented to arbitrators, particularly in circumstances involving bidding, transfer, and promotion. An employer's liability for gender discrimination can be diminished when involuntary transfer is conducted in accordance with the requirements of the seniority provision of the labor agreement.[303] It is proper, for example, to credit an employee returning from pregnancy leave with seniority accumulated at her previous work station before transferring the employee to a new classification. Management's decision to grant the pregnant female seniority credit was driven by the need to comply with Title VII, the civil rights law being contrary to the collective bargaining agreement.[304]

Arbitrator Charles E. Swenson ruled in favor of the *City of St. Cloud*[305] when the union contended that the City bypassed two senior qualified female employees in order to assign a junior male to work out of classification. Arbitrator Swenson's decision was guided by (a) the necessity of assigning the burden of proof upon the union, and (b) the union's lack of both direct and/or circumstantial evidence supporting its gender discrimination claim. The union failed to provide clear documentation that sexist remarks were made about the women, waited until post hearing briefs to present its contention that the Home Rule Charter was violated,[306] and erred in its assessment that the women should have been trained in the higher classification instead of promoting a junior male.

Similarly, *Toledo Edison Company*[307] acted within its contractual rights by not assigning the journeyman job sooner to the female grievant. The grievant chal-

---

[303] *Stockton Unified School District*, 33 C PER 75 (Henderson, 1977).

[304] *United Telephone Company*, 66 LA 1 (Foster, 1976).

[305] *City of St. Cloud*, BMS 9006.5 (Swenson, 1990).

[306] *Hayes International Corporation*, 79 LA 999 (Valtin, 1982).

[307] *Toledo Edison Company*, 94 LA 905 (Richard, 1990). See also *County of Bucks*, 19 LAIS 3608 (Symonette, 1991); *Social Security Administration, Milwaukee*, LAIRS 18465 (Gundermann, 1987); *Crown Zellerbach Corporation*, 79 LA 170 (Bernhardt, 1982); and *Airco, Incorporated*, 70 LA 760 (France, 1977).

lenged that she faced gender discrimination because she was not assigned jobs necessary to achieve journeyman. Arbitrator William L. Richard found that the antidiscrimination clause of the contract was not violated since management retained the right to design and control the apprenticeship program. *Toledo Edison* strengthened its no discrimination contention by awarding the grievant credit for prior education and experience and by giving the grievant the benefit of the doubt. She was assigned early placement on Conditional Journeyman status. Arbitrators have supported management's decision to bypass senior men and women when gender is a BFOQ,[308] when the senior employee(s) fails to show adequate proof that he/she is qualified to perform the job,[309] when the union does not provide adequate proof of disparate treatment,[310] and when a valid business need exists. A drop in sales is business need enough to allow management to forgo the filling of a vacancy even though an affirmative action plan calls for a senior female to fill the job opening.[311]

Arbitrator James C. Duff concluded that the *Youngstown Hospital Association*[312] violated the no-sex-discrimination clause of the contract on three counts when it assigned the painter job to a junior male. The female grievant's former supervisor "unequivocally exhibited discriminatory animus through his questions of and comments to the grievant." To be precise, the former supervisor asked the grievant what she would do with the wages of a painter, wages that could support a family. The gender bias of the former supervisor was further supported by his misconduct toward another female employee working in the grievant's area. Next, gender discrimination was exhibited by management when the painting test given the female grievant differed from the painting test given the junior male. The grievant was required to use a paint roller and the junior male was not. Finally, the former supervisor complimented the grievant about the high quality of her painting during the qualification examination. But in his notes, the complimenting supervisor wrote: "passed the written exam but actual painting portion was not up to standard." Arbitrator Duff awarded the grievant a thirty day trial period on the painter's job. If she proved qualified, the grievant's wages were to be paid retroactive to the date of her improper rejection.

---

[308] *Gloversville Central School District*, 92 AIS 15 (Williams, 1977).

[309] *New York City Board of Education*, 44 AIS 9 (Stockman, 1973).

[310] *Stayton Canning Company*, 75 LA 2 (Axon, 1980).

[311] *Lockheed-Georgia Company*, 87-2 ARB 8499 (Goodstein, 1987). Affirmative action and seniority is also considered in *Babcock and Wilcox Company*, 66 LA 729 (High, 1976); *Airco, Incorporated*, 70 LA 760 (France, 1977); and *County of Santa Clara*, 71 LA 290 (Koven, 1978).

[312] *Youngstown Hospital Association*, 79 LA 324 (Duff, 1982); see also *Tonawanda Union Free School District*, 134 AIS 2 (Babiskin, 1980).

The *Wayne-Westland Community Schools*[313] did not discriminate on the basis of gender when it selected the male candidate based upon the genuine belief that an effective counselor program required a balance of sexes within the school. However, the district violated the seniority provision of the labor agreement because the two candidates were equal on the four selection criteria: experience, competency, qualifications, and length of service. In a different case, Arbitrator Herman ruled that all else being equal the senior female should have been assigned the counselor job.[314]

Arbitrator Carl F. Stoltenberg ruled that *Norristown School District*[315] did not violate the seniority nor the human rights provision of the labor agreement by transferring the senior male counselor. Like *Wayne-Westland Community Schools*, *Norristown's* transfer decision was based upon management's genuine belief that a balanced work force served the needs of the students. *Norristown* refused to transfer junior female grievants in order to achieve a racial balance. Rather, *Norristown* set aside the racial issue and transferred its teachers in order to attain gender balance. In another school seniority/transfer grievance, Arbitrator James C. Duff found it proper to bypass a senior male and transfer a junior female into the girls' physical education job. Locker room presence was a job requirement.[316]

The seniority right of the male physical education teacher seeking recall overwhelmed the need for a women in the girls' physical education job where teaching schedules allowed a female instructor to supervisor the girls' locker room.[317] The union prevailed in an involuntary transfer case at *Penn Delco School District*.[318] The employer's contention that a gender-based BFOQ applied to the involuntary transfer of the senior male to a middle school was dismissed by Arbitrator John M. Skonier. The district argued that locker room supervision assignment justified a BFOQ calling for female coaches to be assigned to the girls' athletic teams and male coaches to the boys' teams. The parties had established a binding practice which overcame the district's BFOQ. It had been the practice to assign male coaches to female teams, and vice versa. The practice at the middle and high school had been to assign a noncoaching instructor of the appropriate gender to supervise the locker room. Citing the same BFOQ, Arbitrator Skonier sustained the male grievant's request for transfer to the high school

---

[313] *Wayne-Westland Community Schools*, DIG 103329 (Cook, 1977). See also *Safeway Stores, Inc.*, 8 LAI 24 (Stratton, 1980); *Warwick School Committee*, 137 AIS 3 (Bornstein, 1981); and *City of Winnipeg*, 22 LAC(3d) 332 (Freedman, 1985).

[314] *Saginaw Community Hospital*, LAIG 2577 (Herman, 1980).

[315] *Norristown School District*, 14 LAIS 4163 (Stoltenberg, 1987). The balanced staff concept does not justify the denial of an employee's seniority right unless a BFOQ is shown; see *Detroit School District Board of Education*, 31 AIS 1 (Herman, 1971).

[316] *Erie School District*, 764 GERR 21 (Duff, 1978).

[317] *Rock Wood District*, 13 LAIS 2035 (Dean, 1985).

[318] *Penn Delco School District*, 91 PSEA 0078 (Skonier, 1991); see also *South Washington County School District 833*, 12 LAI 253 (Karlins, 1984).

coaching job where a noncoaching female was available to supervise the girls' locker room.

In 1971 Arbitrator H. Herman Rauch considered the recall rights of senior women who believed they were denied jobs because of their gender. *Research Products Corporation*[319] correctly decided to recall qualified junior males to perform jobs that senior females could not perform. However, the company erred when it hired new male employees to take jobs for which the senior women were available and willing to work. In his findings and comments Arbitrator Rauch said,

The Agreement provides, in effect, that when the Company chooses to increase the work force, senior employees, regardless of sex, who are on layoff, if qualified and capable of performing the work which the Company wants performed, must be recalled first. The Agreement . . . gives the individual "qualified and capable" woman . . . the right to determine for herself if she wishes to be recalled from layoff to perform such work.

Many employers have so-called affirmative action plans, some of which come into conflict with the seniority provision of the contract. Arbitrator John P. Owens considered just such a situation at *IMC Chemical Corporation*[320] in 1979 and ruled in favor of management. Arbitrator Owens complied with the no-discrimination clause of the labor agreement by requiring the parties to confer constructive seniority to female employees as of the date they would have been hired had it not been for "severe injury" due to gender bias. Arbitrator Owens concluded that his award was proper under the seniority provision of the contract because the conflict between the two portions of the agreement needed to be resolved in favor of an award in compliance with the law. The union evidence favoring its interpretation of the seniority clause was not cogent, and judicial citations upheld the employer's remedy of retroactive seniority.

Arbitrator Richard Mittenthal considered the requirements of a consent decree that conflicted with the bidding rights of senior male workers.[321] The consent decree was aimed to correct the under-representation of women in the job classification opened for bid. Arbitrator Mittenthal ruled in favor of management since the male grievant's qualifications were relatively equal to those of the female worker awarded the bid. Arbitrator Walter N. Kaufman found no evidence of gender discrimination and sustained *Federal-Mogul Corporation's*[322] decision

---

[319] *Research Products Corporation*, 56 LA 308 (Rauch, 1971); see also, *Independent School District No. 720* (Lloyd, 1976). Recall rights are also considered in *Litton Systems, Inc.*, 296 AAA 13 (Ipavec, 1983) and *Lowell Area School Board of Education*, 152 AIS 9 (Straw, 1982).

[320] *IMC Chemical Corporation*, 73 LA 215 (Owens, 1979).

[321] *LTV Steel Company*, 15 LAIS 3756 (Mittenthal, 1987).

[322] *Federal-Mogul Corporation*, 90-1 ARB 8147 (Kaufman, 1989). See also *Youngstown Hospital Association*, 79 LA 324 (Duff, 1982); *Western Michigan University*, DIG 101933 (Roumell, 1980); *Whitesboro Central School District*, 126 AIS 16 (Carey, 1980);

to award the tumbler operator job to a junior male whose prior employment rendered him with qualifications "head and shoulders" above the female grievant. The senior female had ten years' seniority, but no experience driving a forklift or two-ton truck. Arbitrator Kaufman ruled that the labor contract's call for a 90-day trial period did not negate management's right to grant the bid to the most qualified employee from the start, nor did the call for a trial period require the employer to dismiss the bid of the junior male with nine months' seniority. The union was unable to prove gender discrimination because Federal-Mogul Corporation hired and promoted many women, had previously assigned forklift and truck-driving duties to a woman, and because an honest error on the bid award notice was irrelevant. In its bid award notice the employer had incorrectly noted that the grievant's bid was rejected on the basis of her seniority.

TRAINING

Title VII outlaws intentional and unintentional sex discrimination by any employer, labor organization, or joint labor-management committee in the admission or employment in any apprenticeship, training, or retraining program. This prohibition against gender bias in training programs covers on-the-job training. Because gender bias in training programs frequently has its greatest impact upon future working conditions, promotion opportunities, and pay, the courts have been asked to evaluate complaints of discrimination in training programs on the basis of circumstantial evidence. In 1990 the Eleventh Circuit Court of Appeals found sexual bias in a training program administered by the Georgia Department of Human Resources. The Appeals Court found that management denied female workers an equal opportunity to attend training programs, or to work assignments situated in locations conducive to learning and a fair opportunity for human growth. To be precise, male employees transferred into the training program at the same time as female employees were offered new position choices with learning opportunities while qualified women were denied the new position choices. Other direct and circumstantial evidence of gender bias in this same training program came in the form of office space allocation. Junior males were consistently provided with better office space than senior qualified women, making the men's working conditions more acceptable and promotion more likely for the male workers.[323]

Evidence of race and sex discrimination against a black female employee was established by showing that she was qualified for the job, was demoted two

---

Indianapolis Power and Light Company, 75 ARB 8228 (Dolson, 1975); and *Federal Paper Board Company*, 76-2 ARB 8550 (Larkin, 1976).
[323] *Nicholson v. Georgia Department of Human Resources*, 54 FEP 737, 918 F.2d 145 (1990).

grades, and was denied training opportunities granted to white male workers.[324] In a different case, a violation of civil rights law was documented when the New York City Housing Authority denied adequate training and a fair evaluation to a probationary female employee who refused to submit to her supervisor's request for sexual favors.[325] In *Griffin v. Omaha*,[326] the Eighth Circuit Court found that a black female police recruit was improperly dismissed from recruit training because she could not meet firearms standards. Uncontradicted testimony from firearms experts revealed that it is unusual for a recruit to fail firearms qualification. And, the black female recruit qualified at the state police training center over one weekend.

But, not all circumstantial evidence proves the existence of gender discrimination in training programs. In *Cobb v. Anheuser-Busch Inc.*[327] subjective criteria used to decide who receives training did not, standing alone, establish a pattern or practice of gender bias. The East Missouri District Court ruled that female employees were properly denied training because the subjective criteria used by management to guide the selection of trainees was job relevant, identified training needs that varied from individual to individual, and cut both men and women from the training program on the basis of subjective training need.

Proof of gender bias by co-workers against a female trainee did not compel Arbitrator W. Crozier Gowan, Jr. to rule in favor of the union at *Amoco Texas Refining Company*.[328] The union charged that male co-workers systematically avoided assisting the female trainee, even though she asked for assistance. But because the grieving trainee was unable to identify critical equipment or detail their purpose and function, Arbitrator Crozier agreed that management had just cause to discharge the grievant even though she had been retained in a training program longer than normal. Management had elected to extend the grievant's trainee status due to the gender bias exhibited by the grievant's co-workers. Arbitrator Gowan released the employer from the union's gender discrimination complaint on two grounds. Said Arbitrator Gowan:

A charge of sexual discrimination as made in this case is serious. It is not to be taken lightly but by the same token it should not be considered proved upon casual or less than convincing evidence. This is not to say that a standard of beyond a reasonable doubt is required but is to require at least a preponderance of the evidence.

It seems to the Arbitrator that an essential element in any case of alleged discrimination is not only that it occurred but that it occurred on the part of the Company who is the party complained of. In this case it cannot be denied there were acts of discrimination and that these acts formed a pattern of conduct reasonably designed to discourage

---

[324] *Parker v. Secretary, Housing & Urban Development*, 51 FEP 910, 891 F.2d 316 (1989).

[325] *Carrero v. New York City Housing Authority*, 51 FEP 596, 890 F.2d 569 (1989).

[326] *Griffin v. Omaha*, 40 FEP 385, 785 F.2d 620 (1986).

[327] *Cobb v. Anheuser-Busch Inc.*, 54 FEP 451, EMo. Dist. 87-982C(1) (1990).

[328] *Amoco Texas Refining Company*, 71 LA 344 (Gowan, 1978); see also *Continental Telephone Company of the South*, 83-2 ARB 8593 (Maxwell, 1983).

Grievant's continued employment on the Ultracracker Unit. However, it must be determined if these were the acts of the Company. Clearly, they were the acts of employees and that may, but does not necessarily, require a finding that they were also the acts of the Company. For this pattern of discrimination to fall on the shoulders of the Company there must be some positive showing that the acts were condoned, endorsed or encouraged by the Company. For that to be true it must be shown that the Company knew of the acts of harassment because it cannot condone, endorse, or encourage that which is unknown. However, mere knowledge does not in and of itself make a complete case that the acts were condoned, endorsed or encouraged. Additional evidence to that effect would be required. The point being made here is that the entire chain of proof begins with knowledge. Without it there is no case of any kind.

The Company offered testimony through witnesses Forest and McAninch which indicated the Company had no knowledge of the various acts of harassment until the "Pictures on the Bulletin Board" incident and that when it learned of this incident and the earlier incidents it initiated an immediate investigation to determine exactly what had happened and who was responsible. Further, it took very positive steps through the personal contact of Process Superintendent McAninch to inform all employees that such conduct would not be tolerated.

The right of management to instruct a school department head about how to run her department, about how to interact with subordinates, and about how to structure the art curriculum was upheld by Arbitrator David Dolnick.[329] The grievant's claims that she had been singled out for extra criticism, that her right to academic freedom had been violated, and that she was confronted with a hostile working environment were dismissed by Arbitrator Dolnick. The determination of academic policy is a right of management.

Arbitrator Peyton M. Williams ruled for the union in *Safeway Stores, Inc.*[330] since the training program undergone by the female grievant was substantially different than the training opportunity provided males. Management's violation of the antidiscrimination clause of the contract was substantiated by evidence from several quarters. First, the female grievant received two warning letters for mistakes while her male predecessor received no warning letters for the same mistakes. Second, the employer appointed a part time "jobber" to train the grievant and limited the time he was to spend with her, an arrangement which deprived the grievant of the opportunity to qualify for advancement. Third, management did not provide the grievant with the proper equipment needed for on-the-job training.

The undersigned believes, and therefore finds, that since the company admittedly disqualified the grievant before she had received comparable training to that of her predecessor for allegedly committing mistakes and offenses which are found to be no more severe than those committed by the predecessor, connotes she had been discriminated against in violation of the first sentence of Section 1.5. He therefore believes and finds, she should be given another opportunity to qualify for the dough mixer position. Addi-

---

[329] *Merriville Board of School Trustees*, 86 AIS 2 (Dolnick, 1976).
[330] *Safeway Stores, Inc.*, 60 LA 670 (Williams, 1973).

tional support for this conclusion stems from the fact that at least a part of the company's reason for disqualifying her was because of her inability to cause the dough to be mixed at consistent temperature, yet the record is clear the mixing machine's refrigeration system was not only often inoperative, but its use was not adequately explained to her. Also, shortly after her disqualification, the mixing machine was replaced with a new one.

Finally, Arbitrator Williams found no evidence of gender discrimination in management's concern for the grievant's ability to handle the job's physical requirements, even if management's attitude appeared cavalier.

WORK RULES

Title VII requires that work rules and employment policy be free of gender discrimination.[331] The courts have consistently looked beyond the letter of written rules and employment policy when deciding if a specific rule is gender neutral. In other words, employers must comply with both the spirit and the letter of Title VII when administering work rules and employment policy. For example, the mere good faith belief that toxic waste is a substantial risk to fetus or potential offspring does not justify a work rule barring fertile and/or pregnant women from jobs that require exposure to hazardous materials in the workplace. For the work rule to withstand a Title VII test, the employer must provide a preponderance of evidence that the no-exposure-to-hazardous-materials rule is justified by actual business experience.[332]

Complying with the letter and spirit of Title VII requires that work rules be interpreted and enforced without regard to gender. Morris Brown College engaged in unlawful disparate treatment by designating a female employee as "full time" and then firing her because she worked a second full-time job outside the college. Upon close inspection, the Eleventh Circuit Court of Appeals in Atlanta found Morris Brown designated male faculty as "part time," a designation that allowed the male faculty to work a second full time job while carrying substantially the same teaching load as the fired female.[333]

Disparate treatment was found by the U.S. Court of Appeals in New Orleans when Liberty Mutual Insurance Company investigated and fired two female adjusters and first year supervisors for violating its work rule against attending law school. The company did not discipline three male employees in the same job classification who where attending law school. The evidence provided to the Circuit Court showed Liberty Mutual's defense, that it did not know that the male employees were attending law school, was without merit. The court found that the company's lack of information about its male employees was caused by

---

[331] *Katz v. Transportation Department*, 31 FEP 1521, 709 F.2d 251 (1983).

[332] *Hayes v. Shelby Memorial Hospital*, 34 FEP 444, 726 F.2d 1543 (1984).

[333] *Thompkins v. Morris Brown College*, 37 FEP 24, 752 F.2d 558 (1985); see also *Matthews v. A-1, Inc.*, 36 FEP 894, 748 F.2d 975 (1984).

uneven enforcement of its no-law-school work rule. Liberty Mutual energetically investigated women thought to be attending law school, while ignoring rumors and allegations about male law school attendees.[334] In another case, the Court of Appeals in Washington, D.C. overturned the discharge of a female employee working for the Defense Intelligence Agency because she attempted to work cooperatively. The attitudes of management and her male co-workers made her the victim of sexist attitudes which precipitated alternate enforcement of the same work rule based upon gender.[335]

It is lawful for an employer to grant greater latitude to a male subordinate than to his female superior. The subordinate's success was attributable to his experience and creativity.[336] Similarly, the Federal Aviation Administration lawfully provided legal counsel to a male manager, but not a subordinate female claiming sex discrimination, on the basis of employment policy calling for the representation of management officials accused of wrongdoing.[337] *Mountain States Telephone*[338] did not violate Title VII by refusing to grant a travel deferment to a female employee on the basis of her chiropractor's recommendation. Extended periods of travel were assigned to male cable splicers on the basis of a bona fide seniority system. Failure to list her in the phone book, failure to tell her that memos were being placed in her file, and unsupported gender bias charges do not support a claim that *Bendix Corporation*[339] systematically reduced the ability of a new female supervisor to deal with her subordinates. The plaintiff could be terminated in accordance with employment policy governing discharge for poor performance.

Arbitrators support the evenhanded administration of work rules,[340] splitting their award or finding for the union when injustice occurs. For example, management may invoke a nonsmoking policy upon all employees working at a newly opened correctional facility for women. Arbitrator Martha R. Cooper said that the "freedom to smoke [is] a privilege, not a protected right."[341] In *City of New Haven*[342] Arbitrator Daniel E. Johnson reduced a ten day suspension to five days. Management's suspension of the female police officer was justified because she made radio transmissions disrespectful to her supervisor, failed to comply with orders, was insubordinate, and failed to follow police force employment policy three times. Arbitrator Johnson found it necessary to reduce the

---

[334] *O'Connell v. Liberty Mutual Insurance*, sub. nom., *Chescheir v. Liberty Mutual Insurance*, 32 FEP 1344, 713 F.2d 1142.

[335] *McKinney v. Transportation Department*, 38 FEP 364, 765 F.2d 1129 (1985).

[336] *Hill v. Kmart Corporation*, 31 FEP 269, 699 F.2d 776 (1983).

[337] *McKinney v. Transportation Department*, 38 FEP 364, 765 F.2d 1129 (1985).

[338] *Goicoechea v. Mountain States Telephone & Telegraph Co.*, 39 FEP 288, 700 F.2d 559 (1983).

[339] *Andre v. Bendix Corporation*, 38 FEP 1819, 774 F.2d 786 (1985).

[340] *3 M Company*, 8 LAI 778 (Grabb).

[341] *Department of Corrections, State of Delaware*, 20 LAIS 3897 (Cooper, 1992).

[342] *City of New Haven*, 10 LAI 2041 (Johnson, 1983).

grievant's suspension because it was difficult for the female police officer to comply with work rules in a male-dominated department; because the supervisor was hypersensitive to the grievant's actions; because the grievant's actions would have been acceptable if she had been a male officer; and because the supervisor reacted negatively to the grievant being a woman. Citing the grievant's eight year discipline free service and a lack of proof that the grievant had actually broken a work rule prohibiting the taping of conversations, Arbitrator Thomas E. Greef reduced discipline to a five day suspension. The *City of St. Petersburg*[343] suspended the grievant for eight days because she verbally harassed nonunion employees and threatened to tape record conversations.

The *San Mateo County Restaurant-Hotel Owners Association*[344] did not have just cause to terminate a female bartender for failing to know bartending rules, failing to follow bartending rules, and for using the bar telephone for outgoing calls. While gender discrimination was not proved, Arbitrator V. Wayne Kenaston found for the union because the bar owner testified that girl bartenders were not going to be employed anymore and because the owner failed to follow progressive discipline before discharging the grievant. Relying upon the reasonable man theory, Arbitrator Kenaston wrote: "[i]t is the Arbitrator's view that the true test under a contract of the type involved here is whether a reasonable man, taking into account all relevant circumstances, would find sufficient justification in the conduct of an employee to warrant discharge." Overwhelming testimony from several observers convinced Arbitrator Kenaston that the grievant had satisfied the clean bar work rule.

---

[343] *City of St. Petersburg*, 88-2 ARB 8427 (Greef); *Armira Corporation*, 11 LAI 938 (Hart, 1983).
[344] *San Mateo County Restaurant-Hotel Owners Association*, 59 LA 997 (Kenaston, 1972).

Chapter 6

Sexual Harassment

The U.S. Supreme Court's determination of sexual harassment in *Meritor Savings Bank v. Vinson*[2] was issued on June 19, 1986. The Supreme Court ruled on four aspects of sexual harassment in *Vinson*. First, *Vinson* confirmed the existence of a cause of action under Title VII for sexual harassment. Second, a victim advancing a sexual harassment claim need not have suffered tangible economic loss as a result of the employer's actions. The existence of an intimidating, hostile, or offensive work environment sufficiently verifies sexual harassment. Third, it is the question of welcome or unwelcome sexual advances on which an application of Title VII hinges, not whether sexual advances were voluntarily tolerated by the victim. Finally, vicarious employer liability under common-law agency principles for the misconduct of supervisors is not governed by any per se rule. The first three rulings of the High Court appear to be solid legal foundations. The Court registered a five to three to one split on the fourth point, however, making it the most confusing and legally suspect.

The Supreme Court's view of just what constitutes a hostile working environment, first enunciated in 1986 *Vinson* was reaffirmed in 1993 by *Harris v. Forklift Systems*.[3] The Supreme Court listed several relevant factors to be considered in determining the existence of a hostile working environment in *Harris*, indi-

---

[1] Portions of this chapter can be found in Vern E. Hauck and Thomas G. Pearce, "Sexual Harassment and Employer Response," *Labor Law Journal*, Vol. 38, No. 12, December 1987; Vern E. Hauck and Thomas G. Pearce, "Sexual Harassment and Arbitration," *Labor Law Journal*, Vol. 43, No. 1, January 1992, 31-39; and Vern E. Hauck (ed.), *Sex Harassment Handbook*. Washington, D.C.: BNA Books, 1994.

[2] *Meritor Savings Bank v. Vinson*, 40 FEP 1822, 477 U.S. 57 (1986). See also *HuRkanen v. Operating Engineers*, 62 FEP 1125 (1993), and *Burns v. McGregor Electronics Industries, Inc*, 61 FEP 592 (1993).

[3] *Harris v. Forklift Systems*, 63 FEP 225, 114 S.Ct. 367 (1993).

cating that no single factor is controlling. According to *Harris*, the determination of a hostile working environment rests upon "the frequency of the discriminatory conduct; its severity; whether it is physically threatening or humiliating, or a mere offensive utterance; and whether it unreasonably interferes with an employee's work performance." *Harris* affirms that a hostile working environment shall be determined by examining all circumstances within the employment environment. Though helpful, *Harris* leaves a number of unresolved issues because it does not provide a foolproof standard for determining employer liability in sexual harassment cases.

In *Vinson* the Supreme Court concluded that employers are not automatically liable for sexual harassment by their supervisors because common-law agency principles are not transferable in all their particulars to Title VII. In *Harris* the High Court reaffirmed its position in *Vinson* that a sexually hostile working environment may be established without severe injury or clear psychological strain. *Harris* held that a hostile working environment exists "so long as the environment would reasonably be perceived, and is perceived, as hostile and abusive." An important element of *Harris* is buried at the trial court level where the so-called "reasonable woman" standard was used to decide that the victim and any reasonable woman would be offended by the statements and innuendos of the boss.

Quoting *Vinson*, *Harris* holds that Title VII is violated where the sexual conduct is "sufficiently severe or pervasive to alter the conditions of the victim's employment and create an abusive working environment." Even though *Harris* makes it clear that the victim need not suffer a nervous breakdown in order to establish the existence of a hostile working environment, *Harris* does not spell out a precise standard for determining a hostile environment.

One more important digression is worthy of mention at this point. As a practical matter, most sexual harassment grievances do not involve a complaint of sexual harassment by the victim. And, most sexual harassment grievances do not involve sexual harassment by a supervisor or representative of management. Rather, most sexual harassment grievances involve complaints raised by employees who are disciplined for harassing the victim(s). On the other hand, private discussions with Human Rights practitioners by the author reveals that many sexual harassment complaints against and between supervisors are filed a the various Human Rights Commissions rather than under labor agreements. The American Arbitration Association (AAA) Model Sexual Harassment Claims Resolution Process presents a comprehensive program which makes it much easier for victims to complain about sexual harassment at the beginning or when the sexual harassment is first experienced, for the questioning of working conditions related to sexual harassment, and for the resolution of sex harassment complaints once they are filed by the victim.[4]

---

[4] American Arbitration Association Model Sexual Harassment Claims Resolution Process, Effective May 1, 1993.

LEGAL HISTORY OF SEXUAL HARASSMENT

The principle that the conditioning of concrete employment benefits on unwelcome sexual favors is against the law first appeared in 1974 when a claim of sexual harassment under Title VII gained lower court approval. Eventually the victim won her claim because her supervisor made it blatantly clear that she must bow to his sexual demands to hold her job.[5] Again in 1977, a victim won her case because the evidence of sexual harassment was overt. A causal relationship existed in *Williams v. Saxbe*[6] between the victim's rejection of her supervisor's sexual overtures and her subsequent termination for poor performance.   The *Williams* hearing officer found that no serious performance deficiencies were attributed to the victim prior to the rejection of her supervisor's advances. Only after her refusal to acquiesce did the victim's written performance appraisal deteriorate.[7]

On the other hand, if the actual submission to sexual advances was not made a condition of continued employment or advancement, the courts were likely to hold there to be no actionable harm in flirtation.[8] The lower courts dismissed a number of these early cases, even though unwelcome advances or solicitations for sexual favors existed, simply because submission to unwelcome advances was never presented to the victim as a condition of employment. For example, a victim could not force an undeserved promotion by threatening to file a sex harassment claim;[9] nor could an unqualified employee retain a job by filing a sex harassment claim. One of the early courts dismissed overt sexual advances toward the victim where no causal job relationship existed between the rejected sexual advances and the victim's assignment to an inferior job. The victim was initially discharged based upon her poor performance reviews and subsequently reinstated on technical grounds after a disciplinary layoffs.[10]

In *Rabidue v. Osceola Refining Company*,[11] the trial judge held that the plaintiff was not substantially affected by the vulgarity of her supervisor and that sexually explicit posters displayed in the supervisor's personal office had a *de minimis* effect on the plaintiff's separate work station. Title VII was not violated

---

[5] *Barnes v. Train*, 13 FEP 123, DDC (1974); *sub. nom. Barnes v. Costle*, 15 FEP 345, 561 F.2d 983 (1977). See also *Boutros v. Canton Regional Transit Authority*, 62 FEP 369 (1993); *Nash v. Electrospace Systems, Inc*, 63 FEP 765 (1993); *Kopp v. Samaritan Health System, Inc*, 63 FEP 880 (1993); and *Ezolo v. Wolf, Block, Schorr, Solis-Cohen*, 60 FEP 849 (1992).

[6] *Williams v. Saxbe*, 12 FEP 1093, 413 F Supp. 654 (1976).

[7] *Heelan v. Johns-Manville Corp.*, 20 FEP 251, 451 F.2d 1382 (1978); *Clark v. World Airways, Inc.*, 24 FEP 305, Dist DC (1980).

[8] *Walter v. KFGO Radio*, 6 FEP 982, 518 F.Supp. 1309 (1981).

[9] *Bundy v. Jackson*, 24 FEP 1155, 641 F.2d 934 (1981); see also *Rogers v. EEOC*, 4 FEP 771, 406 US 957 (1972) and *Hayden v. Cox Enterprises*, 28 FEP 1315, 534 F Supp. 1166 (1982).

[10] *Tomkins v. Public Service Electric & Gas Company*, 16 FEP 22, 568 F.2d 1044 (1977); see also *Katz v. Dole*, 31 FEP 1521, 709 F.2d 251 (1983).

[11] *Rabidue v. Osceola Refining Company*, 42 FEP 631, 805 F.2d 611 (1986).

where words and conduct were amenable to more than one interpretation, particularly where not all plausible interpretations presented a cause of action.[12]

There is a great deal of similarity between the *de minimis* standard and the matter of welcome sexual advances in *Vinson*. In both situations, employees can fatally compromise their Title VII claims by practicing the very deficiencies in the work environment of which they complain. In *Gan v. Kepro Circuit Systems*,[13] the complaining employee's speech and conduct were held to have welcomed and encouraged the conditions later alleged to constitute sex harassment. The employee's Title VII claim was viewed as *de minimis* in *Gan* because her speech was profane and her behavior was lewd and sexually suggestive. The court felt that the explicit banter and gestures that characterized the workplace in *Gan* were in a considerable part the product of the employee's own conduct.

Speech and conduct that are not explicit can also flaw a sexual harassment claim. The courts have been unwilling to find Title VII violated above the *de minimis* level when a sexual affair soured just before the employee filed a sex harassment claim. The employer was exonerated by testimony that numerous liaisons openly existed on the job where frequent and detailed discussion of personal intimacies regularly characterized the conversation between workers.[14]

The Supreme Court's decision that sex harassment can be created by a hostile or offensive working environment standing alone is also well grounded in case law. The victim's unwillingness to submit to sexual demands did not result in the loss of any tangible economic benefits in *Bundy v. Jackson*.[15] Quite to the contrary, Bundy had made a formal sexual harassment complaint before she was promoted. Bundy's only basis for complaint was an allegedly hostile, intimidating, and offensive work environment. That is, she asserted that Title VII was violated because the employer created or condoned a discriminatory work environment. To be exact, supervisors considered the making of sexual advances toward Bundy and her co-workers a normal fact of life on the job; you won some and you lost some. The court found no need for Bundy to complain in order to establish the existence of a sexually hostile working environment. The facts of the case establish that Bundy neither accepted nor rejected the sexual advances of her supervisors; she simply endured them.

One of the practical implications of the case law leading to *Vinson* is that it does not matter whether all employees find a hostile environment equally objectionable. A work environment becomes impermissibly hostile when male supervisors regularly address questions about sexual activity and preferences to female subordinates, even if some of the women do not mind.[16]

---

[12] *EEOC v. Olin Corporation*, 30 FEP 889, 699 F.2d 1172 (1982).

[13] *Gan v. Kepro Circuit Systems*, 28 FEP 639, E.D. Mo. (1982); see also *Ukarish v. Magnesium Elektron*, 31 FEP 1315, D.C. NJ. (1983).

[14] Evans v. Mail Handlers, 32 FEP Cases 634, D.C. DC. (1983).

[15] *Bundy v. Jackson*, 24 FEP 1155, 641 F.2d 934 (1981).

[16] *Morgan v. Hertz Corporation*, 27 FEP 990, 542 F Supp. 123 (1981).

EMPLOYER LIABILITY FOR SEX HARASSMENT

Three potential sources of sexual harassment create different legal responsibilities for employers: supervisors, co-workers, and people outside the organization. In general, the law assumes that the more discretionary influence a person has over the job benefits of an employee, the greater the opportunity to impose odious sexual conditions of employment. There is a correspondingly greater duty of management to act to eliminate supervisory harassment and a correspondingly greater liability if management does not act.

When it comes to sexual harassment by supervisors, the employer is liable under EEOC Guidelines regardless of whether the victim complains, whether the acts complained of were authorized, and whether the employer knew or should have known about the sexual advances.[17] Management is liable when a senior manager ratifies the conduct of a supervisor through failure to investigate a harassment complaint[18] and take good faith corrective action.[19] Management is liable for sexual harassment by supervisors even if the victim does not follow formal company complaint procedures aimed to bring sexual harassment to management's attention.[20] However, discipline meted out to a supervisor who engages in sexual harassment must equate to the discipline meted out to non-supervisors who engage in similar misconduct.[21]

Employers have an affirmative obligation to show that everything reasonably possible has been done to eliminate sexual harassment in the workplace. Toward this end, the employer's mere adoption of a well worded policy against sexual harassment is not enough. The employer must raise the subject of eliminating sexual harassment affirmatively, train and/or retrain supervisors,[22] place employees on explicit notice of policies and procedures, and verify that employees are aware of the company policy and procedure against sexual harassment. A union grievance process can fulfill a large portion of the employer's "due process" obligation.

The degree of employer liability for harassment initiated by co-workers is considerably less than for supervisors, precisely because co-workers are not in a position to impose adverse conditions of employment. Normally the victim of co-worker harassment can reject the sexual overtures without fear of reprisal. Title VII places an incrementally greater obligation on the victim of co-worker harassment to notify management and to give the employer the chance to correct

---

[17] C.F.R. 1604(c) 1980 and *Karibian v. Columbia University*, 63 FEP 1038 (1994). See also *Purington v. University of Utah*, 62 FEP 354 (1993); *Karibian v. Columbia University*, 3 FEP 1038 (1994); and *Nash v. Electrospace Systems, Inc.*, 63 FEP 765 (1993).

[18] *Munford v. James T. Barnes & Company*, 17 FEP 107, 441 F Supp. 459 (1977).

[19] *Craig v. Y & Y Snacks, Inc.*, 33 FEP 187, 721 F.2d 77 (1983).

[20] *Cummings v. Walsh Construction Company*, 31 FEP 930, 561 F.Supp. 872 (1983); *Horn v. Duke Homes, Division of Windsor Mobile Homes*, 37 FEP 228, 755 F.2d 559 (1985).

[21] *King Soopers, Inc.*, 101 LA 108 (1993).

[22] *Edwards AFB, California*, 93 FLRR 2-1055 (Bunker, 1992).

the problem. The employer is responsible for acts of sexual harassment by co-
workers where management knows or should have known of the conduct unless
the employer can show that it took immediate and appropriate corrective action.[23]

The limited prospect of exercising effective control over nonemployees miti-
gates the employer's liability for sexual advances by vendors, clients, and customers. Management does have some discretion about which employee is assigned to a particular work station, and the employer should avoid placing workers in circumstances where the prospect of harassment from nonemployees is
unduly high. The employer may limit liability for sexual advances from nonemployees by taking immediate corrective action as soon as the harassment is
known.[24]

WELCOME ADVANCES

According to *Vinson*, employees who "welcome" sexual advances are not covered by Title VII. In *Vinson* the focus was upon the degree to which a supervisor's alleged misbehavior was welcome, not the degree to which the employee
voluntarily endured the advances of her supervisor. It is important to understand
that the degree to which alleged sexual misconduct might be welcome is, in part,
indicated by the employee's own behavior, attire, and/or speech.

The Supreme Court agreed unanimously that Vinson's conduct, attire, and
speech indicated that any unseemly sexual escapades that may have transpired at
the bank were not necessarily "unwelcome" on Vinson's part and therefore might
not constitute harassment within the meaning of Title VII. Vinson had been the
recipient of several promotions and salary increases based upon her performance. Vinson had not availed herself of a complaint procedure her employer had
in place at the time of the alleged sexual advances by her supervisor. Moreover,
during the two and one-half years that Vinson said she had endured the harassment of her supervisor, she twice declined offers of transfer and advancement
from the alleged harassment situation at the branch office where she worked.
Arguably, Vinson mitigated the employer's liability under Title VII because she
wore sexually provocative dress and engaged in sexually indelicate speech. In
sum, a woman's voluntary involvement in a relationship characterized by sexual
banter or personal intimacy may not matter; but if she has welcomed sexual at-
tentions, she may have difficulty in proving the existence of a truly hostile, intimidating, or offensive work environment. Overt acts of behavior, indelicacy of
speech, inappropriately revealing or defining style of dress can be presented in

---

[23] C.F.R. 1604.11(d) 1980; *Durant v. Owens-Illinois Glass Company*, 31 FEP 228, 656
F.2d 89 (1981). See also *Saxton v. AT&T*, 63 FEP 625 (1993); *Martin v. Nannie & New-
borns Inc.*, 62 FEP 1275 (1993); and *Weiss v. Coca Cola Bottling Company of Chicago*,
61 FEP 773 (1993).
[24] C.F.R. 1604.11(e) 1980; *EEOC v. Sage Realty Corporation*, 24 FEP 1521, 507 F
Supp. 599 (1981).

litigation by the employer to avert a claim of sexual harassment by an alleged victim who might otherwise prevail.

REASONABLE WOMAN STANDARD AND SEX HARASSMENT

When it comes to sexual harassment, the general test is whether the statement or action is offensive to the victim.[25] However, just what constitutes a sexually offensive statement or action varies between groups of individuals, between individuals within groups, and between the sexes. Because of the vast differences between individuals, the courts have fashioned a so-called reasonable woman standard which differs from the so-called reasonable man, reasonable person,[26] and reasonable homosexual[27] standards.

In 1991 the Ninth Circuit Court elected not to follow the classic reasonable man concept as an objective measure for the establishment of a hostile working environment. Instead, in *Ellison v. Brady*[28] the Ninth Circuit adopted a reasonable woman standard and focused its inquiry upon whether a reasonable woman would consider the conduct sufficiently unpleasant that it creates a sexually abusive working environment.

While the *Ellison* standard has not been directly adopted by the Supreme Court, the High Court has ruled upon the lower courts application of the reasonable woman standard in *Harris*. Both the trial court and the court of appeals, in *Harris*, agreed that the bosses' comments and innuendos were offensive to the victim, and would be offensive to a reasonable woman. Then these two lower courts found for management by concluding that the comments and innuendos were not so severe as to seriously affect the psychological well-being or injure the victim. The U.S. Supreme Court disagreed.

Arbitrator Thomas Levak cited *Ellison* in *City of Havre, Montana*[29] when he explained the reasonable woman standard. According to Arbitrator Levak, "what that means is that a man who makes comments or makes approaches to a female must determine how a woman would reasonably take his comments or approaches, not how his male co-workers feel she should take them." The reasonable woman standard can make a significant difference in how a sexual harassment complaint is viewed by the courts, the parties, and arbitrators. Simply put, statements or actions that are sexually offensive to a reasonable woman are frequently considered acceptable by a reasonable man. The courts and arbitrators are finding it unconscionable to judge a woman's sexual harassment complaint on the basis of a standard of conduct applicable to men.

---

[25] *Ralph's Grocery Company*, 100 LA 63 (1992).
[26] *Dayton Newspapers, Inc.*, 100 LA 48 (1992).
[27] *Fry's Food Stores of Arizona*, 99 LA 1161 (1992).
[28] *Ellison v. Brady*, 54 FEP 1346, 924 F.2d 872 (1991); see also *Robinson v. Jacksonville Shipyards*, 54 FEP 83, 760 F.2d 1486 (1991), and *Austen v. Hawaii*, 55 FEP 685 (DC Haw. 1991).
[29] *City of Havre, Montana*, 100 LA 866 (1992).

JUDICIAL REVIEW OF SEX HARASSMENT ARBITRATION

Thousands of arbitration awards are issued each year, and with a few notable exceptions, neither the courts, nor any other tribunal, elects to review or vacate any arbitral award. In the same vein, over 125 published arbitration awards have considered sexual harassment since 1945, and few have actually been vacated. Clearly, arbitration of sexual harassment complaints presented by union and nonunion employees is desirable, but there are problems.

The dilemma surrounding arbitration awards involving sexual harassment evolves from the conflict between group rights protected by labor law and individual rights protected by civil rights law. The problem is that arbitration awards that evaluate sexual harassment and do not deal with the law are subject to judicial review and correction.[30]   Legally speaking, the final and binding nature of labor arbitration established in labor law by the so-called *Steelworkers Trilogy*[31] is seriously challenged in civil rights law by *Gardner-Denver*.

It is generally conceded that the authority of the arbitrator stems from the collective bargaining agreement, and courts should not question arbitrators authorized to interpret the agreement. But, when the agreement does not provide guidance or when Title VII conflicts with the agreement, the authority of the arbitrator is less certain and *Steelworkers* provides only limited guidance. The *Gardner-Denver* decision by the Supreme Court provides a partial answer to this dilemma. The arbitrator is required, as called for in *Steelworkers*, to follow the terms of the agreement and not civil rights law. Thus, if there is conflict between the contract and Title VII, the arbitrator, according to the Supreme Court, must follow the agreement. But, where the contract is silent or the contract requires following the law, the arbitrator can, and perhaps must according to *Gilmer v. Interstate/Johnson Lane Corporation*,[32] turn to Title VII.[33]

Some courts have ignored the final and binding nature of arbitration set out in *Steelworkers* by overturning arbitral remedies that reinstate discharged sex harassers on the basis that the remedy violates public policy. Because civil rights law forbids the toleration of sexual harassment, reviewing courts cannot author-

---

[30] *Fry's Food Stores of Arizona*, 99 LA 1161 (1992). See also *Hirras v. National Railroad Passenger Corporation*, 63 FEP 970 (1992) and 63 FEP 972 (1994); *Williams v. Katten, Muchin & Zavis*, 63 FEP 792 (1993).

[31] *Steelworkers v. Warrior & Gulf Navigation Company*, 46 LRRM 2416, 363 US 574 (1960); *Steelworkers v. Enterprise Wheel & Car Corporation*, 46 LRRM 2423, 363 US 593 (1960); and *Steelworkers v. American Manufacturing Company*, 46 LRRM 2414, 363 US 564 (1960). See also *Milwaukee Area Technical College*, 40 AIS 8 (1973).

[32] *Gilmer v. Interstate/Johnson Lane Corporation*, 55 FEP 1116, 895 F.2d 195 (1991).

[33] *Bowen v. U.S. Postal Service*, 112 LRRM 2281, 459 US 212 (1983); *Hines v. Anchor Motor Truck*, 91 LRRM 2481, 424 US 554 (1976); *Hirras v. National Railroad Passenger Corporation*, 63 FEP 970 (1992) and 63 FEP 972 (1994); *Williams v. Katten, Muchin & Zavis*, 63 FEP 792 (1993); and *Perugini v. Safeway Stores*, 56 FEP 333 (1991) (a union's failure to pursue a sex harassment charge may breach the duty of fair representation).

ize mild punishment or a lack of punishment altogether which some arbitrators have elected to assign to a sex harasser. That is, reviewing courts feel compelled to overturn arbitration awards involving sex harassment when it can be determined that the punishment and the crime are not relatively coequal. On the other side of the dilemma, *Steelworkers* mandates that the reviewing court shall not substitute its judgment for that of an arbitrator who is assigned the task of interpreting the parties' bargained-for rights.[34] Unless fraud or a serious miscarriage of justice occurs, the reviewing court has been directed by *Steelworkers* and progeny not to interfere with an arbitrator's award.

Four sex harassment cases illustrate the dilemma faced by courts reviewing arbitration awards under this public policy exception. The deference of reviewing courts to *Steelworkers* can be found in *Communication Workers v. Southeastern Electric Cooperative*.[35] The court refused to vacate the arbitrator's award even though the grievant had sexually assaulted a female customer by touching her buttock, fondling her breasts, and forcing a kiss. The arbitrator reinstated the sex harasser and ordered a one month suspension on two counts: (a) the grievant's nineteen year good work record warranted a penalty less than outright termination, and (b) the record provided by the parties was absent any oral or written warning that the grievant would be disciplined for any sex-related offense. In a similar case, *Chrysler Motors v. Allied Industrial Workers*,[36] the reviewing court refused to overturn an arbitrator's award which reduced dismissal to a thirty day suspension. Here again, the reviewing court concurred with the arbitrator's finding that a reduction of discipline for sexual harassment was proper. The grievant had no previous warning that he would be discharged for sex harassment, and the grievant showed every likelihood that he could be rehabilitated through Chrysler's system of progressive discipline.

Going the other way, the oldest and most atypical case involving the application of the public policy exception to sexual harassment awards is *Stroehmann Bakeries v. International Brotherhood of Teamsters, Local 776*.[37] In *Stroehmann* the Third Circuit Court elected to uphold the lower court's decision to vacate an arbitration award that reinstated a sex harasser who had been terminated by the employer. The decision of the reviewing courts to vacate in *Stroehmann* was based upon the arbitrator's inadequate assessment of the evidence submitted on the record, and the arbitrator's failure to properly determine the credibility of witnesses. *Newsday v. Communications Workers, Local 915*[38] is the fourth case. In *Newsday* the Second Circuit upheld a district court decision to vacate. Two arbitration awards are involved in *Newsday*. The reviewing

---

[34] *Daily Labor Report, No. 6*, p. A-10 & A-11, January 10, 1994.

[35] *Communication Workers v. Southeastern Electric Cooperative*, 132 LRRM 2381, 882 F.2d 467 (1989).

[36] *Chrysler Motors v. Allied Industrial Workers*, 139 LRRM 2865, 959 F.2d 685 (1992).

[37] *Stroehmann Bakeries v. International Brotherhood of Teamsters*, Local 776, 140 LRRM 2625, 969 F.2d 1437 (1992).

[38] *Newsday v. Communications Workers*, Local 915, 135 LRRM 2659, 913 F.2d 840 (1990).

court chose to uphold management's request to vacate because the evidence verified that the grievant had engaged in a pattern of sex harassment. The individual incidents of sex harassment in *Newsday*, which had been presented to the arbitrators on a case-by-case basis, were grounds for discharge when taken as a whole even though each grieved incident, taken alone, called for progressive discipline.

How do the parties lower the probability that reviewing courts will vacate an arbitration award involving sex harassment? Judicial review of arbitration awards is more likely to end favorably when the arbitrator considers EEOC Guidelines, complies with applicable court interpretation of sexual harassment law, and renders an award that is drawn from the language of the labor contract and the law of the shop.[39]

TERMINATION UPHELD FOR SEX HARASSMENT

In a typical case, Arbitrator Barry J. Baroni sustained the discharge of a male employee who engaged in a pattern of sexual harassment of female co-workers at *Shell Pipe Line Corporation*.[40] The male grievant violated the collective bargaining agreement by engaging in a pattern of unwanted advances, unwanted verbal abuse, and unwanted physical abuse. Arbitrator Baroni agreed with management's assessment that it was immaterial that one of the three women who was victimized did not complain; her failure to issue a complaint did not make the grievant's advances any less unwelcome. The union documented that other employees had engaged in sexual harassment and only received ten-day suspensions, contending that the grievant should therefore receive no more than a ten-day suspension. Arbitrator Baroni dismissed the union's contention on the basis that the hostile environment confronting the three women differed substantially from the earlier incident cited by the union. In the same vein, *Steuben Rural Electric Corporation*[41] was found to have just cause to discharge a long term male employee who openly admitted to asking sexually explicit questions and requesting sexual favors from three female co-workers. Arbitrator Judith A. LaManna sustained the discharge because the grievant knew about company policy against sexual harassment,[42] knew he had erred, and knew that company policy permitted discharge for sexual harassment. Arbitrator LaManna also noted that the grievant's harassment was severe, presented the possibility of immediate danger to co-workers, and there was no evidence that the grievant would change his behavior despite warnings and psychological counseling.

---

[39] 403: 521 FEP Manual; 405: 6681; 68117 FEP Manual; and *City of St. Paul*, 100 LA 105 (1992).

[40] *Shell Pipe Line Corporation*, 97 LA 957 (1991).

[41] *Steuben Rural Electric Corporation*, 98 LA 337 (1991).

[42] *Dayton Newspapers, Inc.*, 100 LA 48 (1992).

In *Hannaford Brothers*[43] Arbitrator Joseph Chandler found discharge justified because the grievant adversely impacted production with repeated obscene gestures and comments to female co-workers. Similarly, harassing employees have been discharged when profanity impacts the employer's public image,[44] is coupled with a poor work and attendance record,[45] and when vulgar speech occurs seventeen times in twenty-seven months from an employee who refuses counseling[46] and is not apologetic.[47] Arbitrators have upheld discharge when a single obscene gesture is extremely lewd,[48] when the victim's testimony is credible, perhaps even substantiated by a lie detector test,[49] and when a grievant claims sexual harassment in order to entrap co-workers or avoid termination.[50]

RETALIATION BY THE SEX HARASSMENT VICTIM

The right of an employee, including a supervisor, to be free from the fear of unjustified reprisal for what is considered sexual harassment by the victim was considered by Arbitrator Roy Francis. The company, *General Dynamics*,[51] had just cause to suspend the female grievant for fifteen days because she took matters into her own hands. The victim wrote and mailed a letter to her supervisor's wife describing his alleged sexual comments and indecent wall posters. Arbitrator Francis concluded that the grievant's suspension was justified because her off-the-job conduct was aimed to influence her supervisor's on-the-job behavior; because the supervisor's posters had minimal impact compared to the outrageous, vulgar, childish, disgusting, and possibly libelous contents of the grievant's handwritten letter; and because the grievant's behavior was insubordinate. In a similar case, Arbitrator Sharon K. Imes agreed that just cause existed to discipline a supervisor/grievant who punched an employee in the mouth after confronting the subordinate with his involvement in the mailing of condoms and pornographic materials to the grievant's home.[52] Arbitrator Imes reasoned that

---

[43] *Hannaford Brothers Company*, 93 LA 721 (1989); *Tampa Electric Company*, 87-2 ARB 8320 (1986).

[44] *Grey Eagle Distributors*, 93 LA 25 (1989).

[45] *DOD, Army, Tooele Army Depot, Utah*, 83 FLRR 2-1396 (1983).

[46] *Stanley G. Flagg and Company*, 15 LAIS 4129 (1988); see also *Stockham Valve & Fitting*, 13 LAIS 1141 (1986); *IBP, Inc.*, 89 LA 41 (1987).

[47] *Flexsteel Industries*, 94 LA 497 (1990); *McDonnell Douglas Corp.*, 94 LA 585 (1989); *State of Minnesota*, BMS 8903.12 (1988); *Hertz Corp.*, 361 AAA 4 (1988); *Harsco Corp.*, 90 LA 1230 (1988); and *Borg-Warner Corp.*, 78 LA 985 (1982).

[48] *State of Maine*, LAIG 3645B (3224).

[49] *VA, Medical Center, West Roxbury, Maine*, 89 FLRR 2-1322 (1988); *Cuyahoga County Hospital*, 15 LAIS 3392 (1987); *State of Ohio, Department of Corrections*, 14 LAIS 4034 (1987); *Porter Equipment Company*, 86-1 ARB 8275 (1986).

[50] *AeroJet General Corp.*, 87-1 ARB 8275 (1987); *Schlage Lock Company*, 87-1 ARB 8088 (1986); *Rockwell International Corp.*, 12 LAIS 1177 (1985).

[51] *General Dynamics*, 100 LA 180 (1992).

[52] *Wisconsin Power and Light Company*, 99 LA 493 (1992).

the supervisor who was victimized should receive the same discipline – a written warning – as the subordinate who mailed the explicit materials.

SUSPENSION OF HARASSER UPHELD

Suspension, not discharge, of employees for sex harassment has been sustained when the offense complained of involves a single relatively minor incident[53] and when the employer has no policy or training program governing sex harassment.[54] Some arbitrators have approved suspensions when the alleged sexual harassment is, in reality, horseplay[55] or the co-workers are friends who had casual physical contact before the sex harassment complaint arose.[56] Employee acts that are inadvertent, such as looking into a female locker room or making lewd gestures meant for a worker other than the victim, also warrant suspension.[57]

Suspension is proper when a subordinate brags about sleeping with a female supervisor,[58] when a victim withdraws a charge for excessive sex harassment,[59] and when unwelcome advances of a less offensive nature take place over a five year period of time without complaint by the victim.[60] While a clean work record generally favors the grievant,[61] an otherwise clean work record cannot be cited to avoid suspension or discipline for extremely lewd speech or behavior.[62] By the same token, a poor work record may be used to substantiate a company

---

[53] *City of Corpus Christi*, 16 LAIS 3951 (1988); *Washoe County, Nevada*, 88-2 ARB 8415 (1988); *DOD, Naval Hospital, Guam*, 87 FLRR 2-1479 (1987); *Bexar County Hospital, Texas*, LAIG 3870 (1987); *VA Medical Center, Fort Howard, Maryland*, 87 LA 405 (1986); *Island Creek Coal Company*, 87 LA 844 (1986); *A.T.& T., Information Systems*, 327 AAA 3 (1986); *DOD Hill AFB, Utah*, 86 FLRR 2-1832 (1985); *DOD Redstone Army Arsenal, Alabama*, 84-2 ARB 8422 (1984); *Federal Bureau of Prisons, Medical Center, Missouri*, 82 FLRR 2- 2109 (1982); *DOD Hill AFB, Logistics Center*, LAIRS 12370 (1979).

[54] *Michigan State University*, 1281 GERR 1329 (1988); *Powermatic/Houdaille, Inc.*, 71 LA 54 (1978).

[55] *State of Ohio DOT*, 90 LA 783 (1988); *GTE Florida, Inc.*, 16 LAIS 1096 (1989); and *Vons Grocery Company, Store 141*, 88-2 ARB 8611 (1987).

[56] *DOD Fort Rucker, Alabama*, 87 FLRR 2-1137 (1987).

[57] *Island Creek Coal Company*, 87 LA 844 (1986); *Mobil Oil Corp.*, 87-1 ARB 8201 (1986); *Todd Shipyards Corp., San Francisco*, 86-1 ARB 8072 (1985); *Consolidated Coal Co.*, 288 AAA 2 (1982).

[58] *Federal Bureau of Prisons, Arizona*, 86 FLRR 2-2135 (1986).

[59] *Chicago Social Security Administration*, 84 FLRR 2-2078 (1983).

[60] *DOD Charleston Naval Shipyard, SC*, 86 FLRR 2-1819 (1986).

[61] *City of Fairview, PA*, 201 AIS 12 (1986), and *Sugardale Foods, Inc.*, 86 LA 1017 (1986).

[62] *Fairmont General Hospital*, 16 Indus. Rel. Rep. 13.7 (1985); *Chicago Social Security Administration*, 81 LA 459 (1983).

claim that sex harassment is unacceptable and that discipline is proper.[63] Indeed, evidence of gender harassment is also evidence of an employee's poor work record.

DISCIPLINE OVERTURNED OR REDUCED

Unions have been successful in having discharges for sexual harassment overturned or reduced to suspensions when sex harassment is minor, company policy outlawing sex harassment is clear and known to employees, and the employer fails to follow normal progressive discipline.[64] Arbitrator Thomas P. Gallagher reduced discharge to reinstatement without back pay because *Honeywell Inc.*[65] failed to follow its own work rule calling for progressive discipline. Suspension was proper because management warned the grievant twice to discontinue his inappropriate ethnic and sexual remarks to female co-workers. Arbitrator Gallagher ruled that a spontaneous birthday kiss was beyond the range of acceptable behavior, but viewed otherwise friendly bantering and mild flirtations between employees to be of little consequence.[66] In *Dow Chemical Company*[67] the employer had publicized its policy against sex harassment and discharged a black male for misconduct consisting of sexual banter and kidding of three female co-workers. The grievant had been off work for two years when Arbitrator A. Q. Sartain reinstated him because the employer's warning to desist was unclear, because the misconduct was not extreme, and because management failed to follow progressive discipline.

Arbitrator Walter N. Kaufman overturned discharge for sexual harassment where the assistant manager had an otherwise clear sixteen-year service record. The grievant was aware of the company policy against sexual harassment when he referred to one female employee's nipples and forcefully tugged at the sweatpants of another female worker. Arbitrator Kaufman reasoned that reinstatement without back pay was proper because the off-color sexual joke told by the grievant was not understood by the female victim. She asked her father, a minister, what the off-color joke meant and the father complained to management. Arbitrator Kaufman was of the opinion that the test for sex harassment is whether the statement was offensive to the female employee, not her father. And since she did not understand the off-color joke, it could not have been overly offensive. Furthermore, the other female employee whose sweatpants got tugged contributed to the problem by engaging in a running joke with the grievant. She had not complained when the grievant tugged on her sweatpants previously.[68]

---

[63] *DOD Robins AFB, GA*, LAIRS 17589 (1986).

[64] A majority of arbitrators have sustained discharge without normal progressive discipline when sex harassment is excessive.

[65] *Honeywell Inc.*, 95 LA 1097 (1990).

[66] *Eagle-Picher Industries, Inc.*, 101 LA 473 (1993).

[67] *Dow Chemical Company*, 95 LA 510 (1990).

[68] *Ralph's Grocery Company*, 100 LA 63 (1992).

In 1982, Arbitrator George Gillespie defined sexual harassment and ruled that the employer did not have just cause to terminate an employee with twelve years of unblemished service.[69] According to Gillespie, sexual harassment is "the continual or chronically development [sic], on a one on one basis, of an intimate, unsavory climate resulting from purposeful sexual action(s) or clear statement(s) of desire to induce sexual favors from another person." Even though five female co-workers complained of annoyance at the grievant's sexual advances, Arbitrator Gillespie found the alleged victims' testimony noncredible and the work climate normal. The need for workplace sociability outweighed the inadvertent touch and wink of the grievant.

The reluctance of arbitrators to discharge employees when the victim engages in welcoming speech or behavior parallels judicial interpretations of Title VII.[70] For example, Arbitrator Erwin Ellmann, in *Heublein, Inc.*,[71] overturned discharge when an affair soured before the female co-worker claimed sexual harassment. In another case, a bus driver was reinstated because the mentally ill female passenger voluntarily engaged in welcoming behavior; because the testimony from the passenger's social worker favored the bus driver; and, because the bus driver had a clean work record.[72] In *RMS Technologies*[73] discharge was overturned because female co-workers retrieved the *National Lampoon* from the trash where the grievant had thrown the magazine before it was seen by the employee claiming sex harassment. In *National Oats Company*[74] discharge was reduced to a six-week suspension because the victim first led the grievant to believe that love notes were welcome and then the victim complained when the grievant attempted a kiss. Arbitrator Clifford Smith ruled that the grievant's attempted kiss did constitute sexual harassment. Another arbitrator sustained a five-day suspension when a co-worker first encouraged and then discouraged the grievant's advances.[75]

The discharge of a male employee for his off-duty conduct was reduced to a written reprimand by Arbitrator Howard M. Bard. In *KIAM*,[76] the company's sex harassment policy was known to the grievant, but that policy failed to define, describe, or provide relevant examples of sexual harassment. Further, *KIAM* sex harassment policy did not prohibit employees from sending letters and flowers nor from trying to date co-workers while off-duty. Arbitrator Bard concluded that the employer's statement about a possible disciplinary layoff did not constitute adequate warning to the grievant that his behavior could result in summary

---

[69] *Southern New England Telephone Company*, 13 Indus. Rel. Rep. 18.1 (1982).

[70] *Paragon Cable Manhattan*, 100 LA 905 (1993).

[71] *Heublein, Inc.*, 87-1 ARB 8220 (1987); *City of Seattle*, 15 LAIS 3629 (1987); *DOD Norfolk Naval Shipyard, VA*, 82 FLRR 2- 8035 (1982); and *DOD Marine Corps Logistics Base, Barstow, CA*, 82 FLRR 2-2174 (1982).

[72] *Metropolitan Regional Transit Authority, Akron, Ohio*, 13 LAIS 2122 (1986).

[73] *RMS Technologies*, 94 LA 297 (1990).

[74] *National Oats Company, Inc.*, 90-1 ARB 8257 (1990).

[75] *State of Ohio, Corrections*, 90 LA 478 (1987).

[76] *KIAM*, 97 LA 617 (1991).

discharge. Written reprimand was selected by Arbitrator Bard because the grievant's off-duty behavior did contribute to a hostile working environment, but was not excessive enough to warrant the preclusion of progressive discipline.

In *Duke University*,[77] Arbitrator Harwell D. Hooper reinstated a supervisor without back pay who had sexually harassed a female employee after their long term consensual sex relationship ended. The university's decision to terminate the supervisor was not sustained because neither the grievant nor any other female employee would testify against the supervisor; because the arbitrator held that discharge should not be sustained on the basis of hearsay evidence; and because a clear and convincing proof of sex harassment was not presented on the record by management. Arbitrator Hooper elected to reinstate the supervisor without back pay, however, because the grievant had admitted to hugging and kissing female employees.

Like terminations, suspensions and written warnings are frequently overturned when the victim is guilty of the acts complained of, such as when postmarital adjustment and fear cause the victim to overreact to simple horseplay,[78] when touching and mild jokes are a normal office practice among co-workers,[79] and when the victim makes obscene phone calls to the grievant.[80] In a different case, the nurse was justified in dealing with sex harassment when she slapped a male patient who tried to reach under her dress.[81] Finally, arbitrators universally agree that an employee who is wrongfully accused of sexual harassment should be reinstated with back pay and benefits.[82]

TEACHERS AND SEX HARASSMENT

Clearly, a teacher or janitor who victimizes a student faces discharge.[83] Nevertheless, one of the more noteworthy findings in this book is that harassing employees in a position of authority, but without ability to directly impact the victim's tenure, frequently have their discharges commuted to suspensions. For example, in *DOD Fort Gordon, Ga.*[84] a teacher with a thirty year clean service record received five days suspension instead of discharge for touching the breasts of six students. In *DeVry Institute of Technology*,[85] a clean work record contributed to the instructor's reinstatement because the complained of behavior

---

[77] *Duke University*, 100 LA 316 (1993).

[78] *King Soopers, Inc.*, 86 LA 254 (1985).

[79] *DOD Scott AFB, IL*, LAIRS 15931 (1984); *Zia Company*, 84 FLRR 2-2205 (1984); and *City of St. Paul*, 100 LA 105 (1992).

[80] *HHS Food and Drug Administration, East Orange, NJ*, LAIRS 15178 (1983).

[81] *VA Medical Center, Butler, PA*, 86 FLRR 2-1814 (1986).

[82] *Carswell Air Force Base*, 100 LA 876 (1993).

[83] *Norwalk, CT, Board of Education*, 11 LAIS 2176 (1984); *Minnesota Independent School District 200*, 1154 GERR 337 (1986).

[84] *DOD Fort Gordon, GA*, 11 PPA 10.2 (1982).

[85] *DeVry Institute of Technology*, 87 LA 1149 (1986).

occurred before the grievant was warned not to ask female students to pose in the nude. And in *City of Clover Park*,[86] the custodian's discharge was reduced to reinstatement without back pay because other employees testified on behalf of the custodian and the student intern did not appear as a witness at the hearing.

The failure of a male friend, the grievant, and the female student victim to testify caused Arbitrator Charles H. McHugh to dismiss one of two sexual harassment charges against a grievant in *Vermont State Colleges*.[87] However, Arbitrator McHugh supported the college's decision to issue a written reprimand to the grievant regarding his sexual harassment of another female student. Arbitrator McHugh reasoned that the college properly based its written reprimand of the security officer upon his inappropriate contact with female students, the officer's insubordinate behavior, his knowledge of sex harassment policy, and a legitimate belief that a lesser sanction would not deter the grievant's future conduct.

In another unusual case, an employer's threat to file a sexual harassment complaint was not found to violate the labor agreement. The district's threat to file a sexual harassment charge against the teacher had the desired effect of changing his behavior which consisted in using a female mannequin in the classroom.[88] Arbitrator Stanly Michelsteiter found that the district's threat was not barred by the contract. Arbitrator Michelsteiter ruled that the mannequin's existence in the classroom for seventeen years had not created an offensive atmosphere amounting to sexual harassment. Managers of independent contractors,[89] flight instructors,[90] social workers,[91] counselors,[92] and adults supervising minors[93] have been discharged and/or suspended for making inappropriate sexual advances and comments to their subordinates, students, and patients.

DE MINIMIS STANDARD IN SEX HARASSMENT ARBITRATION

When a sex harassment claim is based upon the consideration of co-worker or supervisory acts that are more psychological than economic in effect, the courts often employ the notion of a *de minimis* exception to Title VII.[94] Taken as group, the *de minimis* cases, all decided between 1978 and 1984, suggest that there is a threshold of impact that must be shown in order for a victim to prevail

---

[86] *City of Clover Park, WA*, 89 LA 76 (1987); see also *Houston Lighting and Power Company*, 80 LA 940 (1983).

[87] *Vermont State Colleges*, 100 LA 1193 (1993).

[88] *Madison Metropolitan School District*, 90-2 ARB 8444 (1990).

[89] *Plain Dealer Publishing Company*, 99 LA 969 (1992).

[90] *Pan Am Support Services, Inc.*, 89-1 ARB 8306 (1988).

[91] *Stearns County, MN*, 13 LAIS 2093 (1986), and *Vons Grocery Company*, 11 LAIS 1259 (1984).

[92] *Ramsey County, MN*, 86-1 ARB 8201 (1986).

[93] *DOD Dependents Schools, Livorno, Italy*, 82 LA 761 (1983).

[94] *Hoseman v. Technical Materials, Inc.*, 37 FEP 498,554 F Supp. 659 (1982).

in a Title VII case. When tangible economic damage can be shown, establishing the existence of sexual harassment is not a problem.

Arbitrators have distinguished between excessive and nonexcessive sexual harassment, a distinction resting upon the reasonable woman standard, discussed below, and the *de minimis* cases just mentioned. The threshold of impact applied in the reasonable woman standard and in the *de minimis* cases is not achieved at arbitration when evidence of sexual harassment is too circumstantial and weak;[95] when a female employee's epithet consisted of shop-talk aimed to avoid serious injury to a co-worker;[96] when a victim remains silent for four years before making the sexual harassment complaint;[97] when vulgar language occurs between employees of the same sex;[98] and when national and/or industry practice favors discipline short of termination.[99] For example, discharge was judged too severe in *City of New Hope*[100] for a single off-duty incident that would not likely recur.

Termination for behavior that borders on *de minimis* is likely to be reduced to a suspension when the employer ignores due process,[101] disregards the victim's demeanor, and disregards the grievant's side of the story.[102] Suspension is more appropriate when the employer fails to educate illiterate employees about sexual harassment,[103] or when a work rule announcement against sex harassment is insufficient; e.g., displaying a government human rights poster is not sufficient warning.[104] Written warnings are proper for minor sexual harassment by employees with poor work records[105] as long as the written warning is issued as soon as sexual harassment is discovered.[106]

Unique remedies for sexual harassment have also been fashioned by the parties and upheld. Arbitrators have revoked involuntary transfer after rejection of the supervisor's sexual advances,[107] okayed "improvement plans" to end the telling of dirty jokes to flight attendants,[108] and agreed with calls for obligatory apology.[109] There are limits to arbitral remedy, however, particularly when the

---

[95] *Howmet Aluminum Corp.*, 88-1 ARB 8020 (1987) and *City of St. Paul*, 100 LA 105 (1992).

[96] *T. J. Maxx*, 98 LA 952 (1992).

[97] *Hyatt Hotels Palo Alto*, 85-2 ARB 8409 (1985).

[98] *Hermes Automotive Manufacturing Company*, 87-2 ARB 8471 (1987).

[99] *Boys Markets, Inc.*, 88 LA 1304 (1987).

[100] *City of New Hope MN*, 89 LA 427 (1987).

[101] *Weber Aircraft, Inc.*, 86-1 ARB 8200 (1985); see suspension revoked when victim did not testify, *VA Medical Center, Birmingham, AL*, 82 LA 25 (1984).

[102] *Stroehmann Bakeries*, 98 LA 873 (1990).

[103] *State of Maine*, 15 LAIS 4107 (1987).

[104] *Santa Clara County*, 88 LA 1226 (1987).

[105] *VA Medical Center, St. Cloud, MN*, 85 FLRR 2-1376 (1985).

[106] *Philip Morris, USA*, 94 LA 826 (1990).

[107] *Alpha Beta Company*, 12 LAIS 1134 (1985).

[108] *Customs Service, Atlanta, GA*, 85 FLRR 2-1450 (1985).

[109] *J. J. Jordan Geriatric Center*, 94 LA 484 (1990); *Philadelphia Gas Works*, 90-1 ARB 8061 (1989).

requested remedy involves discipline of nonbargaining unit people, such as inmates. [110] In *Delta College*,[111] for example, the union's request for demotion of a supervisor was rejected because the supervisor was not a union member.

---

[110] *County of Oakland*, 94 LA 451 (1990).
[111] *Delta College*, 212 AIS 2 (1987).

Chapter 7

Pregnancy and Childbearing

The Pregnancy Discrimination Act of 1978 (PDA)[1] extended Title VII coverage to women being discriminated against on the basis of pregnancy or related conditions. To be more precise, female employees are entitled to Title VII guarantees against sex discrimination and those same guarantees are extended to pregnant employees, or employees with related conditions, seeking to be hired, promoted, retained, or allowed fringe benefits. For example, females seeking work may not be asked questions about pregnancy, childbearing preferences, nor childcare.[2] However, an employer's concern for the safety of passengers constitutes ample business need for an airline policy that removes pregnant flight attendants from flight duty.[3] Airlines have been precluded from discharging flight attendants who fail to comply with company policy requiring notification of pregnancy on discovering it.[4]

TERMINATION AND TRANSFER FOR PREGNANCY

In general an employee may not be terminated or transferred for pregnancy. Terminating pregnant employees instead of placing them on leave of absence violates Title VII even when they are later rehired without loss of benefits.[5] Indeed, Title VII allows an employer to treat pregnant women more favorably

---

[1] 42 USC 2000e(k).
[2] *King v. Trans World Airlines*, 35 FEP 102, 737 F.2d 255 (1984).
[3] *Levin v. Delta Air Lines*, 34 FEP 1192, 730 F.2d 994 (1984).
[4] *Pan American World Airways, Inc.*, 53 FEP 707 (11th Cir. 1990).
[5] *EEOC v. Hacienda Hotel*, 50 FEP 877 (9th Cir. 1989).

than other workers.[6] In 1992 the Eighth Circuit Court ruled that PDA entitles pregnant women the same treatment at work as non-pregnant women and men.[7] In *Tamimi v. Howard Johnson Co.*,[8] the employer violated Title VII by adopting a mandatory work makeup rule upon learning of an employee's pregnancy. However, the courts have considered the discharge of pregnant employees to be lawful when termination is based upon one or more nondiscriminatory reasons rather than pregnancy, such as excessive absenteeism[9] or poor job performance.[10]

Arbitrator Janet L. Gaunt ruled that the termination of a female meteorologist by the *National Weather Service*[11] for failure to accept an involuntary transfer violated the labor agreement and the pregnancy disability provisions of Title VII. The merits of the case confronted Arbitrator Gaunt with alleged disparate treatment between members of the same gender as well as reverse pregnancy discrimination. The grievant was transferred because she was not pregnant while two pregnant women were excluded from involuntary transfer. Both pregnant females ranked higher and would normally have been transferred before the grievant. Said Arbitrator Gaunt:

An interesting feature of this case is the fact it involves alleged disparate treatment between members of the same sex. Generally, an allegation of sex discrimination cannot be maintained in such circumstances, but no such limitation applies to pregnancy discrimination . . . a difference in sex is not necessary for pregnancy discrimination to occur. All that need occur is for a woman affected by pregnancy to be treated differently than "other persons," which under Section 701(a) of Title VII can be male or female. 42 U.S.C. 2000e-(a).

For all of the foregoing reasons, I am convinced that while the selecting official may have been well intentioned, the kinds of generalized assumptions he made about pregnancy's likely impact on the ability of [pregnant] MIGs Reid and Azizuddin to perform the Billings [Montana] job did not suffice to establish a BFOQ defense or even that of business necessity. Instead, they reflect precisely the kind of disparate treatment the PDA was intended to prohibit.

In another transfer dispute, the *City of Aurora*[12] did not violate the contractual rights of a pregnant police officer when she was transferred to a light-duty position. Police work is frequently dangerous and management's reasonable concern for the safety of the grievant and her unborn child compelled Arbitrator Marshall A. Snider to agree that the City's transfer of the grievant was justified. Unlike

---

[6] *Aubrey v. Aetna Life Insurance Co.*, 51 FEP 351 (6th Cir. 1989). See also *Toomey v. Clark*, 50 FEP 437 (9th Cir. 1989) and *Harness v. Hartz Mountain Corp.*, 50 FEP 376 (6th Cir. 1989).

[7] *Adams v. Nolan*, 58 FEP 1189 (8th Cir. 1992).

[8] *Tamimi v. Howard Johnson Co.*, 42 FEP 1289 (11th Cir. 1987).

[9] *Eblin v. Whirlpool Corp.*, 36 FEP 1632 (DC Ohio, 1985).

[10] *Hetle v. Dakota Bake-n-Serve*, 21 FEP 740 (DC ND, 1979).

[11] *National Weather Service*, 83 LA 689 (Gaunt, 1984).

[12] *City of Aurora*, 96 LA 1196 (Snider, 1990).

Arbitrator Gaunt, Arbitrator Snider ruled himself without jurisdiction to decide alleged violations of state and federal civil rights law.

UNWED MOTHERHOOD

The application of Title VII to the employment rights of unwed mothers is unclear. For while an employer who terminates or refuses to hire an unwed mother violates Title VII, the courts have allowed termination of pregnant unwed females on a case-by-case basis. For example, an employer unlawfully discharged an employee because she was pregnant and not because she violated norms of conduct by committing the crime of adultery with a superior; the lovers' relationship was known to the employer for seven years, and the pregnant employee was never convicted of adultery. The employer's animus was evidenced by the human resource director's unwillingness to explain to the pregnant employee why she was being discharged, the employer's stated fear that the pregnant employee would press sexual harassment charges against her lover, and documentation that the pregnant employee met the employer's job performance expectations.[13]

The discharge of a pregnant unmarried employee was rejected by the Sixth Circuit Court in *Jacobs v. Martin Sweets Company*.[14] The Sixth Circuit reasoned that pregnancy is unique to women and, therefore, discharge because of pregnancy has a disparate impact upon females. The court set aside the employer's argument that wed and unwed pregnancy should be viewed differently. *American National Bank*[15] violated Title VII by disqualifying a female from work because she had three illegitimate children, the bank's policy not being gender neutral.

The courts have ruled against the claims of unwed mothers who assert that they have been treated differently than unwed fathers who are expectant parents.[16] In *Chambers v. Omaha Girls Club*[17] the employer properly established marriage before children to be a BFOQ. The Omaha Girls Club properly terminated the unwed pregnant staff member because she no longer served as a role model for teenage girls. The court agreed with management's role model theory that a pregnant unwed mother does not make a good role model for teenage girls. Acknowledging that unwed fathers do not look pregnant, the court determined that management's policy was properly based upon the business need to discourage teenage girls from becoming pregnant.

Unwed motherhood is frequently mingled with unmarried cohabitation, raising the need to establish the marital status of pregnant single females. While he was asked to decide the application of a no-spouse rule, Arbitrator A. L. Spring-

---

[13] *Cumpiano Sanchez v. Banco Santander Puerto Rico*, 52 FEP 1444 (1st Cir. 1990).

[14] *Jacobs v. Martin Sweets Co.*, 14 FEP 687, 550 F.2d 364 (1977).

[15] *Davis v. American National Bank*, 12 FEP 1052, DC Tex (1971).

[16] *Grayson v. Wickes Corp.*, 20 FEP 1289, 450 F Supp. 1112 (1978).

[17] *Chambers v. Omaha Girls Club*, 45 FEP 698 (8th Cir. 1987).

field's conclusions in *Public Service Company of New Mexico*[18] point out the significant difference between "cohabitation" and "being married." In his opinion, Arbitrator Springfield states:

> [t]he arbitrator is not persuaded that the marriage rule as written should be construed to include "cohabitation" as being equivalent to "becoming married." The language in the marriage rule was written in about 1955, this being before the changing life-style of the next decade gave rise to a more general acceptance of living together as a meaningful if not generally acceptable arrangement. It seems clearly unlikely that at this earlier time the Company could have foreseen what was to come and therefore included the cohabitation in its concept of marriage. . . . Had it entered into the Company's thinking at the time the rule was promulgated, "husband or wife" would undoubtedly not have been used to designate which employee was to resign. Marriage rules more recently adopted by other companies state quite clearly that the prohibition applied not only to legally married spouses but also to any "partner living with an employee." Such explicit language is not part of the rule being considered here, neither is there any valid basis for implying that had the rule been negotiated by the parties cohabitation would have been included.

In 1978 the marital status of the unwed mother favored management in *University of Rhode Island*.[19] Upon learning of her pregnancy, the single female grievant asked to be assigned family medical insurance rather than the individual coverage entitled to single females without dependents. Arbitrator Thomas S. Hogan ruled that the employer, operating under the laws of the state of Rhode Island, correctly denied family medical insurance to the grievant. Arbitrator Hogan based his award upon the intent of the parties to exempt maternity benefits for single employees. Arbitrator Hogan is quoted: "[t]o hold that the State, by failing to provide maternity benefits for single female employees without dependents, was guilty of discrimination would lead to the ultimate result that all female employees would be entitled to family coverage."

FETAL PROTECTION

In general an employee may not be terminated or transferred to protect an unborn fetus. The U.S. Supreme Court decided unanimously in *United Auto Workers v. Johnson Controls*[20] that an employer may not bar women from working in an automobile battery plant because of possible exposure to lead poisoning. The Court said that Title VII stops employers "from discriminating against a woman because of her capacity to become pregnant unless her reproductive potential prevents her from performing the duties of her job. . . . No one can disregard the

---

[18] *Public Service Company of New Mexico*, 70 LA 788 (Springfield, 1978).

[19] *University of Rhode Island*, 104 AIS 8 (Hogan, 1978).

[20] *United Auto Workers v. Johnson Controls*, 55 FEP 365 (US SupCt., 1991). See also *Grant v. General Motors Corp.*, 53 FEP 688 (6th Cir. 1990); *Hayes v. Shelby Memorial Hospital*, 34 FEP 444, 726 F.2d 1543 (1984); and *Zuniga v. Kleberg County Hospital*, 30 FEP 650, 692 F.2d 986 (1982).

possibility of injury to future children [and Title VII] is not so broad that it transforms this deep social concern into an essential aspect of battery making." The employer carries the burden of proving that discharge of a pregnant employee derives from risks to the expectant mother and unborn child. A good-faith belief, based upon previous experiences with pregnant women, that the pregnant employee should not continue to work is not legitimate grounds for termination.[21]

FAMILY AND MATERNITY LEAVE

Family and maternity leave are closely associated because requests for either type of leave frequently arise in conjunction with childbirth. Upon closer inspection, however, they differ in several key ways. Family leave is available to allow employees time off to care for or establish bonds with newborn children or other important family matters. Individuals requesting family leave are frequently healthy, and employers must offer the same family leave options to both male and female workers.[22]

Maternity leave rights, sometimes called pregnancy leave, are covered by statutes in a majority of the states and do not require male and female employees equal access to time off.[23] For example, the Supreme Court upheld a California law requiring employers to grant up to four months of unpaid leave to pregnant females, temporarily disabled men not being treated the same.[24] And in *Cleveland Board of Education v. LaFleur*,[25] the High Court found a mandatory leave policy requiring pregnant teachers to leave their jobs four or five months prior to childbirth in violation of the due process clause of the Fourteenth Amendment. Unless pregnancy results in an inability to do the job[26] or to complete job training,[27] employers may not require pregnant employees to stop work at a specific time, to remain off the job for a specific time, or to take maternity leave for the worker's so-called own good.[28] Pregnant employees are normally allowed to work as long as reasonably practical for both the employee and the employer.

---

[21] *EEOC v. Service News Co.*, 52 FEP 677 (4th Cir. 1990).

[22] *Maganuco v. Leyden Comm. H.S. District 212*, 56 FEP (7th Cir. 1991); Garner v. *Wal-Mart Stores*, 42 FEP 1141 (11th Cir. 1987); *Clanton v. Orleans Parish School Bd.*, 26 FEP 740, 649 F.2d 1084 (1981); *Abraham v. Graphic Arts International Union*, 26 FEP 818, 660 F.2d 811 (1981); *Langley v. State Farm Fire & Casualty Co.*, 25 FEP 1221, 644 F.2d 1124 (1981); and *Maddox v. Grandview Care Center*, 39 FEP 1456, 780 F.2d 987 (1986).

[23] 421:507 FEP Manual.

[24] *California Federal Savings Loan v. Guerra*, 42 FEP 1073 (US SupCt, 1987).

[25] *Cleveland Board of Education v. LaFleur*, 6 FEP 1253, 414 U.S. 632 (1974).

[26] *Fields v. Bolger*, 33 FEP 1109, 723 F.2d 1216 (1984) and *Woolridge v. Marlene Industries Corp.*, 49 FEP 1455 (6th Cir. 1989).

[27] *Marafino v. St. Louis County Circuit Court*, 31 FEP 1536, 707 F.2d 1005 (1983).

[28] *EEOC v. Service News Co.*, 52 FEP 677 (4th Cir. 1990).

Employers need not extend pregnancy leave beyond the period of physical disability resulting from pregnancy or related medical conditions,[29] and women who leave work due to pregnancy or childbearing may not be eligible for unemployment benefits.[30] Title VII requires that access to maternity leave be available on the same basis as sick leave for other medical conditions covered by disability leave plans. The law requires that pregnant woman be allowed to return to their jobs on the same basis as other disabled workers, and women who elect to breast-feed their newborn at work have the constitutional right to do so.[31] Furthermore, *Pallas v. Pacific Bell*[32] calls for employers to remain liable for employment practices that perpetuate discriminatory maternity leave policy that was legal before the passage of PDA. The EEOC holds that maternity leave is a fringe benefit covered by EPA.

Most arbitrators agree that when a conflict emerges between the specific terms of the labor contract and the law, the arbitrator is obligated to follow the contract and allow the parties to turn their dispute over to the courts. Arbitrator Marvin L. Schurke was confronted with just such a conflict in *Merrill Area Joint School*.[33] According to the agreement between the parties, employees absent from work due to pregnancy or childbirth were not entitled to sick leave. Arbitrator Schurke found the law unclear, himself without authority to consider sex discrimination, and ruled that management correctly complied with the parties' past practice of granting unpaid leave to pregnant teachers. The parties had not contemplated the question of temporary disability when they negotiated the applicable collective bargaining agreement. Citing *Geduldig v. Aiello*,[34] Arbitrator Sinclair Kossoff found that management correctly denied sick leave pay to a pregnant employee who experienced a "normal delivery," using the policy statement of the American College of Obstetricians and Gynecologists as a guide for defining normal delivery (*Geduldig* was overturned by PDA).[35] Arbitrator Kossoff ruled that the grievant was not "ill" within the meaning of past practice and the contract agreed to by the parties.

In 1975 *Samsonite Corp.*[36] did not discriminate on the basis of gender when it limited pregnancy sick leave to six weeks. The contract entitled all employees to twenty weeks of sick leave for any medical condition except pregnancy. In his opinion, Arbitrator Harold P. Knight stated: "[s]ince qualified female employees would receive benefits of twenty weeks for any accident or sickness disability,

---

[29] *Schafer v. School District of Pittsburgh, Pa.*, 52 FEP 1492 (3rd Cir. 1990).
[30] *Wimberly v. Labor & Industrial Relations Comm. of Missouri*, 42 FEP 1261 (US SupCt 1987).
[31] *Dike v. School Board of Orange County* (5th Cir. No.805005, 80-5058, July 17, 1981).
[32] *Pallas v. Pacific Bell*, 56 FEP 1022 (9th Cir. 1991).
[33] *Merrill Area Joint School District No. 1*, 63 LA 1106 (Schurke, 1974).
[34] *Geduldig v. Aiello*, 8 FEP 97, 417 U.S. 484 (1974).
[35] *Miller Brewing Co.*, 64 LA 389 (Kossoff, 1975).
[36] *Samsonite Corporation*, 65 LA 640 (Knight, 1975); see also *Lakeside Center Association*, 82-2 ARB 8376 (Ellmann, 1982), and *Wausau Board of Education*, 64 AIS 8 (Marshall, 1975).

except for pregnancy sickness disability, it appears to be a classification of sickness matter rather than a discrimination based on sex."

Arbitrator Zel S. Rice II concluded that the party's past practice to disallow paid sick leave for pregnancy, childbearing and related medical conditions was contrary to the contract, the master labor agreement, and Wisconsin state law.[37] Arbitrator Rice found "[t]he Employer's practice has been to not allow earned sick leave benefits to be used by employees who were disabled because of pregnancy. . . . Were there no other factors present in this particular case, the arbitrator would deny the grievance. . . . However, there are other factors present in this case." Arbitrator Rice found the labor contract specifically banned discrimination against any teacher with respect to a condition of employment. This contractual provision was further supported by Wisconsin statutes outlawing discrimination in conditions of employment. Management knew that the grievant's physician had determined her unable to return to teaching duties due to medical complications caused by pregnancy. Arbitrator Rice dismissed the employer's testimony that the union made no reference to conditions of employment before the arbitration stage of the grievance process.

Relying upon a separability clause which required that all provisions in the labor agreement comply with general law, Arbitrator William J. LeWinter concluded that the parties intended to comply with State Human Relations Acts which provided that "a disability plan which expressly denies benefits for disability arising out of pregnancy is one which discriminates against women employees because of their sex."[38] Arbitrator LeWinter ruled that the pregnant teacher was discriminated against under state law and was entitled to thirteen days of accumulated sick leave to cover an absence caused by maternity disability.

Juanita County School District[39] could not bar a teacher from returning from maternity leave simply because the teacher failed to provide a forty-five day written notice prior to her intended date of return to work. And, the *American Federation of Government Employees, Council 242*[40] successfully regained the job of a Public Health Service employee who failed to return from approved maternity leave on schedule. The merits of the grievance revealed to Arbitrator John E. Sands that the grievant submitted three separate requests for unpaid maternity leave, and that two of the three requests were approved by management. Nevertheless, the grievant was removed from her job for alleged insubordination because she failed to return to work at the end of the approved portion of her requested maternity leave. Had the employee returned from maternity leave as originally agreed, insubordination would not have occurred.

---

[37] *Muskego-Norway School District*, 71 LA 509 (Rice, 1978). See also *Southwestern Portland Cement Co.*, 81-2 ARB 8526 (Jones, 1980).

[38] *Apollo Ridge District*, 77 PSEA 0955 (LeWinter, 1977). See also *Independent School District 564*, 708 GERR 25 (Fogelberg, 1977).

[39] *Juanita County School District*, 94 PSEA 0077 (Mountz, 1993).

[40] *HHS, Public Health Service, Food and Drug Administration*, 86 FLRR 2-1955 (Sands, 1986).

Even though the grievant remained on the third unapproved maternity leave, Arbitrator Sands favored the union based upon evidence that management's decision to terminate the grievant was entirely without nexus to the efficiency of the service. Arbitrator Sands reasoned that the grievant requested and received approved maternity leave twice, and that the grievant's third request for maternity leave was not unreasonable. That is, management did not convince Arbitrator Sands that the grievant's termination was for just cause, the employer changing its maternity leave approval program while the grievant was engaged in childbearing. The grievant was treated differently than other employees requesting leave without pay, was not provided progressive discipline, and management failed to choose a lesser penalty appropriate to the employee's error. In addition the grievant had a good work record, and was considered by her supervisor and peers to be a noteworthy employee. Indeed, testimony in behalf of the grievant given by her peers and lower-level supervision, substantiating the grievant's good work record, was cited by Arbitrator Sands as additional reasons to favor the union's grievance.

Paid sick leave for childbearing is a major employee benefit and is a protected condition of employment that must comply with both the contract and statutory guidelines. In 1975, in *Pacific Gas and Electric Company*,[41] Arbitrator Adolph M. Koven ruled in favor of the union, writing:

Preliminarily, it should be noted that the Company does not deny that if the EEOC guidelines were followed the Union would prevail in this grievance since those guidelines provide that pregnancy must be treated like any other disability. . . .

There is no specific provision of the Contract relating to the question of sick leave for the normal termination of pregnancy. However, it is clear that the provisions of the Contract regarding unpaid leaves of absence for pregnant women have been changed by the Company in order to comply with EEOC guidelines. That is to say, the provisions which required pregnant women to show that "urgent and substantial" reasons exist which would call for a leave of absence after a normal pregnancy was changed by the Company in order to comply with EEOC guidelines so that an employee is now automatically entitled to six months of sick leave at the termination of her pregnancy. The essence of the Company's argument is that the Union bargained away the right to sick leave pay at the end of pregnancy in exchange for the more liberal leave of absence benefits. . . . In the absence of convincing evidence that the Union bargained away the right to sick leave at the termination of a normal pregnancy, the Company's quid pro quo theory is unconvincing.

Arbitrator David R. Bloodsworth reached much the same conclusion as Arbitrator Koven in *Andover School Committee*.[42] Arbitrator Bloodsworth noted that sick leave coverage for pregnancy-related disabilities was covered by the labor

---

[41] *Pacific Gas and Electric Company*, 65 LA 504 (Koven, 1975); see also *Clio Education Association*, 61 LA 37 (McCormick, 1973).

[42] *Andover School Committee*, 86 AIS 6 (Bloodsworth, 1977); see also *Burgettstown School District*, 76 PSEA 0560 (Mullin, 1976) and *West Branch District*, 74 PSEA 1091 (Mussman, 1974).

contract. To be precise, Arbitrator Bloodsworth concluded that the district's refusal of sick leave to a teacher between the time she gave birth and the start of her maternity violated the contract. The union prevailed because the labor contract did not contain any exclusion of sick leave coverage. The record provided at the hearing showed no intent by parties to exclude sick leave coverage for pregnancy or maternity.

PREGNANCY, MATERNITY, AND EQUAL PAY

The principle that women on maternity leave are entitled to the same employment benefits as other employees was considered by Arbitrator Eli Rock in *Unionville Chadds District*.[43] The grievant had exhausted her sick leave allowance before taking one month of childbearing leave, and the employer refused to pay the grievant the difference between her wage and the "wage necessary to provide a substitute." Arbitrator Rock found virtually no difference in pay between the two wage standards and no reduction in rank for the grievant. Arbitrator Rock based his decision on the arbitral standard that he was without power to add to the provisions of the labor agreement.

In *Veterans Administration Medical Center, Fayetteville*[44] Arbitrator Joseph A. Sickles sustained management's decision to transfer a pregnant x-ray technologist away from her premium-pay position while a male co-worker remained in premium pay status. The grievant did not object when she was transferred for eight months to a non-premium-pay position which removed her from radiation exposure; then she took two months of sick leave after which she returned to premium pay status. Arbitrator Sickles found that the incident cited by the grievant on the record to justify her complaint involved a co-worker, a man who moved directly from the premium pay position he occupied to approved sick leave. This incident differed from the grievant's because the grievant went from premium pay to non-premium pay status and then to sick leave. Arbitrator Sickles found no condition that would require a man to be removed from x-ray exposure. Arbitrator Sickles ruled that sex discrimination would potentially exist had the incident cited by the grievant as a comparison involved a man being transferred from a premium pay to a non-premium pay position and then to sick leave.

Unions have successfully challenged management's action when women on maternity leave are not afforded equal pay for equal work. Arbitrator Carl P. Stoltenberg favored the union when the *Marion Center District*[45] improperly placed employees returning from maternity leave on the salary scale at a level below that which experience would warrant. Among the principles followed by Arbitrator Stoltenberg was the need to follow a previous arbitral award issued

---

[43] *Unionville Chadds District*, 82 PSEA 2032 (Rock, 1982).

[44] *Veterans Administration Medical Center, Fayetteville*, LAIRS 15156 (Sickles, 1983).

[45] *Marion Center District*, 80 PSEA 1328 (Stoltenberg, 1981).

under identical circumstances. The previous arbitration award equated years of service with salary placement. Arbitrator Stoltenberg ruled that the grievant was entitled to the same salary level she would have acquired had she not gone on maternity leave. That is, time on annual leave, including maternity leave, was equated with a year of service to the district.

HEALTH INSURANCE, FRINGE BENEFITS, AND PREGNANCY

Title VII requires that pregnant employees receive the same insurance and other fringe benefits as other employees.[46] In addition, the EEOC holds that maternity rights involve fringe benefits and fringe benefits are covered by EPA. For example, an employer who provides pension accrual, profit-sharing plans, health and life insurance premium payments, and disability leave to other employees on medical leave must provide the same fringe benefits to women on pregnancy leave.[47] Moreover, an employer may not elect to provide reduced maternity benefits to male employees. In 1983 the U.S. Supreme Court decided that a health insurance plan that put a cap on maternity benefits for the wives of male employees violated PDA "because the protection it affords to married male employees is less comprehensive than the protection it affords to married female employees."[48]

Gender discrimination may occur and the principle that all employees must receive the same fringe benefits may be violated when one partner in a married co-worker arrangement is allowed a buy-out under the Flexible Benefits Program. Arbitrator John M. Skonier ruled that *Ridley School District*[49] could place the wife's fringe benefit program on her husband's policy at no additional cost to the grievant and need not buyout the wife's Flexible Benefit Program because the wife was thereby receiving the same fringe benefits as other workers. Arbitrator Skonier reasoned that a requirement to pay the wife's buy-out request would amount to a pay bonus not granted by the labor contract. The principle of equal fringe benefits is not violated by an employer who provides no health insurance to its employees and who offers no medical insurance for pregnancy. An employer must pay for medical complications stemming from an abortion as well as for abortion when the life of the expectant mother is endangered. One potential loophole in Title VII was pointed out by the Sixth Circuit Court in *Fleming v. Ayers & Associates.*[50] A female worker's newborn child had serious medical

---

[46] *EEOC v. Wooster Brush Co.*, 33 FEP 1823 (6th Cir. 1984); *Aubrey v. Aetna Life Insurance Company*, 50 FEP 1414 (6th Cir. 1989); and *Morgan v. Safeway Stores Inc.*, 50 FEP 1339 (9th Cir. 1989).

[47] 421:504 FEP Manual.

[48] *Newport News Shipbuilding & Dry Dock Co. v. EEOC*, 32 FEP 1, US SupCt, (1983). See also, *EEOC v. Atlanta Gas Light Co.*, 36 FEP 1671, 751 F.2d 1188 (1985). For reverse situation see *Hillesland v. Pacar, Ore.* CtApp. No. A32125, July 16, 1982.

[49] *Ridley School District*, 94 PSEA 0113 (Skonier, 1993).

[50] *Fleming v. Ayers & Associates*, 57 FEP 330 (6th Cir. 1991).

conditions and the employer discharged the woman to avoid paying high future medical costs. The Cincinnati Court of Appeals ruled that PDA does not extend to children of employees and the employer's actions regarding the dependent was not gender-related. That is, the employer would have discharged the female worker regardless of the gender of the child.

Arbitrator Edwin R. Render concluded that *Burkhart-Randall*[51] acted correctly when management refused to allow payment of expenses from normal pregnancy under a new major medical plan, the employer opting to pay expenses of normal pregnancy under older and preexisting group health coverage. The union sought protection from the doctrine of *expressio unius est exclusio alterius* by contending that the employer should be required to pay the new increased maternity benefits because the company negotiator failed to exclude maternity coverage from the new major medical program, a conclusion with which Arbitrator Render did not concur. Following several well-known arbitral decision rules in his discussion, Arbitrator Render stated:

> Ample support for the Company's position is further supplied by precedent. Other Arbitrators have held that where maternity insurance benefits are overlooked by the parties during negotiations, no change is affected in the benefits, even though other insured items were the subject of extensive bargaining. *Morse Chain Co.*, 69-2 ARB 8443 (Shipman 1968). Where the terms of the written contract are clear and unambiguous, parol evidence of proposals, negotiations and even oral promises will not effect an alteration. *Howdaille Industries Inc.*, 61-1 ARB 8020 (Shipman 1960); *Container Corp. of American*, 33 LA 825 (Williams 1959); *Chromally American Corp.* 69-2 ARB 8102 (Autrey 1967). The failure of the parties to reach an agreement to vary the terms of the old contract leaves prebargaining conditions unchanged. *Master Vibrator Co.*, 67-1 ARB 8282 (Kasper 1969).
>
> The fact that the Company spokesman may have carelessly failed to mention the exclusion of normal maternity benefits from the Major Medical Insurance Plan is particularly harmless in view of the contemporaneous failure of the Union negotiators to broach the subject. The protection of members of both sexes, as the Union has asserted, is an important responsibility of the Union. Union negotiators are therefore charged with the adjunct duty to bargain on behalf of all classes of its membership. The Union has entirely failed to establish that any representative of the Company purposefully concealed the exclusion of maternity benefits during negotiations; no evidence of bad faith in any form has been introduced by the Union. In fact, the evidence yields indications to the contrary. Company officials themselves made independent inquiries regarding the additional cost of including maternity benefits in the major medical plan (company exhibit 3), and even made personal notations to remind themselves to raise the fact of exclusion at the bargaining table.

Arbitrator Render wrapped up his discussion by pointing out that no implied oral promise existed to require the company to pay increased maternity insurance costs. The parties negotiated for a major medical plan without rate changes for several normal medical expenses, one of which was maternity coverage, and the

---

[51] *Burkhart-Randall*, 68 LA 57 (Render, 1977). For opposite, see *Gear Corp. of Sterling, Inc.*, 76-1 ARB 8125 (Sembower, 1976).

written contract superseded and replaced any other understandings evolving from the bargaining table. Arbitrator Render concluded that the parties needed to change their maternity insurance coverage at the bargaining table rather than as a result of arbitral remedy.

MATERNITY AND PREGNANCY SICK LEAVE PAY

The application of EPA and Title VII to the accident and sickness benefit plan at *Goodyear Aerospace Corporation*[52] was considered by Arbitrator Paul N. Lehoczky in 1973. Twenty years earlier, in 1953, the parties had agreed to an accident and sickness benefit plan calling for male employees to receive $10 more per week in benefits than female employees. The $10 differential remained in effect until 1970 when the parties agreed that all employees would received the same $85 weekly benefit. Arbitrator Lehoczky stated:

In 1963 Congress passed the Equal Pay Act. Its passage was followed by a series of interpretative bulletins, one of which pertains to this issue. Section 800.116 Equality and Inequality Of Pay In Particular Situations, states under:
(d) Contributions to employee benefit plans. If employer contributions to a plan providing insurance or similar benefits to employees are equal for both men and women, no wage differential prohibited by the equal pay provisions will result from such payments, even though the benefits which accrue to the employees in question are greater for one sex than the other. The mere fact that the employer may make unequal contributions for employees of opposite sexes in such a situation will not, however, be considered to indicate that the employer's payments are in violation of section 6(d), if the resulting benefits are equal for such employees.
This order was issued on April 4, 1967. Note that the order clearly states that it is not a violation of the Equal Pay Act to make equal contributions resulting in unequal benefits.
Title VII of the Civil Rights Act of 1964 became effective on July 2, 1965. As in the case of the Equal Pay Act of 1963 the Commission designated to enforce the Act, commonly referred to by its initials as the E.E.O.C., issued a series of Guidelines. Its Guidelines of 1965 states under paragraph 1604.7:
(a) Title VII requires that its provisions be harmonized with the Equal Pay Act [section 6(d) of the Fair Labor Standards Act of 1938, 29 U.S.C. 206(d)] in order to avoid conflicting interpretations or requirements with respect to situations to which both statutes are applicable. Accordingly, the Commission interprets section 703(h) to mean that the standards of "equal pay for equal work" set forth in the Equal Pay Act for determining what is unlawful discrimination in compensation are applicable to Title VII.
This means that the principle of "equal cost but unequal payments" has been accepted by E.E.O.C.
On August 10, 1970, the parties signed a new "pension, Insurance and Service Award Agreement." In it, the applicable arrangement was shifted from an "equal cost but unequal pay" arrangement to an "unequal cost but equal pay" arrangement. Under its provi-

---

[52] *Goodyear Aerospace Corporation*, 60 LA 1011 (Lehoczky, 1973).

sions males and females receive the same weekly benefit, in this instance, $85 per week. This new arrangement, however, is not in conflict with the E.E.O.C. interpretations either, because it is sanctioned as "proper" in the Equal Pay Act interpretative bulletin of 1967.

The union's request that back pay be granted retroactive to July 2, 1965 for female workers who received lower accident and sickness benefit payments than their male counterparts was denied. Arbitrator Lehoczky denied back pay retroactive to July 2, 1965 for female employees who sought equal access to overtime, equal bumping rights, and equal bidding rights that would allow women to perform duties in violation of the Ohio Female Protective Laws. The Ohio Supreme Court overturned the statute restricting the right of women to perform work involving frequent lifting or repeated lifting of weights exceeding twenty-five pounds on March 15, 1972 (about seven years after Arbitrator Lehoczky's award).

In another health insurance grievance all teachers at *Independent School District No. 484*[53] were given the option of choosing either family or individual health insurance coverage. The grievant selected the family coverage option in order to include his child by a previous marriage, and sought attribution for his wife, also a teacher in the same school, in the amount of the premium which the district would have spent for his wife had she been able to choose individual coverage. Arbitrator Martin E. Conway agreed that the district acted properly and did not discriminate on the basis of gender by its refusal to make attribution to the grievant's wife. Arbitrator Conway did not find any evidence of discrimination on the basis of gender, marital status, or any other status because all teachers had the same option, all options were in compliance with civil rights law, and did not favor husbands, wives, or any other class of teacher. In his discussion, Arbitrator Conway ruled that the grievance involved a matter of express contract language rather than a question of equity.

---

[53] *Independent School District No. 484*, 68 LA 325 (Conway, 1977).

Bibliography

Allegretti, Joseph G., "National Origin Discrimination and the Ethnic Employee," *Employee Relations Law Journal*, Vol. 6, No. 4, 1981, 544-560.

American Bar Association, Rules 3.1 through 3.9 from *American Bar Association Model Rules for Professional Conduct*, 1995.

Anderson, Howard J. (ed.), *Primer of Equal Employment Opportunity* (Washington, D.C.: BNA Books, Inc.), 1978.

Appleby, Gavin S., "The Practical Labor Lawyer," *Employee Relations Law Journal*, Vol. 10, No. 4, Spring 1985, 736-744.

Basic Patterns in Union Contracts, Tenth Edition, Staff Editors of Collective Bargaining Negotiations & Contracts (Washington, D.C.: BNA Books, Inc.), 1983.

Bass, Bernard, *Organization Psychology* (Boston: Allyn and Bacon), 1965.

Bingham, Lisa B., "Employee Free Speech and Wrongful Discharge," *Labor Law Journal*, Vol. 45, No. 7, July 1994, 387-401.

Black, Henry C., *Black's Law Dictionary, Fifth Edition* (St. Paul, Minn.: West Publishing Company), 1979.

Bornstein, Tim, "To Argue, To Brief, Neither or Both: Strategic Choices in Arbitration Advocacy," *The Arbitration Journal*, Vol. 41, No. 1, March 1986, 77-81.

Brady, Teresa, "National Origin Discrimination in the Workplace: What It Is and How Employers Can Avoid It," *Labor Law Journal*, Vol. 45, No. 10, October 1994, 645.

Cain, Joseph P., and Stahl, Michael J., "Modeling the Policies of Several Labor Arbitrators," *Academy of Management Journal*, Vol. 26, No. 1, 1983, 140-147.

Code of Ethics and Procedural Standards for Labor-Management Arbitration, 15 LA 961.

Cohen, George H., "The Professional Responsibility of the Advocates, Part II," *Proceedings of the Thirty-Eighth Annual Meeting National Academy of Arbitrators*, Ed. Walter J. Gershenfeld (Washington D.C.: BNA Books, Inc.), 1986.

Coulson, Robert., "Title Seven Arbitration in Action," *Labor Law Journal*, Vol. 27, No. 3, 1976, 141-151.

Decker, Kurt H., *The Individual Employment Rights Primer*. Amityville, N.Y.: Baywood Publishing Company, 1991.

Drews, D. W., and Blanchard, R. E., "A Factorial Study of Labor Arbitration Cases," *Personnel Psychology*, Vol. 12, 1959, 303-310.

Edwards, Charles A., "Direct Evidence of Discriminatory Intent and the Burden of Proof: An Analysis and Critique," *Washington and Lee Law Review*, Vol. 43, No. 1, Winter 1986, 1-35.

Edwards, Harry T., "Arbitration of Employment Discrimination Cases: A Proposal for Employer and Union Representatives," *Labor Law Journal*, Vol. 27, No. 5, May 1976, 265.

___, "Arbitration of Employment Discrimination Cases: An Empirical Study," in *Proceedings of the 28th Annual Meeting of the National Academy of Arbitrators* (Washington, D.C.: The Bureau of National Affairs, Inc.), 1976, 59-92.

___, "Arbitration as an Alternative in Equal Employment Disputes," *The Arbitration Journal*, Vol. 33, No. 4, December 1978, 23-27.

Elkouri, Frank, and Elkouri, Edna A., *How Arbitration Works*, 3rd ed. (Washington, D.C.: The Bureau of National Affairs, Inc.), 1973.

Frank, Jerome, *Courts on Trial: Myth and Reality in American Justice*. (Princeton University: Princeton University Press), 1950.

French, Linda J., "Arbitral Discovery Guidelines for Employers," *UMKC Law Review*, Vol. 50, No. 2, Winter 1982, 145-149.

Freshman, Clark, "Beyond Atomized Discrimination: Use of Acts of Discrimination Against 'Other' Minorities to Prove Discriminatory Motivation Under Federal Employment Law," *Stanford Law Review*, Vol. 43, No. 193, November 1990, 241.

Fruchter, Benjamin, *Introduction to Factor Analysis* (New York: D. Van Norsstrand Company), 1954.

Furlong, Gary, "Fear and Loathing in Labor Arbitration: How Can There Possibly Be a Full and Fair Hearing Unless the Arbitrator Can Subpoena Evidence?" *Willamette Law Review*, Vol. 20, No. 3, Summer 1984, 535-566.

Goodman, Jane and Croyle, Robert T., "Social Framework Testimony in Employment Discrimination Cases," *Behavioral Sciences & the Law*, Vol. 7, No. 2, 227-241.

Greene, Linda S., "Tokens, Role Models, and Pedagogical Politics: Lamentations of an African American Female Law Professor," *Berkeley Women's Law Journal*, Vol. 6, 1991, 81-92.

Gullett, C. R., and Goff, W. H., "The Arbitral Decision-Making Process: A Computerized Simulation," *Personnel Journal*, Vol. 59, No. 8, 1980, 663-667.

Hauck, Vern E., "The Efficacy of Arbitrating Discrimination Complaints," *Labor Law Journal*, Vol. 35, No. 3, March 1984, 175.

Hauck, Vern E., and South, John C., "Arbitrating Discrimination Grievances: An Empirical Model for Decision Standards," *Policy Studies Journal*, Vol. 16, No. 3, Spring 1988, 511.

Highet, Keith, and Kahale, George III, "International Decisions," *The American Journal of International Law*, Vol. 86, 1992, 363-367.

Hill, Marvin F., Jr., and Sinicropi, Anthony V., *Evidence in Arbitration* (Washington, D.C.: The Bureau of National Affairs, Inc.), 1986.

Hollon, Charles J., and Bright, Thomas L., "National Origin Harassment in the Work Place: Recent Guideline Developments from the EEOC," *Employee Relations Law Journal*, Vol. 8, No. 2, 1982, 282-293.

Holzhauer, James D., "The Contractual Duty of Competent Representation," *Chicago-Kent Law Review*, Vol. 63, No. 2, 1987, 255.

Jones, James E., Jr., "The Development of Modern Equal Employment Opportunity and Affirmative Action Law: A Brief Chronological Overview," *Howard Law Journal*, Vol. 20, No. 1, 1977, 74-99.

Kagel, Sam, "Legalism – and Some Comments on Illegalisms – in Arbitration," *Proceedings of the Thirty-Eighth Annual Meeting National Academy of Arbitrators* (Washington, D.C.: BNA Books, Inc.), 1986.

King, Craig H., "Employment Discrimination: The Burden of Proof," *Southern University Law Review*, Vol. 13, No. 1, Fall 1986, 98-99.

Kovarsky, Irving, *Discrimination in Employment* (The University of Iowa: Center for Labor and Management), 1976.

Kovarsky, Irving, and Albrecht, William, *Black Employment: The Impact of Religion, Economic Theory, Politics, and Law* (Ames: The Iowa State University Press), 1970.

Labor Arbitration Reports, Cumulative Digest and Index, Staff (Washington, D.C.: Bureau of National Affairs, Inc.), Sections 106 and 107, all volumes.

Labor Management Relations Act, 1947, Public Law 101 – 80th Congress, as amended by the Labor-Management Reporting and Disclosure Act of 1959, Public Law 86-257.

McKay, Robert B., *Reapportionment: The Law and Politics of Equal Representation* (New York: Simon and Schuster), 1965.

McKelvey, Jean T. (ed.), "The Profession of Labor Arbitration," in papers from the *First Seven Annual Meetings, National Academy of Arbitrators* (Washington, D.C.: BNA Books, Inc.), 1957.

Mealey, Linda A., "English-only Rules and 'Innocent' Employers: Clarifying National Origin Discrimination and Disparate Impact Theory Under Title VII," *Minnesota Law Review*, Vol. 74, 1989, 387-436.

Munafo, Rachel R., "National Origin Discrimination Revisited," *Catholic Lawyer*, Vol. 34, No. 3, 1991, 271-288.

Oppenheimer, Margaret, and LaVan, Helen, "Arbitration Awards in Discrimination Disputes: An Empirical Analysis," *The Arbitration Journal*, Vol. 34, No. 1, 1979.

Pettigrew, T. F., "The Ultimate Attribution Error: Extending Allport's Cognitive Analysis of Prejudice," *Personality & Social Psychology Bulletin*, Vol. 5, 1979, 461-476.

Prasow, Paul, and Peters, Edward, *Arbitration and Collective Bargaining* (New York: McGraw-Hill), 1970.

Prasow, Paul, and Peters, Edward, *Arbitration and Collective Bargaining: Conflict Resolution in Labor Relations, Second Edition* (New York: McGraw-Hill), 1983.

___, *Arbitration and Collective Bargaining: Conflict Resolution in Labor Relation*, 2nd ed., (New York: McGraw-Hill), 1983.

Public Law 88-352, as amended. 401:2301 FEP Manual (Washington, D.C.: BNA Books, Inc.), "Question and Answers Dealing with the Uniform Guidelines on Employee Selection Procedures" [29 CFR 1607 (1987)].

Sacks, Howard S., and Kurlantzick, Lewis S., "The Problem of the Missing Witness: Toward an Educator-Facilitator Role for Labor Arbitration," *Industrial Relations Law Journal*, Vol. 5, No. 1, 1982, 87.

Saks, Michael J., "Expert Witnesses, Nonexpert Witnesses, and Nonwitness Experts," *Law and Human Behavior*, Vol. 14, No. 4, August 1990, 291-313.

Samowitz, Cary B., "Title VII, United States Citizenship, and American National Origin," *New York University Law Review*, Vol. 60, May 1985, 245.

Sanchez, John E., "Religious Affirmative Action in Employment: Fearful Symmetry," *Detroit College of Law Review*, Vol. 3, 1991, 1020.

Schoonhoven, Ray J. (ed.), *Fairweather's Practice and Procedure in Labor Arbitration* 3rd ed. (Washington, D.C.: BNA Books, Inc.), 1991.

Seitz, Peter, III., "The Citation of Authority and Precedent in Arbitration (Its Use and Abuse)," *The Arbitration Journal*, Vol. 38, No. 4, December 1983, 59-60.

Stone, Morris, and Baderschneider, Earl R. (eds.), *Arbitrating of Discrimination Grievances: A Case Book* (New York: American Arbitration Association), 1974.

Sullivan, Donna J., "Advancing the Freedom of Religion or Belief through the U.N. Declaration on the Elimination of Religious Intolerance and Discrimination," *The American Journal of International Law*, Vol. 82, 1988, 487-520.

Thomas, Oliver S., "The Application of Anti-discrimination Laws to Religious Institutions: The Irresistible Force Meets the Immovable Object," *Journal of the National Association of Administrative Law Judges*, Vol. 12, No. 2, Fall 1992, 83-111.

Thornton, Robert J., and Zirkel, Perry A., "The Consistency and Predictability of Grievance Arbitration Awards," *Industrial and Labor Relations Review*, Vol. 43, January 1990, 294-307.

Twomey, David P., *A Concise Guide to Employment Law: EEO & OSHA* (Cincinnati: South-Western Publishing Company), 1986.

Volz, Marlin M., and Goggin, Edward P. (eds.), *How Arbitration Works, Fourth Edition 1985-87 Supplement* (Washington, D.C.: Bureau of National Affairs, Inc.), 1988.

Words and Phrases, Permanent Edition, Staff (St. Paul, Minn.: West Publishing Company), Vol. 10A, 1968, 31.

Youngdahl, James E. "Arbitration of Discrimination Grievances," *The Arbitration Journal*, Vol. 31, No. 3, September 1976, 145.

Zack, Arnold M., and Bloch, Richard I., *Labor Agreement in Negotiation and Arbitration* (Washington, D.C.: The Bureau of National Affairs, Inc.), 1983.

Zazas, George J., "The Case for Establishment of Formal Standards," *Proceedings of the Thirty-Eighth Annual Meeting National Academy of Arbitrators* (Washington, D.C.: BNA Books, Inc.), 1986.

Index

About the Author

VERN E. HAUCK was Professor of Industrial Relations at the School of Business and Public Affairs at the University of Alaska at Anchorage and is a professional labor arbitrator. He is the author of several books, including *Arbitrating Race, Religion, and National Origin Discrimination Grievances* (Quorum, 1997).

ISBN 1-56720-107-5

EAN

9 781567 201079

90000>

HARDCOVER BAR CODE